German Foreign Policy 1917–1933
Continuity or Break?

German Foreign Policy
1917–1933

Continuity or Break?

MARSHALL M. LEE
WOLFGANG MICHALKA

BERG
Leamington Spa / Hamburg / New York
Distributed exclusively in the US and Canada by
St. Martin's Press, New York

Berg Publishers Limited
24 Binswood Avenue, Leamington Spa, CV32 5SQ, UK
Schenefelder Landstr. 14K, 2000 Hamburg 55, West Germany
175 Fifth Avenue/Room 400, New York, NY 10010, USA

British Library Cataloguing in Publication Data
Lee, Marshall M.
    German foreign policy 1917–1933: continuity
    or break?
    1. Germany—Foreign relations—1918–1933
    I. Title   II. Michalka, Wolfgang
    327.43   DD240
    ISBN 0–907582–52–4

Library of Congress Cataloging-in Publication Data
Lee, Marshall M.
    German foreign policy, 1917–1933.

    Bibliography: p.
    Includes index.
    1. Germany—Foreign relations—1918–1933. 2. Germany—
Foreign relations—1871–1981. I. Michalka, Wolfgang.
II. Title.
DD240.L39   1987   327.43   85–22833
ISBN 0–907582–52–4

Printed in Great Britain by Billings of Worcester

Contents

To Esther, Bill and Elizabeth
and Helga, Basti, Stefi, Matthias and Anna

The Continuities of German Foreign Policy

One must really face up to the *result of the past war*. It is the defeat, the *elimination of Germany as a European Great Power* after the failure from the outset of its unconscious attempt — I purposely say *unconscious* attempt — to compete with England for world rule. If one wants to *fight* for world rule one must make long-term preparations with ruthless logic. One must not vacillate or pursue a policy of peace but adopt out and out power politics. One aspect of this is that the ground on which one stands, both at home and abroad, must be firm and unshakeable. We unconsciously strove after world rule — I can of course say this only among friends, but anyone who looks at the matter reasonably clearly and historically can have no doubt — *before* we had consolidated our position on the Continent. What Bismarck initiated he was unable to strengthen and consolidate because of his dismissal, and among his followers there was only one man who saw things with crystal clarity and that was the late Field-Marshal Graf von Schlieffen.

> W. Groener, situation report, given at the General Headquarters on 19 May 1919 (BA/Militärarchiv, N 42/12)

. . . rebuilding of the armed forces is the most important prerequisite for attaining the goal: Reconquest of political power. Universal military service has come back. First the leadership of the state must see to it, however, that those liable for service are not poisoned, even before they enter, by Fascism, Marxism, Bolshevism or that they do not succumb to that poison after having served.

How is political power to be used after it has been won? Not yet possible to tell. Perhaps conquest of new export possibilities, perhaps — and indeed preferably — conquest of new living space in the east and ruthless Germanization of the latter. It is certain that the present economic conditions can be changed only through political power and struggle. All that can be done now — land-settlement — stops gaps.

Armed forces remain the most important and most socialistic institution of the state. They are to remain non-political and above parties. The domestic struggle is not their business, but that of Nazi organizations. Different from Italy, no amalgamation of army and SA is intended. The most dangerous period is that of the rebuilding of the armed forces. Then we shall see, whether Fr[ance] has *statesmen*; if so, she will not leave us time but will fall upon us (presumably with eastern satellites).

Adolf Hitler, according to notes made by Lieutenant General Liebmann, 3 February 1933 (*FZG* II, 4 (1954) p. 435)

Foreword

During our collaboration we have discovered many things, but perhaps the most fascinating was the divergence in outlook and method of two scholars from different countries. While we share similar political and social views, the difference in academic and scholarly styles between the American and the German often produced tension. It was not always clear, for instance, what each of us understood by the same event. Indeed, the distinctions between the German and the American historical consciousness proved dramatic.

This project reconfirmed the fact that writing history is never free from the influences of national origin. In our case, however, such tensions proved creative, for they forced each of us to look again at historical events, struggling to see them through a different lens. We attempted to minimize the effects of national influences through a constant — and now years-long — dialectical process of discussion, confrontation and interpretation which we feel yielded a productive and satisfying harmony of views.

During the course of this work, many people gave generously of their time and counsel. Their advice was welcome and criticism was taken to heart. We wish to thank in particular: Volker Berghahn (Warwick), William Carr (Sheffield), Jost Dülffer (Cologne), Carole Fink (North Carolina/Wilmington), Lothar Gall (Frankfurt/M.), Peter Grupp (Political Archives of the Germany Foreign Ministry), Klaus Hildebrand (Bonn), Jon Jacobson (Irvine), Peter Krüger (Marburg), Paul Gordon Lauren (Montana), Gottfried Niedhart (Mannheim), Reinhard Schiffers (Bonn), and Klaus Schwabe (Aachen).

In addition, we would like to express our appreciation to the libraries of Pacific University, Mannheim University, the University of Frankfurt/M., and Darmstadt University, for their assistance in tracking down references. To Pacific University must go a special note of thanks for supporting this project on the American end.

Finally, our thanks to Mrs Sibylle Schwerdner-Platz and Mrs Barbara Story for their secretarial skills in helping to prepare the first two drafts of this book.

Forest Grove, Oregon, 1986   M.L./W.M.

1

Introduction

A quarter of a century after their appearance, the works of A. J. P. Taylor and Fritz Fischer continue to arouse scholarly interest and debate over the question of the continuities in German history.[1] Agree with them or not, Taylor and Fischer have performed a great service by setting off a controversy which has not only enlivened the historical profession but enriched our understanding of Germany's past. Taylor maintained that Hitler and National Socialist foreign policy could only be understood within the framework of traditional German politics and were, in fact, the logical extension of long-conceived German foreign policy goals.[2] Fischer's examination of the war aims policy of the Wilhelmine Empire and the origins of the First World War produced an important but equally controversial thesis. Germany, he argued, was not only responsible for the outbreak of the First World War, but in addition had pursued aims strikingly similar to those subsequently pursued by Hitler and his supporters. As part of a policy of calculated risk in pursuit of grandiose imperial goals, German strategists welcomed war in 1914, willing 'to let the iron dice roll'. Fischer boldly asserted, moreover, that Hitler's aggressive goals were strikingly similar to those of Germany's strategists in 1914. He viewed his book as a 'contribution towards the problem of the continuity of German policy from the First World War to the Second'.[3]

1. A. J. P. Taylor, *The Origins of the Second World War* (London, 1961); F. Fischer, *Germany's War Aims in the First World War* (New York, 1963), originally published in Germany as *Griff nach der Weltmacht: Die Kriegszielpolitik des Kaiserlichen Deutschland. 1914–18* (Düsseldorf, 1961). Defending himself against his detractors, Fischer broadened and deepened his critique of Germany's prewar foreign policy in his *War of Illusions. German Policies from 1911 to 1914* (New York, 1975), published in Germany in 1969, under the title *Krieg der Illusionen* (Düsseldorf, 1969).
2. C. R. Cole, 'Critics of the Taylor View of History', in *The Wiener Library Bulletin* 22(1968); E. M. Robertson, ed., *The Origins of the Second World War* (London, 1971); W. R. Louis, ed., *The Origins of the Second World War: A. J. P. Taylor and His Critics* (New York, 1972); G. Niedhart, ed., *Kriegsbeginn 1939. Entfesselung oder Ausbruch des Zweiten Weltkrieges?* (Darmstadt, 1976), pp. 1–16; and now also W. Hoffer, 'Wege oder Irrwege der Forschung? Erneute Auseinandersetzung mit "erneuten Betrachtungen" von A. J. P. Taylor', in W. Pols, ed., *Staat und Gesellschaft im Politischen Wandel. Beiträge zur Geschichte der modernen Welt* (Stuttgart, 1979) pp. 523ff.
3. Fischer, *War Aims*, p. xxii.

3

Taylor's thesis outraged those who saw in Hitler something special, a departure from traditional European diplomacy and statecraft, while Fischer's critique sent a shock-wave through the ranks of his German colleagues.[4] Fischer and Taylor added a new dimension to a decades-long debate raging off and on within the ranks of German historians.[5] Where some scholars saw lines of continuity in German history chiefly in intellectual terms, as illustrated in the works of Krieger, Kohn, Stern, and Mosse,[6] now the argument was joined on the much more tangible level of diplomacy and statecraft.[7]

The confrontation between Taylor and Fischer and their critics demonstrated beyond reasonable doubt that Germany's role in the origins of both world wars could not be measured accurately unless set against the background of Prussian-German history since 1860 at the very latest.[8] Against this background certain features of recent German

4. See in this context T. S. Hamerow, 'Guilt, Redemption, and Writing German History', in *AHR* 88, 1(1983), pp. 53–72.

5. H. Kohn, *The Mind of Germany: The Education of a Nation* (New York, 1960); L. Krieger, *The German Idea of Freedom: History of a Political Tradition* (Boston, 1957); G. Mosse, *The Crisis of German Ideology: Intellectual Origins of the Third Reich* (New York, 1964); F. Stern, *The Politics of Cultural Despair: A Study in the Rise of the Germanic Ideology* (Berkeley and Los Angeles, 1961).

6. On the Fischer controversy itself, see the summary and analysis of A. Sywottek, 'Die Fischer-Kontroverse. Ein Beitrag zur Entwicklung historisch-politischen Bewusstseins in der Bundesrepublik', in I. Geiss and B. Wendt, eds., *Deutschland in der Weltpolitik des 19. und 20. Jahrhunderts* (Düsseldorf, 1973), pp. 19ff; A. J. Moses, *Politics of Illusion. The Fischer-Controversy in German Historiography* (London, 1975); K. Hildebrand, 'Imperialismus, Wettrüsten und Kriegsausbruch 1914 (I)', *NPL* 20 (1975), pp. 160ff; V. R. Berghahn, 'Fritz Fischer und seine Schüler', *NPL* 19 (1974), pp. 143ff.

7. On the debate about continuity in recent German history, the following titles are noteworthy: A. Hillgruber, *Kontinuität und Diskontinuität in der Deutschen Außenpolitik von Bismarck bis Hitler* (Düsseldorf, 1969), which is now available in many collections, among others Hillgruber's own *Großmachtpolitik und Militarismus im 20. Jahrundert. 3 Beiträge zum Kontinuitätsproblem* (Düsseldorf, 1974); A. Lüdtke, 'Zur Kontinuitätsfrage. Schwierigkeiten mit Konzeption und Methode', in *Das Argument 70: Kritik d. bürgerlichen Geschichtswissenschaft* (I), 1972; J. C. G. Röhl, *From Bismarck to Hitler. The Problem of Continuity in German History* (London, 1970); K. Hildebrand, *The Foreign Policy of the Third Reich* (Berkeley, 1973); idem, 'Hitlers Ort in der Geschichte des preussisch-deutschen Nationalstaates', in *HZ* (1973), pp. 584–632; W. Alff, *Materialien zum Kontinuitätsproblem der deutschen Geschichte* (Frankfurt, 1976); G. Ziebura, *Grundfragen der deutschen Außenpolitik seit 1871* (Darmstadt, 1975); W. Michalka, 'Nationalsozialismus und Preußen. Ein Beitrag zur Frage nach Kontinuität und/oder Diskontinuität in der neueren deutschen Geschichte', in *Mitteilungen der Gesellschaft der Freunde der Universität Mannheim e.V.*, 26 (1977), pp. 29–39; F. Fischer, 'Zum Problem der Kontinuität in der deutschen Geschichte von Bismarck zu Hitler', in F. Fischer, *Der Erste Weltkrieg und das deutsche Geschichtsbild. Beiträge zur Bewältigung eines historischen Tabus* (Düsseldorf, 1977); K. H. Jarausch, 'From Second to Third Reich: The Problem of Continuity in German Foreign Policy', *CEH*, XII, 1 (1979), pp. 68–82; T. Nipperdey, '1933 und Kontinuität der Deutschen Geschichte', *HZ* 227 (1978), pp. 86–111; F. Fischer, *Bündnis der Eliten. Zur Kontinuität der Machtstrukturen in Deutschland 1871–1945* (Düsseldorf, 1979).

8. See in this connection A. Hillgruber, *Deutschlands Rolle in der Vorgeschichte der beiden Weltkriege* (Göttingen, 1967).

history stood out as much more clearly defined. In the late nineteenth century, the social effects of an accelerating industrial revolution heightened the latent political crisis in Bismarckian Germany, producing national anxiety and threatening to alter the domestic balance of power. The political and social dominance of the traditional ruling elites was no longer secure; this change was of fundamental importance for Prussian-German politics, where the relationship between economic power and political control was particularly close. Under such new pressures, the traditional elites seized on a strategy of consolidation and defense, aimed at preserving an increasingly precarious *status quo*. One immediate result was to underline the interdependence of foreign and domestic policy. Emphasizing this connection, recent scholarship sees persuasive evidence that the continuity of modern German history clearly emerges with the broad foreign policy goals formulated in the *Reichsgründungszeit*. These reflected the values and aims of Germany's political elites and influenced German foreign policy in varying degrees from Bismarck to Hitler.[9] The question of continuity, then, already appears acute at the time of the Wilhelmine Empire, if not earlier. It is one of the most stimulating issues facing the German historian, and in A. Lüdtke's words, 'has become one of the most productive provocations facing historians'.[10]

Historians continue to disagree on the place of the Weimar Republic in recent German history. It is portrayed either as a continuation of the Wilhelmine Empire, and thus little more than a preparatory phase for the Third Reich in the framework of continuity, or as a real break in recent German history and a new beginning for German politics.[11] For this reason, during the last decade scholars have worked toward a synthesis of this crucial 'interlude', a synthesis which should come to terms with the implications for that period of the debate about continuity. Available treatments of Weimar diplomacy touch in varying degrees on this question[12] but the present authors trust that a synthesis of Weimar foreign policy, resting broadly on recent monographic

9. See in this connection particularly H.-U, Wehler, *The German Empire, 1981–1918* (Leamington Spa/Dover, N.H. 1985).
10. Lüdtke, 'Zur Kontinuitätsfrage', p. 105.
11. See the review article by K. D. Erdmann, 'Die Geschichte der Weimarer Republik als Problem der Wissenschaft', *VZG* 3 (1955), pp. 1–20; W. Ruge, 'Zur bürgerlichen Geschichtsschreibung der BRD über die Weimarer Republik', *ZfG* 22 (1974), pp. 677–700.
12. L. Zimmermann, *Deutsche Außenpolitik in der Ära der Weimarer Republik* (Göttingen, 1958); H. Graml, *Europa zwischen den Kriegen* (Munich, 1969); W. Ruge, *Deutschland von 1917 bis 1933. Von der Großen Sozialistischen Oktoberrevolution bis zum Ende der Weimarer Republik* (Berlin, 1974); S. Marks, *The Illusion of Peace. International Relations in Europe, 1918–1933* (New York, 1976); J. Hiden, *Germany and Europe, 1919–1939* (London, 1977); and most recently, Peter Krüger, *Die Außenpolitik der Republik von Weimar* (Darmstadt, 1985).

literature and confronting the question of continuity in recent German history will prove a timely contribution.

An accurate assessment of continuity or discontinuity in Weimar foreign policy begins in 1917, a turning point in international affairs as well.[13] In Germany it brought the culmination of past forces and the apparent realization of traditional foreign policy goals and dreams, spurred on by catalytic events on the Eastern Front and in Russia. Simultaneously, the prospect of realizing their most extreme foreign policy aims unveiled to Germany's leaders new political vistas which promised a qualitative departure from the past. Thus, the Russian Revolution and the territorial gains in Eastern Europe which Berlin anticipated from a favorable settlement with the Bolsheviks, formed the conceptual framework within which Weimar foreign policy evolved. The year 1917, then, serves as the key not only to German foreign policy up to that date, but also to its subsequent development as well.[14]

By the same token, it appears unhelpful to end the examination of Weimar foreign policy abruptly on 30 January 1933, the evening of the National Socialist seizure of power. All historical evidence indicates that National Socialist foreign policy did not start immediately on the morning of 31 January. Beginning well before Hitler, German foreign policy reflected a gradual transition which showed signs of ending only after Hitler assumed power.[15] In addition, only by determining the stages of the transition after the National Socialist seizure of power can one speak convincingly of an evolutionary process rather than a revolutionary break.

13. The importance of the year 1917 for German politics and foreign policy is stressed by Hillgruber, *Kontinuität und Diskontinuität* pp.. 22ff.; Fischer, *Bündnis* pp. 53ff., 358. Fischer, as distinct from Hillgruber, speaks of Germany's foreign policy goals which emerged in 1917–1918 as 'qualitatively new'. See also: G. Schulz, *Revolutionen und Friedensschlüsse 1917–1920* (Munich, 1967), pp. 109ff.; H.-U. Wehler, *The German Empire*, pp. 209–222. Krüger, *Außenpolitik* pp. 18–9.

14. F. Stern, *The Failure of Liberalism. Essays on the Political Culture of Modern Germany* (New York, 1972), pp. xi–xliv; G. Barraclough, 'Mandarins and Nazis', *New York Review of Books* XIX, 6 (1972), pp. 37–43; idem, 'The Liberals and German History', *New York Review of Books* XIX, 7 (1972), pp. 32–8; idem, 'A New View of German History', *New York Review of Books* XIX, 8 (1972), pp. 25–31. More recently, see K. H. Jarausch, 'Illiberalism and Beyond: German History in Search of a Paradigm', *JMH* 55; 2 (1983), pp. 268–84; C. S. Maier, 'The Vulnerabilities of Interwar Germany', *JMH* 56, 1 (1984), pp. 89–99; D. Orlow, 'The Historiography of the Decline of Brüning and the Rise of the Nazis: Comment and Review Article', *CEH* XVII, 1 (1984), pp. 63–71. On the broader, yet no less significant level of general European international affairs, see: J. Jacobson, 'Is There a New International History of the 1920s?', *AHR* 88, 3 (1983), pp. 617–45; Fischer, *Bündnis*, pp. 53ff., 358.

15. For the significance of the year 1933 for German foreign policy, see: K. D. Bracher, 'Das Anfangsstadium der Hitlerischen Außenpolitik', *VZG* 5 (1957), pp. 63–76; C. Bloch, *Hitler und die europäischen Mächte, 1933/1934. Kontinuität oder Bruch?* (Frankfurt a.M., 1966); see also now especially G. Wollstein, *Vom Weimarer*

Introduction

A closely related problem is the need to take into account the mutual dependence of domestic and foreign policy. Although of decisive importance for the republic, this question will — in view of the limitations of space — be dealt with in light of some specific cases, chosen as both critical to an understanding of Weimar foreign policy and also representative of the interdependence with domestic policies.

Finally, given the recent wealth of monographic literature not only on Germany, but on the whole of western Europe, no satisfactory treatment of German foreign policy can ignore the foreign policies of her neighbors and adversaries. Following the German collapse in 1918, the Treaty of Versailles imposed conditions which deprived Germany of much of her previous autonomy in foreign policy.[16] The fact that the Weimar Republic was dependent on the Allies in the immediate postwar years reflects the complexity of international relations following the First World War. The fledgling republic's political and financial dependence on former enemies dramatically demonstrated the limits of German foreign policy, and also the limits of Allied retribution. At the same time, the climate produced by the events of 1918–1919 offered Germany completely new opportunities for political gain unavailable in previous years.

The present authors do not intend to provide a comprehensive history of Weimar foreign policy in all its details. Rather, somewhat in the style of the *pointilliste* whose painting asks the viewer's eye to mix the colors from each individual dot, our intention is to advance an interpretation of Weimar foreign policy which raises as many questions as it answers. It seems that a particularly productive means of accomplishing this end is to consider the central problems of Weimar foreign policy against the background of the debate on continuity and/or discontinuity in recent German history.

Chapter 1 will sketch the preconditions of Weimar foreign policy. In 1917–1918 the foreign policy goals of the German leadership crystallized from mere wishful thinking into a concrete program whose essential elements were realized in the East following the

Revisionismus zu Hitler. Das Deutsche Reich und die Großmächte in der Anfangsphase der nationalsozialistischen Herrschaft in Deutschland (Bonn-Bad Godesberg, 1973); H. Graml, 'Präsidialsystem und Außenpolitik', *VZG* 21 (1973), pp. 134–45. H.-A. Jacobsen, *Nationalsozialistische Außenpolitik 1933–1938* (Frankfurt/M., 1968); G. L. Weinberg, *The Foreign Policy of Hitler's Germany* (Chicago, 1970); Edward W. Bennett, *German Rearmament and the West 1932–1933* (Princeton, 1979); T. Nipperdey, '1933 und die Kontinuität der Deutschen Geschichte', in *HZ* 227 (1978); pp. 86–111; and, of course, Hildebrand, *The Foreign Policy of the Third Reich, passim*.

16. It is fair to question whether, in the modern industrial era, an autonomous foreign policy is at all possible. However, relative to her prewar position Germany was far more limited after the war in the degree of freedom to reach foreign policy decisions.

Russian collapse and the Treaty of Brest-Litovsk. In their scope and quality these goals, which in 1918 briefly became reality, formed a continuous thread woven throughout the foreign policy conceptions of the Weimar Republic. At the same time, the collapse of Wilhelmine Germany, the Treaty of Versailles and the radical shift in the European — indeed global — balance of power, imposed very real limits on German foreign policy.

Chapter 2 analyzes the opportunities open to Weimar foreign policy in the years 1919–1923. Essential in this context were Germany's relations with the two reclusive giants, the Soviet Union and the United States. These two powers, conspicuously aloof from the European arena, represented opposite social and economic extremes, both in theory and in practice. Throughout the Weimar period, the United States and the Soviet Union offered markedly opposed choices for German foreign policy, and these influenced the republic until its final hours. During the period 1919–1923, however, it was the influence of French security policy which served to restrict Germany's freedom to explore the American and Soviet options to the fullest. The former represented a distinct departure from traditional German foreign policy, the latter an element in its continuity.

Chapter 3 is devoted to the foreign policy of Gustav Stresemann from 1924 to 1929. In 1925 the Locarno Pact mediated the influence of French security policy, while Germany's subsequent entry into the League of Nations in 1926 offered her a new forum from which Stresemann could embark upon a more active foreign policy. Its ultimate aims had not materially changed, although new and different diplomatic tactics created the impression of altered goals; yet, once again, the international system and Germany's own internal conditions limited her action in this field.

The Wall Street crash and global economic depression intensified the internal crisis which had never fully subsided in Germany after 1924. **Chapter 4** deals with foreign policy during the years 1930–1933. Under the pressure of economic collapse, the republic resumed a foreign policy which, in its predominantly domestic function, recalled German diplomacy after the fall of Bismarck, when foreign policy was used as compensation for domestic sacrifice. Increasingly strident demands for treaty revision and the emergence of new and more extreme foreign policy goals resulted from the domestic chaos early thirties. It was in this atmosphere that Hitler came to power.

In *Leitmotif* and **Recitative** the question of continuity and/or discontinuity in recent German history reappears, this time in the light of the preceding chapters.

1

The Determinants of Weimar and Traditional German Foreign Policy, 1917–1919

1917 and German Foreign Policy Goals

For Germany, the beginning of the year 1917 held little promise of improvement in what had, during the last twenty-nine months, become a frustrating war of attrition. The *Burgfrieden*[1] had been greeted across the political spectrum in August 1914 as a means of ending long-standing quarrels between disparate German social interests, thus laying to rest (or at least reducing to a minimum) domestic conflict. But it had proved a mere chimera. From the outset the German political and military establishment had sought to create a stable homefront, free from social and political tensions, by appealing to the concept of the *Volksgemeinschaft*. The 'people's community', rooted in the ideal of a conflict-free society, labelled by Hans Ulrich Wehler a 'tissue of grand-sounding phrases',[2] collapsed into empty fiction. What had begun in the West in the fall of 1914 with great promise for German arms had quickly degenerated from a war of movement into static and enervating trench warfare. The *Reichsleitung* could no longer conceal the staggering casualties, nor could it easily justify the extravagant expenditure of human resources. In addition, since 1914 the Allied blockade had more or less successfully sealed Germany off from her sources of strategic resources. Economic mobilization and a sophisticated war economy could for a short time replace most, if not all, of the strategic raw materials denied to Germany, but by 1917 the worsening food shortages caused by the blockade began to take their

1. On the genesis and function of the *Burgfrieden*, see A. Rosenberg, *Entstehung der Weimarer Republik* (Frankfurt/M., 1974), pp. 67ff; S. Miller, *Burgfrieden und Klassenkampf. Die deutsche Sozialdemokratie im ersten Weltkrieg* (Düsseldorf, 1974).
2. Wehler, *The German Empire*, p. 213. On the military dictatorship of Ludendorff and Hindenburg, see M. Kitchen, *The Silent Dictatorship: The Politics of the German High Command under Hindenburg and Ludendorff, 1916–1918* (New York, 1976).

toll of a civilian population as yet unaware of the delicate military situation. While internal troubles mounted early in 1917, the war suddenly took a turn for the worse. With the failure of peace initiatives in 1916, the German leadership ordered the resumption of unrestricted submarine warfare in a desperate bid to knock Britain out of the war, thus also, it was believed, forcing France to sue for peace. Within weeks, however, the fears of those opposed to this decision were confirmed: on 6 April 1917 the United States entered the war on the Allied side.

The failure of Germany to achieve a clear military decision in 1914 had forced Germans of every political hue to contemplate something less than complete victory over Britain and France. Now America's entry into the war seemed to thrust the chance of victory even farther into the background. What could Germany do, domestically or militarily, to bring about a decisive end to the war? That was the question of the hour.

First to react at this critical moment in the summer of 1917 was the military leadership who, from the very beginning, had viewed the war as an opportunity to 'escape forward' (*Flucht nach vorn*). By this they meant to escape forward into a victorious future, which would enable Germany's Imperial elites to bury the impending social and political crisis of 1914 forever in the spoils of a short and victorious war; spoils which would compensate virtually every segment of German society and thus remove the need for social and political reform. Accordingly, the war could only be won at the front, but in the same breath military leaders implied that if Germany lost the war the failure would be on the home front. In this way, the generals planned to evade responsibility for their failure in the field, and by 1917 they determined to lay it squarely at the door of the politicians.[3] Their first victim was Chancellor Bethmann Hollweg, whose growing willingness to consider domestic political reform made him unreliable in the eyes of the generals.[4] The High Command (OHL) secured their domestic political position on two fronts. In so far as they could shift blame for their own military blunders onto the politicians, and the home front in general, they provided themselves with political cover. Simultaneously, they prepared the so-called stab-in-the-back legend, 'which attributed to the political leaders alone the sole responsibility for the

3. Fischer, *Germany's Aims*, pp. 391–2.
4. On the fall of Bethmann Hollweg, see *ibid.*, pp. 391–405; K. Jarausch, *The Enigmatic Chancellor. Bethmann Hollweg and the Hybris of Imperial Germany* (Princeton, 1972); in a general context, see the review essay by K. Hildebrand, *Bethmann Hollweg — der Kanzler ohne Eigenschaften? Urteile der Geschichtsschreibung. Eine kritische Bibliographie* (Düsseldorf, 1970).

military collapse of Germany'.[5] At the same time, the OHL sought a decisive extension of their influence over the domestic political decision-making process, so that within months their position could be described as 'dictatorial'.[6]

Even as Germany's declining military fortunes in the spring of 1917 produced desperate political maneuvers by her generals in Berlin, her strategic position began to change. And the change was in the East. The situation in Russia during the summer and early fall of 1917 became steadily more chaotic. Economic collapse, *putsch* and counter-*putsch*, military disaster, all combined to bring Russia to her knees. Lenin's successful bid for power in October seemed to offer Germany renewed hope, for no one doubted the Bolsheviks' intention to pull Russia out of the war. The possibility of transferring great numbers of troops from the Eastern to the Western front radically altered Germany's military prospects. The Russian Revolution must have appeared to the OHL as divine intervention. For the first time since the successes of 1914, the military situation favored Germany. The Russian Revolution so altered the military situation that failures were forgotten and miscalculations expiated; the domestic crisis subsided and the war aims debate surfaced with renewed fervor.[7]

The resumption of that debate revived old traditional territorial claims deriving from the early days of the war. Intoxicated by their rapid advance in France in August and September 1914, virtually the entire political spectrum had endorsed aims similar to the 'September Program' of Bethmann Hollweg,[8] which demanded sweeping terri-

5. Fischer, *Germany's Aims*, p. 392.
6. Wehler, *The German Empire*, p. 216; Kitchen, *The Silent Dictatorship*.
7. On the war aims debate, see among others: W. J. Mommsen, 'Die deutsche Kriegszielpolitik 1914–1918. Bemerkungen zum Stand der Diskussion', *Kriegsausbruch 1914. Deutsche Buchausgabe des Journal of Contemporary History*, W. Laqueur & C. L. Mosse, eds. (Munich, 1967), p. 60ff; W. Schieder, ed., *Erster Weltkrieg. Entstehung und Kriegsziele* (Cologne, 1969); E. W. Graf von Lynar, ed., *Deutsche Kriegsziele 1914–1918* (Darmstadt, 1964); I. Geiss, 'Die Fischer-Kontroverse. Ein kritischer Beitrag zum Verhältnis zwischen Historiographie und Politik in der Bundesrepublik', in I. Geiss, *Studien über Geschichte und Geschichtswissenschaft* (Frankfurt a.M., 1972); Sywottek, 'Die Fischer-Kontroverse . . .'; T. T. Helde, 'The Fischer Years and After: 1961–1976 or "The Kriegsschuldfrage" Revisited. A Retrospective Essay', in *Reviews in European History* III, 3 (1977).
8. Fischer, *Germany's Aims*, pp. 95–119, 155–83. For an attack on Fischer's analysis of the September Program, see W. C. Thompson, 'The September Program: Reflections on the Evidence', *CEH* XI, 4 (1978), pp. 348–54. Thompson maintains that the September Program represented 'maximum demands... drawn up so that they would be available "for the eventuality of sudden negotiations"'. This does not alter the fact, however, that the September Program embraced all the hopes and desires of official and private German circles on war aims in the fall of 1914. See also G. Ritter, 'Der Kanzler und die Machtträume deutscher Patrioten 1914', in W. Schieder, ed., *Erster Weltkrieg. Ursachen, Entstehung und Kriegsziele* (Cologne, 1969), pp. 107–46; E. Zechlin, 'Probleme des Kriegskalküls und der Kriegsbeendigung im Ersten Weltkrieg', in *ibid.*, pp. 149–64; K.-D. Erdmann, 'Zur Beurteilung Bethmann Hollwegs', in *ibid.*, pp. 205–21.

torial compensation for a victorious Germany. But as the anticipated victory slipped away, the intensity of the war aims discussion subsided. Now, however, with the Russian collapse in 1917, Germany's territorial claims seemed once again within reach, in fact already partially realized. At the core of the September Program was the desire to eliminate France 'for all time' as a significant political and economic force in Europe, coupled with the intent of pushing Russia eastward, away from Germany's frontier. Thus, German continental hegemony would be consolidated from the Atlantic coast of France and the rich mineral fields of the Longwy-Briey basin in the West, to an Eastern gradient stretching roughly from the Baltic to the Black Sea. Thus expanded, Germany could dominate Europe through 'a central European economic association', to include France, Belgium, Holland, Denmark, Austria-Hungary, Poland, and eventually Italy, Sweden and Norway.[9] This association would enable Germany to dominate Central Europe economically and strategically, thus bringing to life the old German dream of *Mitteleuropa*.[10]

But even as the realization of· that greatest territorial ambition approached, a certain anxiety pervaded the atmosphere in Berlin. The territorial demands which up till then had seemed absolutely sufficient to guarantee Germany's future dominance now seemed insufficient, as the truly global implications of America's entry into the war became clear. Could an expanded Germany, even with continental European hegemony, expect to withstand the combined might of the world's two greatest naval powers, Great Britain and the United States, in a future war?

The possibility that both France and Russia could be defeated gave little comfort, therefore, to German strategists. Through their global resources, the two maritime giants commanded virtually unlimited economic potential. In Berlin, planners believed that Britain and America were likely to remain Germany's potential enemies, even if she were victorious in this war. This introduced an additional note of urgency into demands for economic autarky, which would supposedly secure the rapidly expanding geopolitical and strategic interests of the continental German Empire. Given the success of the Allied blockade against Germany, autarky came to play a greater and greater role in the minds of German planners, who envisioned a German *Großraum*, from the Bay of Biscay to the Urals, impervious to a naval blockade. Following the vast territorial acquisitions in the East, this grandiose descendant of the traditional *Mitteleuropaplan* suddenly seemed

9. Ibid., p. 104.
10. On German *Mitteleuropapolitik*, still valuable is H. C. Meyer, *Mitteleuropa in German Thought and Action, 1815–1945* (The Hague, 1955).

within reach. Russia, with her vast agricultural potential and untapped mineral resources, offered the German economy a safeguard against future blockades, as well as virtually limitless possibilities for development.[11]

For Germany's political leadership, therefore, the year 1917 produced a fundamental alteration in foreign policy determinants, resulting in a qualitative change in existing foreign policy concepts. In the place of the old and often revised *Mitteleuropaplan*, which since 1914 had been the clearest expression of German territorial goals, there now appeared a new and far more ambitious vision of an Eastern *Großraum*.[12] This new plan was apparent in the conditions of the Treaty of Brest-Litovsk of 3 March 1918, which recognized the territorial conquests of the Germans in the East.[13] The extent of the German victory and the magnitude of the change in German war aims, and hence German foreign policy, strikes Andreas Hillgruber as a new stage in the evolution of German foreign policy:

> Perhaps most important, because of its elevation to virtual axiom in German *Ostpolitik* in 1918, was the belief commonly shared among the German leadership that it was thoroughly possible to seize all of Russia and to hold this gigantic empire in a state of perpetual dependence on Germany. This was an absolute contradiction to the massive exaggeration of Russia's strength to which the political and military leaders of Germany fell victim in the years prior to 1914.[14]

The strategic economic and military considerations behind a German *Ostraum* or Eastern *Imperium*, although much grander in scope than previous plans, represented only the magnification of elements long present in German foreign policy. Debate on an *Ostimperium*, however, revealed in the thinking of the German leadership an additional facet which introduced a qualitatively new perspective in German foreign policy. Both the *Alldeutscher Verband* and the *Ostmarkverein*, as well as General Erich Ludendorff who, in his relatively innocuous sounding but powerful position as Chief Quartermaster

11. This dominance was confirmed five years later, when Krasin wrote that Russia's relationship to Germany was 'semi-colonial': E. H. Carr, *The Bolshevik Revolution 1917–1923*, vol. 3 (London, 1966), p. 365.
12. In this connection see also Hillgruber *Deutschlands Rolle*, p. 62, as well as Wehler *The German Empire*, pp. 211–2.
13. On Brest-Litovsk, see J. W. Wheeler-Bennett, *Brest-Litovsk. The Forgotten Peace. March 1918* (New York, 1971); W. Baumgart. *Deutsche Ostpolitik 1918. Von Brest-Litovsk bis zum Ende des Ersten Weltkrieges* (Munich, 1966); P. Borocwsky, *Deutsche Ukrainepolitik 1918* (Hamburg–Lübeck, 1970).
14. Hillgruber, *Deutschlands Rolle*, p. 64; see also Fischer, *Germany's Aims*, pp. 563–82, particularly p. 573. See also W. Gutsche, 'Erst Europa — und dann die Welt. Probleme der Kriegszielpolitik des deutschen Imperialismus im Ersten Weltkrieg', in Schieder, *Erster Weltkrieg*, pp. 256–79.

General, had secretly become virtual dictator during the final year of the war, demanded that in the newly-won *Ostland* the Slavs should be driven out mercilessly, in a *'völkische* field-clearing', to prepare Eastern territory for German colonization. In expectation of German conquests, General Ludendorff had already emerged as an outspoken proponent of what would become this new political dimension when he remarked in December 1915: 'Here [in the East] we are winning the breeding ground for the men we shall need for further campaigns in the East. And these campaigns will come, inevitably.'[15] The *völkisch* character of Ludendorff's foreign policy concepts thus anticipated the racial politics of Hitler, cruelly realized two decades later in Germany's war of ideology and racial extermination against the Soviet Union. '[Ludendorff's] choice of words is highly revealing', comments Wehler, 'for already in 1918 the green light was given to a racialist policy of Germanization [in the East].'[16]

With the introduction of this new quality in German foreign policy, preparation for the coming struggle for world domination absorbed more and more energy during the last phase of the war. Publicly, German strategists maintained the illusion that German intentions centered on *Mitteleuropa*. In fact, however, from then on Germany's attention was focused on achieving a continental *Imperium* which would be the bedrock of her global authority.[17] Continental German hegemony would serve as a stepping stone towards fulfilling the long-cherished imperialist dream of overseas expansion and the creation of far-flung colonial and maritime bases.[18] Here, Klaus Hildebrand believes, was an all-embracing policy, whose antecedents lay in past German aims and which offered a solution to recognized German economic and strategic problems; in short, a panacea:

> ... the policy of world power which [had been] debated already in the Bismarckian era found practical expression in the politics of the Wilhelmine Reich.... [W]hat seems decisive here is that, in accordance with the Brest-Litovsk war aims programme (1917–1918), realised under pressure from the 3rd High Command and particularly Ludendorff, broad tracts of land lying directly adjacent to the Reich in the East and belonging to the

15. Ludendorff to Delbrück, 29 December 1915, in E. Zechlin, 'Ludendorff im Jahre 1915', *HZ* 211 (1970), p. 352.
16. Wehler, *The German Empire*, p. 213. See also Marc Ferro, *The Great War, 1914–1918* (London, 1973), p. 141: 'The ethnic and economic map of Europe would be changed. The programme came up a few years later, and can be found point for point in Hitler's *Tabletalk*.'
17. For a comprehensive treatment, see Fischer, *Germany's Aims*, pp. 583–608, particularly pp. 607–8.
18. Woodruff D. Smith, *The German Colonial Empire* (Chapel Hill, 1978), pp. 224–30.

newly established revolutionary Russian state were conquered and placed under German control. In effect, these areas were to create for Germany the nucleus of a position as a world power—for the subsequent extension of the Reich overseas was also a settled matter in the minds of the German imperialists who dictated the 'forgotten peace' of Brest-Litovsk. The plan to achieve world power in two stages, first by creating the continental foundation and then by expanding overseas, which can already be clearly traced in the discussion on war aims during the First World War, finds its precursors in the Wilhelmine Reich and the era of Bismarck.[19]

Such a policy, it was believed, would give Germany equal might with Great Britain and the United States as a world power.

The year 1917 thus seemed to promise sweeping foreign policy and strategic gains dreamt of by the German leadership since Bismarck. But such an aggressive foreign policy aimed at more than mere territorial acquisition. Since Bismarck it had served a domestic function as well by easing social tensions and averting political crisis, while staving off necessary political reform.[20] By diverting the nation's attention to Germany's drive for Great Power status, as well as direct industrial and naval competition with Great Britain after the mid-1890s, the Wilhelmine elites sought to preserve the *status quo*, which translated directly into the preservation of their privileged position within the authoritarian Prussian-German state. Indeed, for almost two decades before the war, Germany's ambitious foreign policy served as a rallying point, drawing such disparate groups as agrarians and industrialists together in a loose political alliance in support of the government. Now, in the winter of 1917–1918, an increasingly desperate military leadership hoped that the promise of imminent victory and the huge gains which would go with it would once again 'integrate' the various parties and classes in Germany, which could be rallied by their 'will for a victorious end to the World War.' 'The functional aspect of Germany's war-aims can scarcely be overestimated', argues Wehler. 'They were without doubt seen by the power-elites as a means of ensuring political and social unity [*Integrationsklammer*], and to this extent, the planner's excesses provide a true reflection of the fact that society in Imperial Germany was socially and politically deeply divided.'[21]

Although Germany's military leaders recognized that the Russian Revolution was at best a mixed blessing, they minimized the possi-

19. Hildebrand, *Foreign Policy*, pp. 7–8.
20. One of the best recent treatments of ther relationship between expansionist German foreign policy goals and internal political crisis in pre-World War I Germany is V. R. Berghahn, *Germany and the Approach of War in 1914* (New York, 1973), *passim*, but especially, pp. 5–24.
21. Wehler, *The German Empire*, p. 211.

bility that revolution in Russia might soon spread to Germany. Germany need not fear a 'revolution from below' if she were victorious, and it was in this context that Ludendorff and his colleagues in the 3rd High Command allowed the war aims issue to surface publically once more in the winter of 1917–1918. Thus the intimate relationship between domestic and foreign policy, between military-strategic planning and socio-political concepts, is clearly visible in 1917–1918. For Germany 1917 was the most critical year since 1914, and for future German policy 1917 threatened change on a scale only dimly perceived at the time.[22] But, just as suddenly as her fortunes had improved in 1917, German hopes for a victorious end to the war vanished in the early summer of 1918. Fresh American troops and a revitalized Allied command under the centralized leadership of Marshal Ferdinand Foch turned Germany back for a second time in the West at the Marne. The failure of Germany's great spring offensive of 1918, the 'Peace Offensive', signalled the end. By September, with German troops in full retreat, Hindenburg and Ludendorff told the Kaiser that further resistance was futile. Defeat in the field and the simultaneous collapse of the military leadership and the Imperial government bewildered and embittered Germans of all classes. These circumstances forced the Foreign Ministry and the government to re-examine German foreign policy. Could a policy conceived in the Bismarckian era as a strategy to ward off domestic crisis and which had produced ever more exaggerated demands for imperialist expansion survive the collapse of the Empire? And if it did survive, was such a foreign policy likely to have any validity in the postwar world? Indeed, did 1918 represent a break in German foreign policy, or did the aims of 1917 survive to influence policy in the Weimar era?

National Interest or Collective Peace? The Versailles Treaty and the Reorientation of the European Balance of Power

The grandiose territorial gains extracted at Brest-Litovsk bolstered the victorious mood in Germany in the spring of 1918 at the opening of

---

22. *Ibid.*, pp. 176.: '. . . successful social policy alongside an increase in parliamentary influence would make it possible to conduct a powerful *Weltpolitik* by first satisfying the workers. In this case internal reform would underpin imperialism as the main priority, for the integration of the social classes was seen as the prerequisite of strength abroad. *Weltpolitik* would, moreover, facilitate an effective social policy through tangible material concessions. Successes abroad were expected to lead to a kind of truce on the home fronts. . . . The true significance of Wilhelmine "world policy" can, it seems, be appreciated only if viewed from the perspective of social imperialism. Its precipitate character should not obscure the fact that it was based on the deliberate and calculated use of foreign policy as an instrument for achieving domestic political ends.'

the 'Peace Offensive' on the Western Front, meant to end the war. Throughout the summer of 1918 official propaganda fuelled German hopes, so that the collapse of November 1918 came as an unassimilable shock to a stupefied population, helplessly witnessing the collapse of the Empire with a mixture of resentment and resignation. Only in the stab-in-the-back legend were many people able to find an explanation for what was otherwise the unacceptable outrage of defeat.[1] Long before the end of the war the OHL had carefully prepared this tale as a self-serving explanation for Germany's military disaster. It also served the purpose of transferring responsibility for the capitulation and the armistice negotiations from the shoulders of the Supreme Command to those of the political leaders.

In view of the hopeless military situation in the West, on 28 September 1918 Ludendorff and Hindenburg demanded that the German government without further delay offer to accept peace terms based on the Fourteen Points of US President Woodrow Wilson. Simultaneously, the military leadership took the initiative in domestic politics. Parliamentary reform, consistently blocked throughout the war by the military leadership, was now supported by the very generals who had until then been its greatest opponents: a cynical attempt to saddle center and left-wing politicians with the blame for Germany's collapse following the abdication of the Kaiser and the armistice.[2]

On 1 October 1918, the moderate liberal Prince Max von Baden assumed the office of Chancellor.[3] For the first time, Germany's political parties exercised considerable influence over the composition of a cabinet. While the ministerial portfolios of Max von Baden's cabinet remained essentially in the hands of the government faithful, his cabinet did include powerful parliamentary leaders: Philipp Scheidemann (SPD), Matthias Erzberger and Adolf Groeber (Center) and Konrad Haußmann (Progressive Party), all of whom served as ministers without portfolio. Of the problems confronting the new government, most pressing were the long-delayed parliamentary reform and an armistace. The former came almost immediately, and by

1. F. Freiherr von Hiller von Gaertringen, ' "Dolchstoß"-Diskussion und "Dolchstoßlegende" im Wandel von vier Jahrzehnten'. in *Geschichte und Gegenwartsbewußtsein. Historische Betrachtungen und Untersuchungen. Festschrift für Hans Rothfels zum 70. Geburtstag*, W. Besson, ed. (Göttingen, 1963); J. Petzold, *Die Dolchstoßlegende. Eine Gerschichtsfälschung im Dienst des deutschen Imperialismus und Militarismus* (Berlin, 1963).
2. See Wehler, *The German Empire*, p. 219.
3. E. Matthias and R. Morsey, *Die Regierung des Prinzen Max von Baden* (Düsseldorf, 1962); A. J. Mayer, *Politics and Diplomacy of Peacemaking: Containment and Counterrevolution at Versailles, 1918–1919* (New York, 1967), p. 62; Gordon A. Craig, *Germany, 1866–1945* (Oxford, 1978), pp. 396–402.

28 October constitutional amendment had dismantled a key element of the Bismarckian political system: at last the chancellor could not govern without the confidence of parliament. Ministerial responsibility no longer flowed to the crown, but instead to parliament. But these reforms came too late; the sailors' mutiny in Kiel heralded the coming revolution. On 9 November 1918, the Social Democrat Philipp Scheidemann proclaimed a German republic. On the following day the 'Council of People's Commissars' assumed government. Prince Max gave way first to Friedrich Ebert, Majority Socialist, who briefly became chancellor, but who soon thereafter became co-chairman of the Council of People's Commissars along with Hugo Haase, leader of the Independent Socialist Party.[4] From the outset, Ebert's government was saddled with the legacy of the lost war, a burden which would fall most heavily on the SPD.

Parallel to the bewildering developments in Germany, negotiations in Compiègne culminated on 11 November in the armistice which brought the First World War to an end.[5] Urged on by the Supreme Command, the revolutionary government signed the articles of armistice, thus submitting to conditions far more harsh than the overoptimistic German planners had expected.[6] The draconian armistice conditions demanded German evacuation of all occupied territory in the West and of Alsace-Lorraine within fifteen days. The left bank of the Rhine, including the three bridgeheads of Cologne, Koblenz and Mainz, remained occupied by Allied troops. The Germans agreed to the immediate release of all Allied prisoners of war; the fate of German prisoners in Allied hands remained undecided. In the East, Germany renounced the Treaties of Brest-Litovsk and Bucharest and agreed to evacuate the eastern territories.[7] The armistice conditions, however, obliged Germany to make restitution only for damages to civilian

4. On the German revolution of 1918–1919 and the government of the 'Council of People's Commissars', see S. Miller and G. A. Ritter, eds., *Die Deutsche Revolution 1918 bis 1919* (Frankfurt a.M., 1969); E. Kolb, *Die Arbeiterräte in der deutschen Innenpolitik 1918–1919* (Düsseldorf, 1962); R. Rürup, *Probleme der Revolution in Deutschland 1918–1919* (Wiesbaden, 1968); E. Matthias, *Zwischen Räten und Geheimräten. Die deutsche Revolutionsregierung 1918–1919* (Düsseldorf, 1970); E. Kolb, ed., *Vom Kaiserreich zur Weimarer Republik* (Cologne, 1972).

5. On the armistice negotiations, see H. Rudin, *Armistice, 1918* (New Haven, Conn., 1944); J. W. Wheeler-Bennett, *The Nemesis of Power. The German Army in Politics, 1918–1945* (New York, 1956), pp. 3–82; Mayer, *Politics and Diplomacy*, pp. 3–116.

6. Actually, with respect to compensation to the Allies, the pre-armistice agreements and the armistice itself turned out to be relatively generous, given the final reparations figures of 1921. See Marc Trachtenberg, 'Reparations at the Paris Peace Conference', *JMH* 51(1979), pp. 40–1. See also Marvin R. Zahniser, *Uncertain Friendship — American-French Relations Through the Cold War* (New York, 1975), p. 215.

7. On the armistice conditions and Germany's reaction, see Wheeler-Bennett, *Nemesis*; Mayer, *Politics and Diplomacy*; O. E. Schüddekopf, 'German Foreign Policy between Compiègne and Versailles', *JCH* 4 (1969), p. 181–197.

property, a point which originated in the Lansing Note of 5 November and which would return to haunt the Paris Peace Conference but on which the Germans placed great hopes.[8]

Almost immediately, the German government began to prepare for the anticipated peace negotiations. Under the leadership of Count Ulrich von Brockdorff-Rantzau, the delegation to the peace conference hoped to preserve the German national state from the anticipated efforts to diminish its size or political unity.[9] In addition, von Brockdorff-Rantzau and his subordinates strove to reconstruct Germany's favorable prewar commercial position among the industrialized nations of the world. Nevertheless, as Leo Haupts points out, the Count grudgingly acknowledged that the war had profoundly altered Germany's power-political position:

> Military force was rejected [as a means of assuring Germany's continued existence], particularly under the assumption that an international system of justice protected the political independence of countries incapable of their own defense and that the positions of the various powers made such a guarantee plausible. The destruction of the political and military Great Power aspirations of the Wilhelmine Reich was accepted as an established fact. German [foreign] policy must seek its way in the future by other means.[10]

During the interval between the armistice and the Paris Peace Conference, the German leadership seemed to live in a world of their own, as yet barely affected by external realities. This air of illusion was evident in the zest with which the Germans seized upon Wilson's Fourteen Points as the most attractive basis for an acceptable peace.[11] General disarmament, national self-determination, international arbitration, and collective agreement for the settlement of political, economic and social problems were principles which the German government now embraced. For tactical purposes, Berlin hoped to

---

8. Trachtenberg, 'Reparations at the Paris Peace Conference', *passim*; Klaus Schwabe, 'Die USA, Deutschland und der Ausgang des Ersten Weltkrieges', in Manfred Knapp, Werner Link, Hans-Jürgen Schröder, and Klaus Schwabe, *Die USA und Deutschland, 1918–1975* (Munich, 1978), pp. 11–61 Krüger, *Außenpolitik*, pp. 40–1.

9. On Brockdorff-Rantzau, the 'Red Count', see U. Wengst, *Graf Brockdorff-Rantzau und die außenpolitischen Anfänge der Weimarer Republik* (Berne and Frankfurt a.M., 1973).

10. L. Haupts, *Deutsche Friedenspolitik* (Düsseldorff, 1976), p. 416.

11. The Germans pinned great hopes on Wilson and House. In recent years, however, Trachtenberg has thrown much light on the degree to which the Americans pursued a peace policy which was highly moralistic and punitive. See Marc Trachtenberg, 'Reparations at the Paris Peace Conference'; idem, *Reparations in World Politics: France and European Economic Diplomacy, 1916–1923* (New York, 1980): idem, 'Versailles after Sixty Years', *JCH* 17 (1982), pp. 487–506. See also Krüger, *Außenpolitik*, pp. 51–4.

make the Fourteen Points the basis for the coming peace negotiations in Paris.[12]

Such will-o'-the wisp visions, however, were joined to a hard-headed attempt to exploit Allied anxiety over Bolshevism. Primarily a tactic to win the sympathy and support of Washington and London, Berlin's repeated references to the danger of Soviet revolution in Germany sought to capitalize on widespread concern in the West that without Allied support the Ebert government would soon fall. The Allied fear of Bolshevism was useful, since Germany's hand might be strengthened at the peace conference if British and American fears could be manipulated.[13] Indeed, the fear of soviet revolution in Germany had been a crucial factor for Allied political leaders in their consideration of an armistice in November 1918, against the advice of their generals, who advocated continuing the war until Germany's armies were destroyed in the field.[14] During the peace negotiations, therefore, Brockdorff-Rantzau made every effort to convince the Allies that Bolshevism would find its ideal breeding ground in the political and economic collapse of Germany; surely, he argued, this could not be in the interests of the West.[15] At the same time, Berlin encouraged negotiations with political and military figures from the victorious coalition,[16] hoping that by talking to American, British, French and Italian representatives perhaps Germany could drive a wedge between the Allies, creating conditions favorable to German peace demands. In these conversations, German representatives continually stressed their support for Wilson's Fourteen Points, in the hope of gaining American support in the coming peace negotiations.

Why exactly did the German delegation feel that American proposals gave a possibility of lenient peace terms? Since the first weeks of

12. Schwabe, in Knapp et al., *USA und Deutschland*, pp. 26–31.
13. See in this connection Paul Kennedy, *The Realities Behind Diplomacy. Background Influences on British External Policy, 1865–1950* (London, 1981), pp. 209–10, 215; Wengst, *Brockdorff-Rantzau*, p. 94 Mayer, *Politics and Diplomacy*, p. 233.
14. K. Schwabe, 'Die amerikanische und die deutsche Geheimdiplomatie und das Problem eines Verständigungsfriedens im Jahre 1918', *VZG* 14 (1971), pp. 1–32; N. G. Levin, Jr., *Woodrow Wilson and World Politics. America's Response to War and Revolution* (London, 1968), p. 139. In the end, however, the Germans were not particularly successful in this regard, for, as Craig points out, it was only in the light of Béla Kun's threatened takeover in Hungary that the Allies paid heed to Germany's domestic conditions: 'But Bela Kun did not last, and the advocates of a Carthaginian peace had their way.' Craig, *Germany*, p. 425.
15. Brockdorff-Rantzau, Memorandum, 21 January 1919, quoted in Mayer *Politics and Diplomacy*, p. 233.
16. See F. T. Epstein, 'Zwischen Compiègne und Versailles. Geheime amerikanische Militärdiplomatie in der Periode des Waffenstillstandes 1918/1919. Die Rolle des Obersten A. L. Conger', *VZG* 3 (1955), pp. 412–45; Schwabe, 'Geheimdiplomatie'; L. Haupts, 'Zur deutschen und britischen Friedenspolitik in der Krise der Pariser Friedenskonferenz. Britisch-deutsche Separatverhandlungen in April–Mai 1919?', *HZ* 217 (1973), pp. 54–98.

1918, the cabinets of Europe had been fully aware of Wilson's Fourteen Points and it was widely assumed (most strongly in Berlin) that the president's proposal would be the basis for peace negotiations. From the spring of 1918, German and American officials met in secret to discuss the possibility of a separate peace. During these contacts American agents encouraged the Germans to formulate their peace proposals around the Fourteen Points.[17] Over and above this, the United States, with its overwhelming economic, military and political potential, had decisively influenced the outcome of the war. Naturally enough, the German leadership envisioned the American proposals as occupying a central position in the coming peace negotiations.[18]

Wilson intended to promote new patterns of international relations which he felt would produce lasting peace. A League of Nations seemed to him to offer the best means of assuring world peace through international organization;[19] it promised not only peaceful settlement of political disputes but, in the event of aggression, the possibility of collective economic or military sanctions against violators of the peace.[20] The Wilsonian spirit of collective cooperation was epitomized in the expression, 'a peace without victors or vanquished', an idea naturally appealing strongly to Berlin. Such a peace, stressing cooperation among nations would, of course, rest on the basis of national self-determination. It was taken for granted by Wilson and his people that these two principles would produce world-wide economic coop-

---

17. Schwabe, 'Geheimdiplomatie', and idem, in Knapp et al., *USA und Deutschland*, pp. 26–31.

18. Krüger indicates that following the armistice the German government navigated almost exclusively by American lights, which was a mistake: 'Nach dem, wenn auch begrenzten, Erfolg der Anknüpfung mit Wilson konzentrierte man sich auf die Vereinigten Staaten, sowohl im allgemeinen — in der Hoffnung auf den Gegensatz zwischen Amerika und der Entente — als auch mit konkreten handelspolitischen und finanziellen Erwartungen.' Krüger laments the fact that the Wilhelmstraße did not consider the implications of its actions against the more global nature of American interests. Krüger, *Außenpolitik*, pp. 51–2. On the German government's hopes for salvation from Washington, Craig sardonically remarks: 'Having placed their faith in the American President and convinced themselves, by an extraordinary feat of wishful thinking, that the decisions made at Paris would be guided by the spirit of reconciliation that he had expressed in the speech announcing the Fourteen Points, they were outraged to discover that the victors intended to apply that older principle of settlement, *vae victis*.' Craig, *Germany*, p. 424.

19. On the nexus of Wilsonian peace plans, particularly those on economic matters and the League of Nations, see Levin, *Woodrow Wilson*, pp. 123–82; Kennedy, *Realities*, p. 211; Trachtenberg, 'Versailles after Sixty Years', pp. 489–93; Raymond J. Sontag, *A Broken World, 1919–1939* (New York, 1971), p. 6.

20. According to Kennedy, however, British diplomats viewed the League as the means by which to *adjust* the treaty settlement. Lloyd George went so far as to remark in the Commons in July 1919: 'I look forward to the League of Nations to remedy, to repair, to redress ... [it] will be there as a Court of Appeal to readjust crudities, irregularities, injustices.' Kennedy, *Realities* pp. 219–20.

eration. The United States proposed to extend the 'open door' to Europe.[21]

It was just these economic points which demonstrated American material interests in Europe. US policy was aimed in the first instance at recovering the massive sums invested in the Allies during the war. The economic and financial influence of the United States in Europe, despite political isolationism, became an essential factor in postwar European, and particularly German, politics.[22] This became clear in the reparations question, where the Americans sought to prevent the Allies from shifting the burden of their war debts owed to the United States onto a defeated Germany. According to Klaus Schwabe, American negotiators were successful in maintaining the separation of war debts from German liability:

> The American negotiators were actually able to prevent the question of Entente debts [to America] from being raised at the Paris [Peace] Conference at all, and in so doing to prevent the extension of German liability to include all war-related costs [i.e., Entente debts].[23]

The peace objectives of the French government appeared to be diametrically opposed to those of America.[24] Publicly, France intended to use the Allied victory to secure at the conference table that which had eluded her in four years on the battlefield. Without question the central goals of French planners were the elimination of Germany as a potential enemy once and for all, together with the protection, indeed institutionalization, of what France saw as her hard-won military advantage over Germany on the European continent. The past and future rivalry between France and Germany, contends G. Schulz, dominated French peace proposals: 'French concerns manifested during the [Paris Peace] conference centered on security guarantees against Germany, considered indispensible in view

21. Walter A. McDougall, 'Political Economy versus National Sovereignty: French Structures for German Economic Integration after Versailles', *JMH* 51, 1 (1979), pp. 10–11; Trachtenberg, 'Versailles after Sixty Years', *passim*.

22. McDougall, 'Political Economy', p. 11. See also Marks, *Illusion*, p. 3: 'Yet America, to whom most states directly or indirectly owed enormous sums of money, had no territorial or economic claims and no financial demands beyond the substantial one of debt repayment, a burden to be levied on the victors, not on the foe.' See also K. Schwabe, 'Die Vereinigten Staaten und der Frieden in Europa, 1919 und 1945', in *Historia Integra. Festschrift für E. Hassinger*, H. Fenske, W. Reinhardt and E. Schulin, ed. (Berlin, 1977), pp. 392f; and Sally Marks, 'The Myth of Reparations', *CEH* 3 (1978), pp. 231–55.

23. Schwabe, 'Die Vereinigten Staaten', p. 395.

24. Levin, *Woodrow Wilson*, pp. 125, 146f; Trachtenberg, 'Versailles after Sixty Years', pp. 489–94. More recently, on French foreign policy immediately following the war, see J. Jacobson, 'Strategies of French Foreign Policy after World War I', *JMH* 55, 1 (1983), pp. 78–95.

of the loss of Russia as an alliance partner, and — directly related — on maintaining a permanent influence over the left bank of the Rhine.'[25] Territorial considerations were thus at the heart of French security demands.[26] In the West, besides Alsace-Lorraine (whose return went without question) French public opinion demanded the Saar, whose strategic value was as much economic as military. At the same time, French hardliners like Raymond Poincaré and General Charles Mangin hoped to detach the Rhineland Republic from Germany and to support it as an autonomous territory under French protection, *desiderata* not entirely shared by either Clemenceau or Marshal Foch.[27] But French aims did not stop with the annexation or political control of German land in the West; France supported cession of German Eastern territory to the newly created states of Poland and Czechoslovakia, so surrounding Germany with an alliance system as to keep her in political and military check.[28]

French negotiators also pursued economic aims as well as territorial aims at the peace conference.[29] Although France evinced a willingness throughout the proceedings to settle for more moderate reparations, in the end she demanded a substantial sum. Reparations served two functions: the most immediate effect would be to supply the French economy with the capital required for reconstruction, contributing, in Walter McDougall's terms, to French domestic stability by 'exporting' financial problems and thus avoiding internal unrest. Less immediate,

---

25. G. Schulz, 'Die Probleme des Friedensschließens und die Verhandlungen der Versailler Friedenskonferenz', in Kolb, *Vom Kaiserreich zur Weimarer Republik*, p. 286.

26. On the meaning of *sécurité* to France, see, among others, Arnold Wolfers, *Britain and France Between Two Wars* (New York, 1966), pp. 20ff. Wolfers and others were given to believe that for France security meant above all the separation of the Rhineland from Germany. But as Robert McCrum has shown, Rhineland separatism was an issue upon which little consensus reigned within either the French government or military circles. Robert McCrum, 'French Rhineland Policy at the Paris Peace Conference, 1919', *The Historical Journal* 21, 3 (1978), pp. 623–48, especially p. 636.

27. McDougall, 'Political Economy', pp. 13–4. McDougall's comments in his article in the *Journal of Modern History* are a superb distillation of his equally superb book, *France's Rhineland Diplomacy, 1914–1924. The Last Bid for a Balance of Power in Europe* (Princeton, 1978), in which he discusses French plans for a separate Rhineland state in great detail. And see K. D. Erdmann, *Adenauer in der Rheinlandpolitik nach dem Ersten Weltkrieg* (Stuttgart, 1966); H. Koller, *Separatismus* (Berlin, 1976); McCrum, 'French Rhineland Policy', *passim*.

28. Kalervo Hovi, *Cordon Sanitaire ou Barrière de l'Est? The Emergence of the New French Eastern European Alliance Policy, 1917–1919* (Turku, Finland, 1975), pp. 11–21, 215–7.

29. McDougall, 'Political Economy', *passim*; M. Trachtenberg, 'Reparations at the Paris Peace Conference', *JMH* 51, 1 (1979), p. 52. Trachtenberg contends that France 'had no desire to use reparations as a way of crushing Germany. . . '. Nevertheless, Trachtenberg never does deny the fact that in French calculations, reparations became a means of limiting German potential. Indeed, the Treaty of Versailles contained numerous provisions, which were intended to restrict Germany's economic position on the Continent far into the future.

but more important in the long run, the financial and economic burden of reparations could set limits to Germany's economic potential.[30] Although, as Marc Trachtenberg shows, 'Clemenceau hoped to base the peace on the effective continuation of the wartime Alliance', if necessary France was prepared to press her territorial and financial claims against Germany despite the objections of her former allies.[31] These four aims, which were designed to leave France in a position of *sécurité* as far as Germany was concerned, colored the peace negotiations and came to have a profound effect on international politics during the succeeding decade.

Great Britain is usually seen as occupying a middle position among the Allies; British peace proposals were neither as lenient as those of the United States nor as severe as those of France.[32] London shared with Paris the desire to reduce Germany's threat as a potential enemy. Yet, at the same time, London's interests coincided with those of Washington, since British economists believed that only an economically stable, anti-Bolshevik, crisis-free Germany represented a genuine guarantee for a peaceful Europe. Then, too, both the US and British businessmen and bankers hoped to resume their prewar volume of trade with their enemy, something which depended heavily on stable political and financial conditions in Germany. For London the timing was critical: the British Empire had already reached its political and economic zenith. Britain would be increasingly occupied with Empire reform and with her own domestic economic crisis. It was in her interests to work toward the most peaceful European climate possible.[33] A return to the traditional British 'balance of power' policy would afford greater diplomatic latitude, so that her energies could be devoted to domestic problems. Already visible here are the outlines of the British appeasement policy during the late 1920s and 1930s.[34]

30. McDougall, 'Political Economy', p. 9.

31. Trachtenberg, 'Reparations at the Paris Conference', p. 28; McDougall, 'Political Economy', p. 14: 'France truly needed reparations, given Anglo-American intransigence on war debts and loans and internal resistance to taxation or devaluation.' See also C. Maier, 'The Truth about the Treaties?', *JMH* 51 (1979), p. 58.

32. Trachtenberg argues that in the matter of reparations Britain in reality pressed for much higher compensation than did France, who, in his view, actually favored more modest reparations, but was pushed by Anglo-American influence into more extreme demands. Trachtenberg, 'Reparations', pp. 36–7. On the ambivalent position of Great Britain, see Levin *Woodrow Wilson*, pp. 146f; and Kennedy *Realities*, pp. 199–220.

33. On the transition of the British Empire to Commonwealth, see A. J. P. Taylor, *English History, 1914–1945* (Oxford, 1965); C. L. Mowat, *Britain Between the Wars, 1918–1940* (London, 1968), pp. 86–8, 109–12; E. J. Hobsbawm, *Industry and Empire* (Harmondsworth, 1971); B. Porter, *The Lion's Share. A Short History of British Imperialism, 1850–1970* (London, 1975), pp. 259–302. A. Orde, *Great Britain and International Security, 1920–1926* (London, 1978).

34. This is the conclusion reached by Kennedy and argued forcefully in a chapter entitled, 'The Politics of Appeasement, 1919–1939', Kennedy, *Realities*, pp. 221–312.

The diverse and often incompatible aims of the Allies produced long and bitter negotiations at the Paris Peace Conference.[35] Gerhard Schulz considers that little could have been done to avert the effects of the rivalry between the different peace programs:

> . . . In truly fateful fashion, errors in organization and planning had a lasting effect on all participants in the conference. War aims were abundant, but their very abundance and scope diminished the chances of carefully considered and measured plans for a peace conference whose authority could rest on its broad basis. . . Neither before nor after the conclusion of armistice was the Peace Conference in any sense prepared for the magnitude of the task before it.[36]

In short, the outcome satisfied none of the victors completely.[37] Disappointment was perhaps greatest among the Americans, while at the time statesmen in France seemed most content.

In the long run, however, it appeared that the United Kingdom had gained most from the long, drawn-out negotiations, while across the Atlantic bitterness grew. America, conscious of a wasted effort, in quick succession refused to ratify either the treaty or US entry into the League of Nations. Dissatisfaction with what appeared an obvious rebuff of American peace proposals, coupled with Wilson's tactical blunders both at the peace conference and in the treaty fight at home, strengthened the American inclination to withdraw from the European mess behind the cover of isolation and George Washington's Farewell Address.[38] Never an 'allied power', the U.S. had preferred the role of 'associated power', a position which facilitated disengagement from the peace process. Having withdrawn, Washington brought hostilities

---

35. Marks, *Illusion*, p. 11; Mayer, *Politics and Diplomacy*, pp. 753–812; D. R. Watson, 'The Making of the Treaty of Versailles', in N. Waites, ed., *Troubled Neighbours: Franco-British Relations in the Twentieth Century* (London, 1971), pp. 67–99; Taylor, *English History*, pp. 133ff; on the contrasting British and French peace proposals, see L. Kochan, *The Struggle for Germany* (New York, 1963), p. 17; see also M. Gunzenhäuser, *Die Pariser Friedenskonferenz 1919 und die Friedensverträge 1919/1920. Literaturbericht und Bibliographie* (Frankfurt a.M., 1970).

36. Schulz, 'Die Probleme des Friedenschließens', p. 286.

37. McDougall, 'Political Economy', p. 12; Trachtenberg, 'Versailles After Sixty Years'; Schulz, 'Die Probleme des Friedensschließens'.

38. Ibid., p. 282: 'Unbestritten ist, daß Wilson während der Konferenz einige seiner wichtigsten Thesen aufgegeben und Teile seiner Kongreßbotschaft vom Januar 1918 revidiert hat. Doch jüngere historische Forschung . . . hat erkannt, dass Wilsons Scheitern in Paris weder auf einem Mangel an Charakter noch auf einem Mangel an Energie oder an geistigen und körperlichen Kräften beruhte. Er scheiterte an objektiven Umständen, denen er ebensowenig wie irgendein anderer Staatsmann dieser Zeit wirkungsvoll genug entgegenzutreten vermochte. Auf den Gang der Verhandlungen aber und auf die Stellung und das Ansehen des amerikanischen Präsidenten wirkte sich verhängnisvoll aus, daß Wilson sich nicht mehr auf die Meinung und auf den Willen der Mehrheit in den Vereinigten Staaten stützen konnte.'

officially to an end by separate bilateral agreements with Berlin, Vienna and Bucharest.[39]

What was the nature of this treaty to which America objected so strongly, and what were its implications for Germany? The fundamental aim of the Versailles treaty system was to strip Germany of its Great Power status and thereby eliminate Germany as a potential aggressor for all time. Several means were employed to this end. Most immediately, Germany suffered the loss of numerous frontier territories, such as Alsace-Lorraine to France, Eupen-Malmédy to Belgium, Upper Silesia and most of Posen and West Prussia to Poland, North Schleswig to Denmark and the Hultschin District to Czechoslovakia. The Saarland was placed under French administration for fifteen years. Important strategic bridgeheads along the Rhine remained occupied by Allied troops, and the Rhineland was demilitarized and occupied by the same Allied forces. Germany's armed forces were reduced to 100,000 men, including 15,000 sailors. Offensive weapons were prohibited altogether, and, finally, her colonies were seized. Moreover, on top of the territorial losses from Germany proper, amounting to one-seventh of the Reich and one-tenth of the population, which were aimed at reducing the country's military potential to an absolute minimum, there were added economic burdens concentrated in the reparations demands of the Allies.

'The reparations clauses were among the least read, most written about, least understood, and most controversial sections of the Versailles Treaty', notes Sally Marks.[40] In addition to immediate and long-term deliveries to the Allies of material goods, Germany faced substantial financial demands from her former enemies. Her only hope lay in the fact that the Allies themselves could not agree on the final amount demanded or on a schedule of payments. Again Marks: 'The quarrel over reparations was so fraught with political implications that the Big Four eventually decided to make Germany responsible for a much narrower but somewhat expanded range of specific categories of largely civilian damages.' Because of their failure to agree, the negotiators accepted reparations in principle but left the precise amounts and manner of payment to be determined by later conferences.

In principle, an indemnity was nothing new in peace settlements.

39. The United States concluded separate treaties with Germany, Austria and Hungary. The German-American peace treaty was signed on 25 August 1921. In these acts there was no mention of either the League of Nations or war guilt. Reparations, however, remained as part of the treaties, in compensation for civil damages suffered in the course of hostilities.

40. Marks, *Illusion*, p. 12; *idem*, 'Myths'. Marks' most comprehensive treatment of reparations can be found in S. Marks, *Innocent Abroad. Belgium at the Paris Peace Conference of 1919* (Chapel Hill, 1981), pp. 170–205.

Traditionally, an indemnity served a twofold function: to reconfirm victory through compulsory surrender of treasure by the vanquished to the victor and to reimburse the victor. An indemnity thus symbolized defeat. But that contemplated by the victors at the Paris Peace Conference served new and different purposes. As with an indemnity, reparations were obviously intended to compensate the victorious Allies for their losses, in particular France and Belgium, whose soil had seen the worst of the fighting and whose economies were seriously crippled as a result. But reparations were not merely symbolic of a lost war; they were linked indirectly to the principle that sole responsibility for the outbreak of war was to be borne by Germany. Reparations, then, became in German eyes symbolic of guilt, a fact strongly suggested by the existence of Article 231 of the treaty, which from its first appearance became known as the 'war guilt clause'. Furthermore, as the Allies began to assess the dimension of economic dislocation in France and Belgium, France felt that reparations should also be a means of permanently limiting Germany's economic, and hence military, potential.

One lesson of the war lost on none of the belligerents was the military and strategic importance of national economy. Before the war, accelerating German economic development had caused grave concern to Britain and France; between 1900 and 1914 German industry outpaced both Britain and France. Even before the war, France was concerned about German industrial development in 1918 she was deeply troubled by the predictions of economists and demographers whose figures unambiguously indicated that, barring extraordinary measures, in a few years Germany would win the peace. There were several reasons for this dark prophecy. The French economy lay in ruins. Concentrated in the Northeastern departments, much of her industry had fallen to the Germans in the opening weeks of the war, or, if not immediately captured, had been damaged or destroyed during the ensuing four years of fighting. The German economy, on the other hand, remained untouched; poised, Allied economists calculated, to convert from wartime to peacetime production and to strike a potentially fatal blow to its struggling French counterpart. Without severe restrictions on the German economy, coupled with vehement efforts to resuscitate the French economy, the outcome was foregone. Reparations, therefore, seemed to promise the only means of averting almost certain disaster.

Had the Germans not allowed themselves to pin such high hopes on Wilson's Fourteen Points,[41] the treaty prepared by the Paris Peace

41. See note 17, above.

Conference might not have seemed so vindictive. Many Germans could not see beyond the contradiction between the actual treaty and the Wilsonian principle of 'peace without victors'. They were unable to reconcile the Fourteen Points with territorial losses resulting from (in German eyes) dubious plebescites; or with the eventual amount and duration of reparations; or with the war-guilt question, biting so deeply into German national pride. For them, the Treaty of Versailles was the *Diktat* of the victors, something which could never be accepted.[42] And more than any other facet of the treaty, the concept of war guilt was despised by the German people, all the more so for its association with reparations.[43] Despite the objections of the Americans, who sought what they called 'impartial justice', the French negotiators succeeded in saddling Germany with collective responsibility for the war. The lasting resentment left by the 'war-guilt clause' Article 231 of the treaty seemed to Germans to give the lie to the Wilsonian principle that the treaty settlement should create a stable and lasting framework for peace. A very real opportunity for long-term peace was missed, laments Haupts:

> The readiness for peace among the Germans was neither heeded, nor seriously considered; although Allied financial experts [at the Peace Conference] all began with the same premise, their deliberations quickly diverged. Power struggles, as well as domestic pressures on each delegate, deprived the Allied statesmen of the room necessary to make a peace with understanding.[44]

At virtually every political level, Germans considered the treaty a searing wound to their national pride and a deep affront to the German character. The unanimous condemnation of the treaty in Germany as a *Diktat* obscured the possibility of political understanding and cooperation between victors and vanquished, which could have reduced the

42. Schulz, 'Die Probleme des Friedensschließens', p. 280: 'Aber in der Friedenskonferenz offenbarte sich eine andersartige Wirklichkeit. Der "Covenant" der verbündeten Nationen des Krieges nahm ein anderes Aussehen an, als ihm zugedacht war, und er hinterließ eine scheinbar unüberwindbare Kluft zwischen den Gegnern des Weltkrieges. Aus ihm ging nicht unmittelbar der Frieden hervor, sondern eine neue Gegnerschaft, die an die Gegensätze der Kriegszeit anknüpfte.'

43. Amid the recent debates surrounding reparations, one traditional scholar has held up particularly well. While some apologists for France and Britain speak of 'astronomical figures bandied about Paris', (Schuker) and the 'truly colossal sum' demanded by France (Kennedy), Hajo Holborn's assessment of almost twenty years ago remains temperate and judicious. Holborn pointed out that the author of Articles 231–2, the young John Foster Dulles, spoke of German responsibility, not guilt. 'Only the German's feverish conviction that the treaty was bound to contain a statement on Germany's sole war guilt made them seize upon Article 231', H. Holborn, *A History of Modern Germany, 1840–1945* (New York, 1969), pp. 564–5.

44. Haupts, *Deutsche Friedenspolitik*, p. 417.

international tensions left by the war.[45] The combination of a genuine longing for peace on the one hand and old power-political interests on the other, produced in Germany the fervent desire for immediate treaty revision, as well as deep feelings of vengefulness. That the victors could not, or would not, balance national interests in the new international system simply transmitted prewar tensions into the post-war world, and, Schulz maintains, thereby allowed nationalism not merely to survive but to increase.[46]

Neither the war nor the Peace Conference had dissipated old tensions; and now those new forces on the political stage — the United States and Soviet Russia — both withdrew from European affairs immediately after the war. As G. Kotowski has said:

> In effect, it felt like the time before 1914. For Briton and Frenchman alike, this meant that they could only maintain their position of world hegemony if they succeeded in subjugating Germany. The opposite idea dominated German thinking, that Germany could only recover her Great Power position if she succeeded in destroying French hegemony.[47]

The new European order fashioned at Versailles thus offered both victor and vanquished opportunities to renew their traditional prewar power politics and to continue the old rivalries more or less unchanged.

With the Treaty of Versailles, Great Britain realized her central war aim: the destruction of Germany as a rival. The sabre-rattling aggressive German Reich which had sought its 'place in the sun' was emasculated. No longer an immediate overseas threat to Britain, Germany's loss of her colonies, her navy and her army reduced her influence from global to continental.[48] Moreover, if an Anglo-American guarantee of French security were avoided and the establishment of a Rhenish separatist state frustrated, Whitehall was optimistic that a continental balance of power could be re-established. As long as Germany was not completely enfeebled — and that was the trick — she remained a significant barrier to Bolshevik advances into Western Europe, as well as a potential counterweight to France.[49]

45. Levin, *Woodrow Wilson*, pp. 154ff; Holborn places responsibility squarely on the shoulders of his countrymen: 'For a Germany that would make Europe's peace the exclusive goal of her foreign policy, opportunities for leadership were by no means closed forever by the Versailles Treaty. John Maynard Keynes was utterly mistaken when he called it a "Carthaginian peace"', Holborn. p. 577.

46. G. Schulz, *Deutschland seit dem Ersten Weltkrieg, 1918–1945*. (Göttingen, 1976), p. 51.

47. G. Kotowski, 'Die Weimarer Republic zwischen Erfüllungspolitik und Widerstand', in H. Rössler, ed., *Die Folgen von Versailles* (Göttingen, 1969), p. 151.

48. Taylor, *English History*, p. 133.

49. Kennedy, *Realities*, pp. 212–20.

At first glance, however, the immediate postwar situation appeared even brighter for France than for Britain. She had accomplished her most obvious goal: the recovery of Alsace-Lorraine. Even more alarmed about German military potential than Britain, France considered German disarmament, coupled with interallied military control, as satisfying a major war aim. Furthermore, France's western frontier was now secured by international guarantee, and the detachment of the Saarland from Germany strengthened her hand against the old enemy in economic affairs. The imposition of reparations, moreover, apparently guaranteed that on the one hand Germany's economy could not become too powerful, while on the other it promised France the necessary capital to reconstruct her shattered economy.[50] Finally, for both Britain and France, the League of Nations would institutionalize and perpetuate their victor status in the postwar order.

Parallel to the treaty, France would build a system of alliances to fill the security gaps in the Versailles settlement. From the ruins of the four fallen empires — the Habsburg, Hohenzollern, Romanov and Ottoman dynasties — there rose a series of secondary and tertiary states in Central and Eastern Europe and among them France fashioned her new alliances. These client states, sanctioned by the Treaty of Versailles, formed a *cordon sanitaire* whose function was twofold: to provide a breakwater in Eastern Europe against which the red tide of soviet revolution could crash harmlessly and, equally important to Paris, to encircle Germany completely with an alliance system linked to France.[51]

The Versailles Treaty system seemed to present Britain and France with substantial realization of their wartime aims, as well as a framework for institutionalizing the Allied victory. But what, if any, advantages did it offer Germany? Despite the very real loss of power and territory, the Versailles system did provide some genuine benefits for the infant republic. Although from a military standpoint the German Reich was virtually defenseless, she still possessed other 'weapons' for deployment in the altered European power constellation and these soon proved effective. Despite the losses, the largest part of her territory was still intact. Although defeated, partly occupied, completely disarmed and diplomatically isolated, the German nation re-

50. As Trachtenberg has amply demonstrated, however, what the public perceived as a victory was in fact a severe setback for Clemenceau and his lieutenant Louis Loucher. When Anglo-American intransigence on reparations forced Clemenceau to accept a higher figure than he had intended, the prime minister found no difficulty in getting public acceptance for a higher figure. Trachtenberg, 'Reparations', *passim* and 'Versailles after Sixty Years', *passim*. Likewise, McCrum shows that when the Anglo-American guarantee treaty fell through, France had to settle for a fifteen-year occupation of the Rhineland. McCrum, 'French Rhineland Policy', p. 636.
51. Hovi, *Cordon Sanitaire . . .?*, pp. 11–21, 215–7.

mained a nucleus constituting the most powerful industrial force on the continent. There were other advantages: as an organ of collective security, the League of Nations offered Germany the same long-term guarantee of security conferred on France. Even the loss of her colonies and consequent restriction of Germany to the European continent had a liberating influence on the long-impaired Anglo-German relationship, soon producing a dramatic improvement in relations. And the same restriction allowed Germany to concentrate on strictly continental affairs, notably in Eastern Europe.

The newly created states of Eastern and Southeastern Europe offered Germany almost unlimited opportunities for economic and political influence. In addition, new options in terms of power politics and alliances opened up in the wake of the treaty, greatly extending the range of German political influence. The collapse of the Habsburg Empire cut the recent ties with Austria making an improvement in German-Russian relations possible for the first time since 1890. Not since the Bismarck era had Germany been able to focus her economic and political attention entirely on continental Europe. Thus, argues Hermann Graml, what seemed at first glance to be the forfeiture of Germany's coveted Great Power status would in the event emerge as an improvement in her diplomatic position:

> Without question, Germany was for the time fettered by the Treaty of Versailles. Nevertheless, the concept of the 'fetters' or 'chains' of Versailles does not suggest that Germany believed herself without freedom of [political] maneuver. The recovery of [political] maneuverability was by no means considered an impossible task.[52]

Sadly, however, the original intention to construct a political order in Europe which would guarantee lasting peace fell prey to national interests. The Versailles Treaty temporarily shored up the fragile British Empire. France, briefly elevated with Anglo-American help to the heights of influence of Europe, appeared to have been granted protection against the Great Power potential of Germany. But the treaty aroused in Germany the will to resist the postwar international order or, at the very least, to work for its revision.

52. Graml, *Europa*, p. 81.

2
The Limits of German Foreign Policy, 1919–1923

Foreign Policy in the Shadow of Domestic Crisis

From the signing of the Versailles Treaty to the end of the Ruhr Crisis, German foreign policy was decisively influenced by domestic affairs. During this period the government had to wage political war on two fronts: the one against the victorious Allies; the other — far more difficult — against the enemies of the republic at home, spanning the entire political spectrum, from unreconstructed monarchists on the Right to Bolsheviks on the Left.

In a climate of acute political tension, there began the transition from monarchy to republic. The fate of the nation seemed suspended between parliamentary democracy and soviet revolution. Amid this confusion, on 9 November 1981, Philipp Scheidemann proclaimed the republic and on the following day the Council of People's Commissars assumed power. Over the objections of the Independent Socialists, the Council decided to convene a National Assembly for the purpose of framing a parliamentary constitution. Nevertheless, throughout Germany, Soviet-style revolutionary governments sprang to life, producing widespread unrest.[1]

Thus arose the paradoxical situation in which the former opponents of Wilhelmine Germany, the Social Democrats, found themselves in the same political bed with the bourgeois parties of the center, indeed, even with the military, in their mutual efforts to save the infant republic from lurching leftwards into a Bolshevik-style revolutionary government. As the result of this 'absurd' alliance, important reforms were sacrificed, even though the SPD had fought for them over decades: for example, socialization of key sectors of the industrial and banking economy, and the general dismantling of the German capitalist system. This was a heavy price indeed, for it meant that the party was irreparably compromised. But the process of change within the

---

1. Kolb, *Arbeiterräte*, passim.

SPD had already begun before the end of the war.

As early as 1916–1917 the Social Democratic Party was shaken by the defection of its left wing. Disaffected left-wing socialists founded the Independent Social Democratic party (USPD), thus heralding the first great split in the German workers' movement. The effect of this division, as Peter Krüger notes, was not immediately apparent during the last days of the war:

> In October and November 1918 the SPD had risen to the position of the leading party in Germany. Nevertheless, the party believed in November that it still had to ally itself with the Wilhelmine establishment, the Army, the Bureaucracy and the Capitalists. Such an alliance enabled the party to overcome the extreme Left, but at the same time, it precluded the possibility of the Socialists achieving any fundamental change in foreign or domestic policies.[2]

The old elites thus benefited from an unbroken continuity from Kaiserreich through revolution to republic. 'Not the revolution', argues Rürup, 'but rather the continuity wrested from the revolution, *that* was the basis of the Weimar Republic'.[3]

The fear that revolution would spread and lead to civil war permeated the deliberations of the Council of People's Commisars. For this reason, the government of Friedrich Ebert, leader of the Council and future president of the republic, concluded an alliance with General Wilhelm Groener, representative of the Army and the traditional elites, with the idea (according to Wehler) of ensuring a peaceful transition from monarchy to republic:

> This pact was intended to provide the new government during the period of the transition before elections, in return for which the mass movement was to be kept in check as an essential requirement in the defence of the *status quo*. For precisely these reasons, it must be regarded as a symbol of the frustration and containment of the revolution.[4]

In aborting domestic revolution, however, the government did not

---

2. P. Krüger, *Deutschland und die Reparationen, 1918/19. Die Genesis des Reparationsproblems in Deutschland zwischen Waffenstillstand und Versailler Friedensschluß* (Stuttgart, 1973), p. 210. See also E. Kolb, 'Internationale Rahmenbedingungen einer demokratischen Neuordnung in Deutschland 1918/19', in L. Albertini and W. Link, eds., *Politische Partien auf dem Weg zur parlamentarischen Demokratie in Deutschland* (Düsseldorf, 1981), pp. 147–76.

3. R. Rürup, *Probleme der Revolution in Deutschland, 1918/19* (Wiesbaden, 1968), p. 5. See also W. Elben, *Des Problem der Kontinuität in der deutschen Revolution. Die Politik der Staatssekretäre und der militärischen Führung vom November 1918 bis Februar 1919* (Düsseldorf, 1965).

4. Wehler, *The German Empire*, pp. 220f.

relieve mounting social pressures. While war ceased at the front, armistice and revolution simply brought it home; world war became civil war as returning soldiers, many still armed and some even organized in *Freikorps* battalions, sought to influence domestic politics.[5]

The German Foreign Ministry, in particular, found its task more difficult in the quasi-civil war of the months after the armistice. The curious relationship of internal and external influences up to the signing of the Versailles Treaty had a profound impact on German foreign policy, crippled by the stalemate in internal conditions. Peter Krüger says: 'The initial concrete foreign policy measures were little more than a reaction to Germany's desperate situation and her helplessness rather than part of a comprehensive foreign policy concept with long-range goals.'[6] With no new foreign policy initiatives formulated by the Council of People's Commissars, the old Wilhelmstraße 'experts' and elites maintained their control over the German foreign policy.[7]

The central task facing German diplomats during the initial phase of the Weimar Republic was to confront the Western Powers and guarantors of the Treaty of Versailles, in the hope of negotiating more liberal peace terms and indeed demonstrating the unrealistic nature of the treaty itself. At the same time, however, prompt and effective measures were needed to combat the efforts of both Bolsheviks and Polish nationalists to annex German territory. This led to a curious situation, in which the Allies' demands for German disarmament and demilitarization conflicted directly with their willingness to use German regulars and *Freikorps* units to secure Germany's eastern borders. Allied insistence on immediate deliveries of reparations in kind, moreover, found the German economy at a particularly delicate stage of conversion from wartime to peacetime production. In Krüger's accurate words:

> Without substantial performance by the economy, payment of reparations was unthinkable; that was probably the most potent argument against the Allies, particularly France, who was simultaneously pressing the patently incompatible demands of full indemnification, together with the longterm weakening of the German economy.[8]

5. See H. Schulze, *Freikorps und Republik, 1918/20* (Boppard, a.Rh., 1969); R.G.L. Waite, *Vanguard of Nazism. The Free Corps Movement in Post-war Germany. 1918–1923* (Cambridge, Mass., 1952).
6. Krüger, *Außenpolitik*, p. 51. See also Krüger, *Reparationen*, p. 57.
7. P.G. Lauren, *Diplomats and Bureaucrats: The First Institutional Responses to Twentieth-Century Diplomacy in France and Germany* (Stanford, 1976); G. Craig, *Germany*, pp. 419–21.
8. P. Krüger, 'Die Rolle der Banken und der Industrie in den deutschen reparations-

The German domestic crisis, marked by general strikes, separatist movements, putsches and 'government by assassination',[9] inhibited exact fulfilment of the conditions in the Treaty of Versailles. In addition, the Reich government intended that the chaos created by the ostensible attempt to carry out every treaty demand to the letter should of itself prove that the requirements of Versailles were impossible to satisfy. It is important to note, therefore, that the 'policy of fulfilment', bitterly ridiculed by the government's domestic political opponents, was ultimately aimed at the relaxation of demands and revision of the Treaty of Versailles.

Amid domestic instability, therefore, the 'policy of fulfilment' was born and symbolized the ambiguous nature of German foreign policy following the signature of the Treaty of Versailles. On the one hand, Berlin was forced to combat internal crisis (partly created by itself) at times by violating the treaty — for example, the use of paramilitary irregulars on Germany's eastern frontiers and in Poland. Ironically, this was encouraged by the self-same Allies who sought to disarm and demilitarize the Reich. On the other hand, Berlin probed for weaknesses both in the treaty itself and in the Allied coalition, hoping to find openings for a more active foreign policy. It was at precisely this initial stage of postwar German foreign policy that the close-knit relationship between domestic and foreign policy was particularly intense. Among the first German initiative toward her chief antagonist — France — were those undertaken by private industrial interests, and it is to the relationship between reparations and private industry that we will now turn.

Reparations and Private Industry

The first initiatives in a more active German foreign policy came from the private industrial sector which, in contrast to the generals and politicians, reacted first and with the most flexibility to the postwar circumstances.[1] Interestingly, it was private industry which was best

---

politischen Entscheidungen nach dem Ersten Weltkrieg', in H. Mommsen, et al., eds., *Industrielles System und politische Entwicklung in der Weimarer Republik* (Düsseldorf, 1974), p. 569.
    9. This term is taken from the title of a book by Hugh Byas, *Government by Assassination* (New York, 1942), in which he describes the political decline of Japan during the 1930s.

    1. The remarkable agility of German industrialists to adapt to postwar conditions and their eagerness to exploit whatever advantages were offered by confusion of demobilization, recession and diplomatic uncertainty are the subject of lengthy analysis in G.

able to mobilize for the transition from war to peace.[2] In response to the pressures of economic mobilization for total war, private industry had entered into a new and critical relationship with the state. Mobilization centralized hitherto decentralized economies, concentrating unparalleled power among a handful of military, political and industrial warlords. As Krüger points out:

> The First World War opened the prospect of an explosive expansion of power. Power was committed; power was at stake. The struggle for power became a struggle for existence. The political leadership did not survive the war; the army lost the war and survived — militarily, if less so politically — only as an institutional nucleus; the economy alone, despite every difficulty, remained intact. . . . Only the economy . . ., motivated by profit, possessed the requisite elasticity to enable it to adapt nimbly to changing conditions. The economy constituted the most important source of power left possible to Germany.[3]

Two severe problems confronted Germany and the German economy. Most immediately, drastic steps were necessary to prevent widespread famine. This was vital for the government to avoid domestic unrest and equally so for the German economy to convert from wartime to peacetime production and begin to exert its influence on world markets. Secondly, it was urgent that the government respond to the immediate economic conditions of the Treaty of Versailles. Since the Allies were in no hurry to decide on either the amount of reparations or the method of their payments, short-term demands for surrender of material goods were substituted for some future cash transfer under a schedule of reparations payments. To meet the problem of feeding the nation, exacerbated by Allied demands for material, German economic and industrial leaders developed strategies which at least in part derived from wartime ideas. The starting-point of the industrialists was the knowledge that the French steel industry depended extensively on German coal stocks in the Ruhr; from the outset, then, very practical grounds for Franco-German economic cooperation were apparent.

Hardly had the guns fallen silent in the west when German industrialists were seeking communication with their French counterparts, hoping to create an industrial cartel to produce French steel with

---

Feldman, *Iron and Steel in the German Inflation, 1916–1923* (Princeton, 1977). Trachtenberg points out that early attempts by French officials to reach an understanding on reparations and financial stabilization were rebuffed by Germany.

2. McDougall, 'Political Economy', pp. 15–16.
3. Krüger, 'Die Rolle der Banken . . .', pp. 568f.

German coal. These early contacts, altogether independent of the German Foreign Ministry, were intended to lead to an official meeting on Christmas Day 1918 in Luxemburg.[4] However, this first attempt to insert a measure of Franco-German economic cooperation into the armistice agreement *post terminum* broke on the rock of official French objections. But the semi-official contacts remained unbroken.

Parallel to the Paris Peace Conference, German negotiators offered their French opposite numbers a plan for the exchange of iron and coal as part of the reconstruction of the industrial districts of Northern France by Germany. Since France had already laid claim to German coal, the Germans hoped that by offering such an exchange — and with it the possibility of formal agreement — they could exploit their temporary advantage over France. The French saw through the scheme, however, rejecting it out of hand: they had no intention of joining such a cartel, preferring rather to depend on higher reparations deliveries by Germany. Thus the military confrontation of the First World War extended into postwar economic and political conflict.

France, well aware that a resurgent German economy would soon overwhelm the French economy — creating French dependence on strategic German resources and, indeed, on the German economy itself — sought to prevent such a situation by means of reparations. The French goal, writes Georges Soutou, remained constant: '. . . to extract the economic advantages from military victory, not by weakening German industry, but rather by exploiting it for [French] reconstruction.'[5] The policy pursued was highly complex. In the first place, German economic expansion was to be curtailed and reparations offered an ideal tool. France accordingly demanded raw material supplies, which would be instrumental in reconstructing and revitalizing her economy and permit her at least to match the German economy. For France, however, 'the problem was not merely economic: the French government had succeeded in inserting a clause in the Versailles Treaty requiring Germany to supply considerable quantities of coal to France; in all probability, the French intended to withhold *minette* ore to coerce Germany into making deliveries. In this way the economic rise of France within Europe would be facilitated and the German recovery delayed'.[6]

---

4. Krüger, *Reparations*, p. 137.
5. G. Soutou, 'Der Einfluß der Schwerindustrie auf die Gestaltung der Frankreich-politik Deutschlands, 1919–1921', in Mommsen et al., *Industrielles System*, pp. 546 and notably p. 453: 'Nach dem Scheitern der Wirtschaftsverhandlungen im Frühjahr 1920 und dem Beinahe-Mißerfolg in Spa ging es nach wie vor, wenn auch mit anderen Mitteln um das von Millerand fixierte Ziel: die wirtschaftliche Entwicklung Frankreichs zu sichern und durch Zusammenarbeit mit Deutschland die wirtschaftliche Früchte des Sieges zu ernten.'

Soon after the Paris Peace Conference, the limits of such strategic calculations became evident.[7] Throughout the immediate postwar years, the success of France's reparations policy could be measured by the relationship between French exactions and the response in actual performance by the German economy. Exhausted by excessive reparations, German industry refused to meet all demands. On both sides, the decisive factors were British and American financial and reparations policies.

While reparations policy crystallized in Paris, German economic planners sought to reformulate their policy toward France, since economic relations between the two countries were central to virtually every issue. The German goal was to resume and intensify Franco-German economic relations. Cooperation here would ease the transition from wartime to peacetime economy; a vigorous German economy could then pursue the aim, by no means unrealistic, of inextricably involving the French economy with their own. Soutou writes:

> Industry sought long-term protection of its interests, harnessing both economic and political resources to the service of their goal, which was to recover the position of economic domination enjoyed by Germany in prewar Europe. In this way, the distinction between politics and economics became less and less clear . . . The influence of the industrialists of the Ruhr revealed itself as the decisive factor in German politics.[8]

The influence of the Ruhr industrialists was certainly important: perhaps not a major factor and scarcely the one and only decisive consideration, but rather one of many.

By formulating policy in primarily economic terms, German planners conjured up an outstanding advantage in dealing with domestic political and economic problems. Arguing that reparations were an economic problem, without political implications, German industrialists successfully advanced the notion within political circles that a

---

6. Ibid., p. 543. *Minette* ore was an easily worked low-grade iron ore from the Longwy-Briey basin. Because of a high phosphorous content, it could only be profitably used in German mills employing the Thomas/Gilchrist process.

7. McDougall, 'Political Economy', p. 13: 'Even as the German state claimed bankruptcy from 1919 to 1923, the inflation gave German business an enormous advantage. Playing on the depreciation of the mark, industrialists borrowed heavily at home while underselling competitors abroad. After 1918, Ruhr firms modernized and expanded, liquidated debts, and captured markets, while French metallurgy could not even exploit the liberated minette of Lorraine. By 1922 the unthinkable was occurring: Germany rebounding, with Anglo-American tolerance, while France had achieved neither financial stabilization, nor economic recovery, nor security.'

8. Soutou, 'Der Einfluß . . .'. p. 546.

solution to the reparations question lay outside politics, that is to say, outside the Reichstag. This strong emphasis on the economic dimension of reparations, as Hermann Rupieper points out, enabled German industry to take over the entire question as a national issue. The middle-class majority in the Reichstag willingly deferred the matter to a handful of industrialists, mostly members of the DVP, who thus influenced questions relating to reparations, frequently blocking developments they considered undesirable. 'In foreign affairs matters took an identical course. Various coalition governments retained representatives of high finance and heavy industry as "experts" available whenever the government developed a position on reparations questions.'[9]

From the German perspective, the most difficult challenge was to submit to reparations while simultaneously working to reduce their amount. At the same time, moreover, efforts at reduction could not be allowed to compromise parallel endeavors aimed at increasing Franco-German economic cooperation. Balancing German policy between these two conditions required the greatest agility since, as has been noted, the ultimate aim was to use economic cooperation to enmesh the French industrial economy to the extent that it would finally be subordinated to that of Germany. From the position of industrial domination over her western neighbor, Germany could then openly demand revision of the Versailles Treaty. But such a strategy would not bear fruit overnight: if great rewards were to be reaped, in the short run the German government would have to keep quiet about its true underlying motives. Thus, as Erzberger noted during the Paris Peace Conference, the undeniable domestic political benefits to the Reich government entailed in the policy of 'fulfilment' could not be disclosed to an increasingly disgruntled populace, since in political terms 'fulfilment' was a promissory note with no fixed date of payment.[10] Undoubtedly, disclosure of the implications and real nature of this policy would have considerably reduced domestic political opposition to reparations payments. Yet such an admission would have further convinced France as to the wisdom of her insistence on security.[11]

9. H.J. Rupieper, 'Industrie und Reparationen: Einige Aspekte des Reparationsproblems, 1922–1924', in Mommsen et al., *Industrielles System*, p. 583.

10. Krüger maintains that *Erfüllungspolitik* was neither a change in the direction of German foreign policy, nor a new tactic: 'Die Absicht der Regierung Wirth, nicht nur neue Verpflichtungen zu unterschreiben, sondern mit Entschlossenheit an ihre Erfüllung zu gehen, war kein grundlegender Wandel der deutschen Außenpolitik, auch gar nicht einmal bloß eine neue Taktik, wie oft gesagt wird, denn schon bei Simons tauchte der Vorsatz auf, die Reparationsforderungen soweit wie irgend möglich zu erfüllen, um ihre Undurchführbarkeit zu erweisen.' Krüger, *Außenpolitik*, p. 132.

11. Ibid., p. 133.

In the wake of the Reichstag elections of June 1920, which dealt a mortal blow to the Weimar coalition and crippled the SPD for years to come, unofficial contacts between German and French industrialists came to an unceremonious end. Tension between France and Germany mounted in the series of conferences of 1920–1921.[12] The conflict centered on reparations. As mentioned, the Treaty of Versailles left the details of reparations — such as assessment of the final amount, methods and schedules of payment — for future settlement. During the latter half of 1919 and early 1920 Germany repeatedly demanded that transfer of material and payments be moderated and delayed. In July 1920, Allied representatives meeting in Spa determined the division of reparations among the injured parties. France, who had suffered the most, would receive 52 percent of all reparations, Great Britain 22 percent, Italy 10 percent, Belgium 8 percent and the remainder would be divided among the other claimants. Although at Spa the Allies could agree on how the reparations pie should be divided, they still were unable to decide on the final sum of reparations, which was left for a future date.

That date arrived in May 1921, when, after countless preparatory sessions, the London Reparations Conference convened and at last set the sum demanded of Germany at 132 milliard gold marks. Yet realistic appraisal of the German economy meant that this sum was divided into two parts. Provision was made that, first, Germany should pay 50 milliard gold marks in at most fifty years, at an interest rate of 6 percent on annual payments of two milliard marks. Only after completion of the first stage would the second phase begin, when the remaining 82 milliard gold marks would be paid. However, not even the most optimistic financial experts imagined that Germany would ever pay this second sum: Allied experts may well have already written it off before the conference in 1921. Nevertheless, it was retained in the final reparations calculations. In 1921, domestic political pressures were simply too strong for Allied negotiators to appear anything but uncompromising toward the Germans. Even so, as Schuker clearly indicates, the final sum represented a massive reduction in reparations demands:

> The Reparations Commission actually reached its determination by revising downward the various estimates of loss submitted until it arrived at a figure that Allied statesmen meeting in conference considered an acceptable political compromise . . . In practice, therefore, the London Schedule signified a reduction of the German debt from the astronomical figures bandied about at the peace conference to a sum which, it would fairly be argued, was

12. Ibid., pp. 103–32.

reasonably consonant with German capacity to pay. This schedule, if implemented, would have required Germany to transfer in cash and kind something on the order of 7 percent of its national income — a figure which, while requiring substantial sacrifice, did not represent an insuperable burden for a nation resolved to limit domestic consumption sufficiently to meet the levy.[13]

Predictably, the expected German protest against excessive reparations demands was rejected. Instead, the Allies countered with the threat of occupying the Ruhr, unless the German delegation accepted the London settlement as final and non-negotiable. Under threat of punitive military action, Berlin acceded to the London ultimatum.[14]

Minister of Reconstruction Walther Rathenau,[15] later Foreign Minister under Chancellor Josef Wirth, considered that the London ultimatum was not only impossible to fulfil but also immoral. He intended to demonstrate that Allied demands could not be satisfied — and so bring about revision — by attempting to discharge reparations requirements down to the last detail, even if in the process German finance and industry were strained beyond the limits of their resources. This was a dangerous and complex game, for Rathenau faced Allied suspicion that the German government was willfully underestimating the country's ability to pay. Although reparations represented severe economic and financial problems to Germany in 1921, any move to delay or postpone payment was seen by Allied politicians and experts as an attempt to default.[16] At the same time, any show of willingness to pay on the part of the German government was likely to provoke a domestic parliamentary crisis.

Nevertheless, the policy of attempted fulfilment of impossible demands offered the only chance for gradual revision of reparations.[17] The process began immediately. As early as the end of 1921, the

13. In this connection, see also S.A. Schuker, *The End of French Predominance in Europe. The Financial Crisis of 1924 and the Adoption of the Dawes Plan* (Chapel Hill, N.C., 1976), pp. 14f.

14. On the London ultimatum, see C.S. Maier, *Recasting Bourgeois Europe. Stabilization in France, Germany, and Italy in the Decade after World War I* (Princeton, 1975), pp. 245f: 'Submission [by the Germans to the London ultimatum] seemed all the more necessary when the Polish-supported Korfanty rebellion in Upper Silesia broke out on May 3. Unless Berlin accepted the London demands, the French would not only occupy the Ruhr, but through the League of Nations commissioners in Upper Silesia would intervene on behalf of Korfanty's pro-Polish uprising. General Seeckt ruled out any direct German military suppression, presumably because the French warned that war in the West would follow. As in 1919, the Germans apparently had to give in — but who would take responsibility for signing the ultimatum?'

15. D. Felix, *Walther Rathenau and the Weimar Republic. The Politics of Reparations* (Baltimore, 1971).

16. Erdmann, 'Weimarer Republic', pp. 228f.

17. McDougall, 'Political Economy', p. 16.

German government of Chancellor Wirth reported to the Allied Reparations Commission ('REPKO' to the Germans) that Germany would be unable to meet payment of the instalments due in the coming year, and therefore requested a reduction in the payments; moreover, the government did not feel sufficiently secure to undertake the tax increase necessary to meet reparations payments.[18] The aim was to convince the Allies that Germany's capacity to pay was considerably less than originally estimated and that the amounts demanded should be correspondingly reduced. In fact, however, Wirth's policy severely damaged the German economy. Derek Aldcroft has vividly described the dislocation of finance and industry resulting from the German reparations policy:

> The cost of meeting her treaty obligations, including reparations, would cost Germany 80% of her total income [in 1921], and in 1922–1923, cost exceeded income. At the same time, domestic expenditures for economic recovery grew. The tax system, which was not effective to begin with, collapsed under such pressure. The result was massive budget deficits and the resort of the government to the issuance of great quantities of paper money, in an effort to meet its obligations. At the same time, the transfer problems became acute. The obligation to meet cash demands forced the government to weaken further its finances. The government sold large quantities of paper to foreign speculators, liquidated the bulk of Germany's gold reserves and paper investments, which had been retained as currency reserves and used the proceeds from the sale of government bonds and landholdings to pay reparations.[19]

The net effect of such a disastrous financial policy, as Aldcroft indicates, was the rapid intensification of inflation and devaluation. The social effects were catastrophic.

The German leaders believed that by this calculated policy of inflation they could demonstrate Germany's inability to pay reparations and so achieve the desired reduction in reparations.[20] But as

18. Ibid., 'Konrad Adenauer offered to accept the chancellorship in the May 1921 crisis, but only if permitted a national ministry including the right-wing parties, dissolution of the Reichstag's socialization commissions, and a return to the nine-hour day. Seemingly, only a nearly dictatorial government pledged to preserve the social status quo and place the German economy on a war footing could enforce strict taxation, repress particularism, and fulfil the treaty.'

19. D. Aldcroft, *Die Zwanziger Jahre* (Munich, 1978), pp. 101f. (English edition: *From Versailles to Wall Street, 1919–1929*, Berkeley, 1977); see also Maier, *Recasting Bourgeois Europe*, p. 249: 'The Wirth government promised an overhaul of German taxes in June 1921 to meet reparation needs. While existing taxes were based upon Erzberger's tough reforms of 1919, they were levied in paper marks and yielded only a fraction of what had originally been intended. Officials now estimated that, in current paper marks values, obligations to the Allies would require levying 50 [milliard] marks out of a total government expenditure of 100 [milliard].'

20. Marks, 'The Myths of Reparations', *CEH* XI, 3 (1978), pp. 231–55.

Krüger points out, 'for Wirth and Rathenau the export economy was the only remaining hope for improving Germany's internal situation but, even more, improving her external situation. From any standpoint, the economic recovery of Germany would go hand in hand with the restoration of Germany as a Great Power'.[21] Still ambivalent toward German recovery, Britain did not discourage this policy,[22] thereby strengthening Germany's position.[23] Suddenly isolated with respect to reparations, France found herself on the defensive and left with no alternative but to follow a hard line. From his arrival at the helm in January 1922, French Prime Minister Poincaré was in no position to consider any reduction in reparations whatsoever.[24] Out of the conflict over reparations and the loser's ability to pay, clear distinctions began to emerge in the political economic strategies of France, Great Britain and Germany, which would shape every successive reparations conference over the next ten years.

In an effort to achieve her objectives, France felt compelled to seize the political initiative.[25] 'From mid-1922,' says Rupieper, 'the French government was no longer prepared to accept a solution to the reparations problem without [productive guarantees] . . . .'[26] It faced a perplexing problem. On the one hand, the Poincaré government, under pressure from both the Chamber of Deputies and public opinion, demanded reparations payments — both in kind and in cash — to support French reconstruction. On the other hand, French strategists soon recognized that only by increasing her exports could Germany meet her annual reparations obligations. But this would undoubtedly lead to Germany recovering her prewar position of industrial and commercial prominence in Europe. 'Such a development', continues Rupieper, 'was not in the interests of French security, the aim of which was to hold Germany suspended in [her postwar economic and political] dependence.' The dilemma defied solution. If France allowed German exports to climb, her own industry would suffer.[27] Yet

---

21. Krüger, *Außenpolitik*, p. 144.
22. Schuker, *French Predominance*, p. 19. Neutral and Allied financial experts strengthened the hope among German leaders that Germany's economic distress would lead to the revision of reparations. In this connection, see Rupieper, 'Industrie und Reparationen', p. 585. For the British view of German and French reparations policies, see ibid, p. 591.
23. Marks, 'Myths'.
24. Schuker, *French Predominance*, p. 23: 'Poincaré remained unwilling to accept any reduction in reparations that would leave France with less than the amount necessary to rebuild its devastated districts — a sum which, according to French calculations, at least equalled their full 52 percent share of [the 50 milliard gold marks].'
25. McDougall, 'Political Economy', p. 17.
26. Rupieper, *Industrie und Reparationen*, p. 588.
27. McDougall, 'Political Economy', pp. 17–18: 'The occupation of the Ruhr can only be understood within the context of France's triple postwar crisis, which found

without German payments, the French financial situation would become difficult, since London and Washington were demanding settlement of British war loans to France. Until the receipt of German reparations payments, a discharge by France of her war debts to Britain would have most certainly led to the fall of Poincaré's government.[28] Indeed, as Krüger indicates, the outcome of this quandary was the precise opposite of French wishes. In exerting pressure on Germany in hopes of forcing a capitulation to her demands, France inadvertantly strengthened the position of western Germany's heavy industry while at the same time playing into the hands of right-wing German politicians.[29]

Meanwhile, inflation accelerated in Germany, virtually eliminating the possibility of reparations payments in 1922, whilst increasing the probability of domestic crisis. Assassination had become a quasi-legal political weapon. On 29 August 1921 Erzberger was murdered by reactionaries who succeeded in eluding the authorities. An old score with a socialist 'traitor' had been settled. But when, on 24 June 1922, rightwing anti-Semitic assassins cut down Walther Rathenau, Germany lost her ablest proponent of reparations revision. Simultaneously, the widening rift between the Reich government and Bavaria necessitated extraordinary measures by the government under Article 48 of the Weimar constitution. After an unsuccessful bid to create a Great Coalition, Chancellor Wirth resigned. On 22 November 1922 Dr. Wilhelm Cuno, Director of HAPAG Line, formed a 'nonpartisan' government, whose first challenge was the London Reparations Conference in December 1922. Strongly influenced by Hugo Stinnes, the Cuno government precipitated a confrontation with the Allies, demanding the early evacuation of Allied occupation forces from the Rhineland, linked to a four-year moratorium on reparations payments. Once these conditions had been met, the Germans blithely suggested, they would be willing to agree to a final lump-sum reparations payment of 12 milliard gold marks. The Allies laughed this proposal out of court. As 1922 drew to an end, Germany had still not met her reparations obligations for the delivery of timber and coal to France. Her total obligation to France in terms of these raw materials amounted to 1.478 milliard gold marks: by January 1923 she was 24

expression in the reparations/war debts, security, and industrial disputes of the 1920s.'
28. Rupieper, 'Industrie und Reparationen', p. 589; see also Maier, *Recasting Bourgeois Europe*, p. 290: 'Poincaré thus had less domestic room for maneuver. His position became even more unenviable when on July 12, the Germans, citing the new fall of the mark after Rathenau's death, asked for an end to all further cash payments through 1924. At the same time the United States Foreign Debt Commission announced that France's obligations could not simply be postponed indefinitely.'
29. Krüger, *Außenpolitik*, p. 144.

million in arrears. On 9 January 1923, despite objections by the British representative, the French, Belgian and Italian representatives of REPKO declared Germany in default. On 11 January, elements of the French and Belgian armies, accompanied by technical experts, advanced into the industrial heart of the Rhineland, the Ruhr.

German default on coal deliveries and on shipments of timber and telephone poles was the legal justification for the occupation of the Ruhr. But in fact France's motive was far more complex: exactly as in Germany, inadequate wartime taxation, whose inequities and ineffectiveness were magnified by postwar events, was producing swiftly rising budget deficits.[30] In response to the occupation the Cuno government, supported by all political parties, ceased reparations deliveries. Advised by the Reichswehr that military resistance was useless, the government declared 'passive resistance' against the Franco-Belgian forces of occupation.[31] Passive resistance was intended to demonstrate that France's policy of forcing payment by seizing territorial hostages would not be worthwhile. Cuno further hoped that, after forcing an end to Franco-Belgian occupation, Germany would be in a position to negotiate a revision of the scope and amount of reparations. As the result of passive resistance, shipments of strategic materials from Germany to France fell off drastically. 'In the first half-year of the occupation of the Ruhr, Karl Erdmann points out, 'less coal and coke was delivered [to France] than in the last ten days before occupation.'[32]

On the other hand, France was seeking to exert extreme pressure on the German economy, not only in order to compel complete payment of reparations, but also, with a show of force, to slow the gradual revision of the Treaty of Versailles.[33] Poincaré, faced with passive resistance, found himself obliged to answer every such act with military force. But if Paris viewed force as an acceptable means of insuring reparations payments, London did not. Eventually, not German resistance, but that of Britain was the decisive factor in the failure of French policy. British politicians, bankers and industrialists vigorously opposed the French policy of productive guarantees both for strategic

---

30. Rupieper, 'Industrie und Reparationen', p. 589.

31. Schuker, *French Predominance*, p. 25: 'The ministries in Berlin determined every feature of this resistance, from noncooperation by the citizenry, railway workers and factory owners alike, to actual sabotage carried out by paramilitary bands. Characteristically, German government agencies were so thorough that they even developed an effective public relations campaign portraying the resistance as spontaneous.'

32. Erdmann, 'Weimarer Republik', p. 240.

33. Marks, 'Myths', pp. 244–45: 'In applying the ultimate sanction of Ruhr occupation, Poincaré was above all making a final effort to force Germany to acknowledge her defeat in World War I and to accept the Treaty of Versailles . . . .' McDougall, 'Political Economy', p. 18.

and for economic reasons. In August 1922, well before the occupation of the Ruhr, the British government had blocked the transfer of German industrial shares to REPKO, because it 'did not wish to be identified with methods similar to [those of] the Soviet Union'.[34]

Nevertheless, in the bitter test of strength presented by occupation, France held the stronger position.[35] The cost to the German government of 'passive' resistance was far higher than the sum of reparations from 1919 to 1923:

> In the short run nobody suffered financially from the Ruhr crisis except the German people. . . . The German government and state enterprises paid off their domestic debts with worthless inflation marks, while leading German entrepreneurs, such as Hugo Stinnes, who had close ties to the business cabinet of Wilhelm Cuno, took advantage of the situation to buy up failing firms and corner a startling percentage of German national wealth. While the German working class suffered from the runaway inflation, the middle class suffered more, both financially and psychologically.[36]

With the economic collapse of Germany only a matter of days ahead, the Cuno government was forced to seek an immediate solution. In a note to the Allies dated 2 May 1923, the government offered the figure of 30 milliard gold marks as the final sum Germany was capable of paying. The offer was of course refused by France, Belgium, Italy and Great Britain as completely inadequate. In addition, however, the German note contained another more far-reaching proposal, which would come to fruition two years later. In an attempt to accommodate French demands for security, the Cuno government proposed a pact among Western powers, which would guarantee Germany's western frontiers. Although in 1923 this proposal produced no immediate response in Paris or London, within two years the idea of a Western security pact took concrete form in the Locarno Treaties.[37] Both Cuno's initiatives having failed, however, and in view of the rising domestic crisis, the German government was left with no

---

34. Rupieper, 'Industrie und Reparationen', p. 590.
35. Krüger is the latest scholar to see in the occupation of the Ruhr the extension of the First World War — '. . . .eine verbissene Auseinandersetzung . . . mit einer kriegsähnlichen Atmosphäre und voller nationaler Leidenschaft' — which many in Germany considered unavoidable if Germany were to be free from the pressure exerted by France. Krüger, *Außenpolitik*, p. 201.
36. Marks, *Illusion*, p. 51. See also Schuker, *French Predominance*, p. 25.
37. Erdmann, 'Weimarer Republik', p. 241; Schuker, *French Predominance*, p. 24: 'Chancellor Cuno, meanwhile, following the advice of American Ambassador Alanson B. Houghton, suggested a four-power non-aggression pact on the Rhine, according to which the signatory powers would agree not to declare war for a generation without a plebiscite.'

other choice but to end passive resistance and seek an understanding with the Allies.[38]

British policy played a decisive role in the German calculations to liquidate passive resistance in the Ruhr.[39] Though taking great care to remain dissociated from France's unilateral action, and quick to point out what the Foreign Office considered to be the injustice of the Ruhr occupation, the British government was far from giving up its closest ally and supporter. The Foreign Office was severely strained by the Ruhr crisis, which highlighted the conflicting interests of its continental policy. Britain had no interest in seeing France, by means of German coal and French iron, become the dominant economic force on the continent, and so succeed to the hegemonic military position in Europe. But neither had she any intention of dropping her claims to German reparations. The almost paralyzing ambivalence of Great Britain, avers Marks, was the crucial factor in the crisis:

> Had Britain committed herself firmly to either side, the Ruhr episode would have ended quickly, but Britain balanced in the middle, unwilling to break with France or to discipline Germany, and kept trying futilely to bring the warring giants together. Lost in technicalities, the British leaders never realized that they were watching an extension of the First World War. Unfortunately it was to prove in some respects as costly and inconclusive as the war itself.[40]

Thus, the Ruhr conflict was the climax of a decade of warfare. The struggle between Germany and her antagonists, whose military phase ended on 11 November 1918, continued unabated for the next five years. Despite Versailles, or perhaps because of it, the Great War was extended by political and economic means, until political, economic and military warfare came together in the Ruhr conflict to bring the war to an end.[41] The crisis signalled the first test, and the subsequent failure, of a collective policy for the peaceful solution of disputes, as defined by the League Covenant. Similarly, it demonstrated that

---

38. 'Allein, die deutsche Widerstandskraft war am Ende, die Reichsregierung hatte ihre Hauptziele nicht erreicht: Im Innern hatte sich angesichts der zunehmenden Uneinigkeit die Konsolidierung von Währung, Wirtschaft und Finanzen als undurchführbar erwiesen, in der Außenpolitik war der Spielraum zwischen innerem und äusserem Druck zu gering, um Frankreich zu widerstehen und eine Bereinigung der Reparationsfrage zu erreichen.' Krüger, *Außenpolitik*, p. 205.

39. Marks, 'Myths'.

40. Erdmann, 'Weimarer Republic', p. 241; Marks, *Illusion*, p. 50: 'Beyond [the British inability to recognize that France needed the coal from the Ruhr, as well as the cash from the reparations payments for reconstruction] they would not see that what was at stake for France was the survival of the Versailles Treaty and indeed the victory in the war. . . .'

41. Ibid.; Marks, 'Myths', p. 245.

economic cooperation was not yet possible, particularly in the case of French and German private industrial interests, despite their promising immediate postwar contacts.

Even more important, the end of the Ruhr crisis spelled victory for prewar national power politics over the Wilsonian ideals contained in the Fourteen Points. Thus the discrepancy between cooperation and self-interest clearly revealed itself in reparations policy. Although in most of its points the Versailles Treaty may have rested on the uneasy and still incomplete foundation of Wilson's program and on the agreement emerging from the exchange of notes preceding the armistice as Krüger indicates, reparations demands nevertheless ran counter to the Wilsonian spirit of conciliation. The domestic consequences for Germany were severe: 'The size and severity of the reparations demands . . . served as a permanent catalyst for the cooperation between the Right and the SPD in German parliamentary politics, the inexhaustible source of agitation against Versailles.'[42] The Allies, particularly France — who, on security grounds, demanded a long-term barrier to German economic growth — resisted German objections that reparations were too severe. Nevertheless, Poincaré's reparations policy failed to produce anything like German industrial or financial dependence on France; on the contrary, it forced German heavy industrial interests and right-wing nationalists into the same bed. Not surprisingly, many ills of the postwar years were put down to reparations. Only American financial influence and assistance, which by 1924 would lead to the eventual stabilization of the German economy, could bring about the conditions for a permanent solution to the reparations problem.[43] But the Wilhelmstrasse was tempted to see its opportunities as lying either in Washington or in Moscow. Let us turn east, then, to consider what possibilities for German foreign policy lay in Russia.

Toward Rapallo: Alternative to 'Fulfilment'?

With the London Ultimatum of May 1921, the German government realized that no quick solution to the reparations question was at hand. In the wake of the London Conference, this became all the more apparent as the American government still showed no desire to influence the course of reparations policy. To a stalemated, and diplomatically isolated Berlin, improvement of relations with the Soviet Union

42. Krüger, *Reparationen*, p. 213.
43. Maier, *Recasting Bourgeois Europe*, p. 304.

seemed the only remaining option for diplomatic initiative.[1]

Progress in this direction, however, was not without considerable effort. During the long-drawn-out talks at Brest-Litovsk, Soviet and German negotiators developed a working relationship which, while far from friendly, constituted a basis for possible future diplomatic approaches. But by mid-1918, following Brest-Litovsk, German–Soviet relations had begun to deteriorate,[2] and, for a variety of complex reasons (among them the assassination of the German ambassador in Moscow, Wilhelm Count von Mirbach-Harff) sank to a new low in the latter half of 1918. After the deportation of the Russian ambassador in Berlin, Adolf Joffe, in November 1918, formal relations between Germany and Soviet Russia ceased to exist. Military defeat, revolution — even in the streets of Berlin — and the appearance of Soviet-style governments modelled on the Russian example, further prevented any significant diplomatic contact. The government of Prince Max von Baden, the Council of People's Commissars and virtually every political party considered the influence of the Bolshevik Revolution as a danger to Germany. The consequence of the 'defensive struggle against Bolshevism' was the survival of the leading conservative Wilhelmine elites and their influence on the infant German republic.

Germany, of course, was not alone in the fight against communist influence and in fact found considerable sympathy for her resistance to internal communist revolution among her bourgeois antagonists in the West. Although the twin goals of subverting reparations and revising the Treaty of Versailles naturally pitted her against her Western counterparts, Germany nevertheless had to face the fact that she was more Western than Eastern, an orientation reflected in her social and political structure. It could not, however, in the short run outweigh the immediate need to break out of diplomatic isolation: despite her basic Western bias, Germany sought an understanding with Soviet Russia.[3]

Having failed to win favorable peace terms, the republic's chief diplomatic task was the earliest possible modification of the Versailles Treaty. German attention, therefore, was almost wholly centered on France and Britain, and indeed, apart from crippling internal upheaval, her concerns were largely dominated by Western influences — Ver-

---

1. Nicholls, *Weimar and the Rise of Hitler*, p. 78: 'Wirth had quickly begun to lose faith in the possibility of concessions from Britain and France [in mid-1921], although he had not renounced fulfilment. Instead he switched his attention to the east, hoping to strengthen Germany's diplomatic position by drawing closer to Soviet Russia.'
2. E. H. Carr, *Bolshevik Revolution*, v. 3, pp. 86ff.
3. Erdmann, 'Weimarer Republik', p. 231.

sailles, occupation, disarmament, reparations, territorial transfers.[4]

The belated appearance of an Eastern policy was perhaps most clearly evident in German relations with the newly emergent Poland. Throughout the summer and fall of 1919, officials of both countries worked to carry out the transfer of territory from Germany to Poland dictated by the Treaty of Versailles. Berlin instructed German bureaucrats in these territories to remain at their desks to insure as smooth a transfer as possible; however, there was a further, long-term motive. If relations with Poland could begin on such a cooperative note, and Berlin could appear to be fulfilling the letter of her Versailles obligations, von Riekhoff shows, the Reich government believed it could preserve a core of German officials in Poland as a starting-point for a systematic *de-facto* revision of the Versailles Treaty:

> . . . Germany tried to exploit her superior bargaining position by attaching some far-reaching political conditions to the provisional agreements. If the German tactics had succeeded, they would, in part at least, have revised some of the terms of the Versailles Treaty. Count Lerchenfeld, a counsellor in the German Foreign Ministry, had quite openly told the *Reichstag* that the German government should encourage German civil servants and teachers to remain in the ceded territory in order to strengthen the German character of the area and to use this provision as a lever to revise the Versailles Treaty terms on the question of optants and liquidations.[5]

The talks soon moved to Paris, a not unwelcome development in Berlin's eyes, since Germany hoped France would prevail on Warsaw to grant some of Germany's requests on matters of the transfer of the corridor. Yet fears of a growing Polish *détente* with Germany and the possible frustration of key elements in the Versailles treaty led the Allies to put a stop to the talks.[6] This tactic was effective, for German-Polish relations quickly began to cool. Losing what little diplomatic leverage she had over the newly-ceded territories, Germany launched

4. See in this connection G.F. Campbell, *Confrontation in Central Europe. Weimar Germany and Czechoslovakia* (Chicago, 1975), pp. 99f.: 'In its broad outlines German policy aimed at the maintenance of order and stability in Central Europe while German governments wrestled with their domestic problems and their negotiations with the Western powers. At the same time German policymakers hoped to prevent the rise of alliances or commitments that would be inimicable to the reassertion of German interests in Central Europe once Germany had recovered from the war.' Carr echoes the same conclusions, *The Bolshevik Revolution*, v. 3, pp. 109f.: 'The realities of the German situation at the end of 1918 were . . . complex. Germany was prostrate and helpless to do anything on her own account. Every decision about Soviet Russia was bound to present itself as a choice between leaning on Russia or leaning on the western allies. The mutual hostility between east and west made the choice unavoidable . . . The choice could not be in doubt.' See *Ibid.*, p. 306 and p. 317: Until the ratification of the Treaty of Versailles, '. . . the Weimar Republic could still scarcely afford to have a foreign policy'.
5. H.v. Riekhoff, *German–Polish Relations, 1918–1933* (Baltimore, 1971), pp. 24f.
6. Ibid., p. 26.

an economic blockade against Poland in January 1920 with the hope of forcing compensation from Warsaw for a variety of German claims. No agreement was reached, and in the end the blockade, while damaging Poland, also hurt German businessmen; nevertheless, they circumvented it by shipping goods via Czechoslovakia, Austria and Scandinavia. Following the partition of Upper Silesia by the League of Nations in August 1922, which took place despite considerable opposition from the local population, relations between Berlin and Warsaw degenerated almost to the point of rupture.[7]

Earlier, in the cooperative period of transition from German to Polish rule, Poland had sought to expand her Eastern frontiers at the expense of Russia. The embattled Red government, already fighting for its life in the civil war against the White forces, nevertheless struck back and open war broke out. Germany saw in this the possibility of new political gains. Poland's expansionist policy provided a common ground for renewed contacts between German and Soviet officials. Soviet anxieties, already heightened by aggressive operations along the Western frontiers, were intensified by increased Western pressure for discharge of prewar Czarist debts.

The combination of anti-Western, anti-Polish sentiment in Berlin and Moscow produced a rapid thaw in relations. The two had initiated informal contacts in the fall of 1919. By the spring of 1921, the former enemies had already settled the prisoner-of-war exchange question, left unresolved since the end of the war, and had resumed trade talks. Despite the fact that official relations still did not exist, these talks rapidly produced concrete results. Out of the prisoner-of-war exchange, a gradual economic understanding developed. In fact, the cultivation of trade with Russia quickly took on new significance for German foreign policy.[8] By February 1920, as Krüger says, 'the European race for Russia was on'.[9] Two of the earliest contestants were Italy and Germany: in the winter of 1920 Rome had already suggested to Berlin a cooperative approach to Moscow. While nothing came of this, 'Germany was from the beginning a significant factor in Western economic initiatives in Russia'.[10]

German economic interests, however, could not agree as to their country's policy in Russia. As Erdmann points out, 'heavy industry in particular, whose most influencial spokesman was Stinnes, placed great

---

7. Ibid., p. 53.
8. Carr, *Bolshevik Revolution*, v. 3., pp. 320, 364. On the subject of German–Soviet economic relations, see W. Beitel and J. Nötzold, *Deutsch–sowjetische Wirtschaftsbeziehungen in der Zeit der Weimarer Republik*, (Baden-Baden, 1979).
9. Krüger, *Außenpolitik*, p. 115.
10. Ibid.

value on opening direct export opportunities in Russia, while manu-
facturing interests, who counted Rathenau among their number, urged
closer trade relations with the West, due to their much greater dependence on Western raw materials'.[11] Such internal differences within the
economic community, however, did not prevent closer cooperation
between Russia and Germany, since even Western-oriented manufac-
turing interests grasped the market possibilities in Russia.

Both Berlin and Moscow welcomed the resumption and intensification of their economic relations which before 1914 had been very
productive indeed.[12] Yet the German–Soviet talks of 1921 revealed
thinking among German industrialists and diplomats which went far
beyond the mere resuscitation of prewar economic relations. Robert
Himmer indicates that Rathenau and his industrialist colleagues,

> . . . desired to establish [in Russia] an economic domination which would
> enable the Reich to weather its postwar burdens and eventually to become a
> world power of the first rank. They pursued this goal through a flexible
> strategy built around, but not limited to, the consortium — a device they
> inspired.[13]

The Germans proposed a foreign syndicate, composed of Germany,
England, America and possibly France, all of whom would contribute
capital to 'a plan for the revival of a number of branches of the Russian
economy'. Although the Soviets objected to the possible compromise
of their sovereignty, discussions continued. Meanwhile, Berlin sought
the support of other Western capitals. British contacts enjoyed by
Rathenau and other prominent German industrialists played an important role in winning London's blessing. Moreover, the consortium
promised to extend British commercial influence, both directly and
indirectly, in Soviet Russia. Surprisingly, the plan also found support
in Paris, where it was greeted as a means of enhancing Germany's
ability to pay reparations.

It is abundantly clear that in promoting the idea of a consortium,
German planners sought to implement aims cherished by Wilhelmine
industrialists and expansionists, and also to recover some of the
influence won and subsequently lost by Germany in Russia in 1918. It
is possible here to speak, as does Hartmut Pogge von Strandmann, of a
'compulsion to continuity' in German foreign policy:

> In this connection [i.e., the economic dimensions of Russo-German rela-

11. Erdmann, 'Weimarer Republik', pp. 231f.
12. Well before the end of the war German and Soviet industrial leaders had already
begun informal contacts. *Ibid.*, p. 91.
13. R. Himmer, 'Rathenau, Russia and Rapallo', *CEH* IX, 2 (1976), p. 149.

tions] it should be pointed out, that Germany's prewar trade with Russia became a central notion [*Leitvorstellung*] behind the resumption of economic and political pressures, one can probably even speak of a certain 'compulsion to continuity' [*Kontinuitätszwang*].⁴

As early as the second half of the war, the importance of economic ties with Russia in the postwar world was already a frequent topic in Germany. After the October Revolution and the Treaty of Brest-Litovsk, German strategists believed that by means of a future *Ostreich* they could dominate the Ukraine economically, and in fact eventually all Russia. In something of an understatement, Pogge von Strandmann maintains that 'the orientation of Germany's prewar industrialists influenced the reformulation of Germany's goals by industrialists during the war'.¹⁵

As early as August 1915, Rathenau had decided that Germany's future lay in closer relations with Russia than with Britain: Russia was 'our future market [*Absatzgebiet*] . . . We have no anti-Russian interests'.¹⁶ Rathenau's conception of German policy in this area began to crystalize well before the end of the war. In May 1917 he advanced the notion of a separate peace between Austria and Russia, so enabling Germany to penetrate Russia economically under cover of Austria.¹⁷ After the war, Rathenau, in a memorandum dated 17 February 1920, again outlined the case for resumption of trade between the two countries.¹⁸ By means of economic ties, Germany should seek to win political influence in Russia, in order to realize what had been accomplished by force of arms in 1917–1918: an economic *Grossraum* under German domination.

Although German penetration eastward took a new tactical form in the proposed consortium, the idea of Eastern economic domination did not represent any new element in German foreign policy goals. The method remained constant: commercial and industrial development. Nor did the function alter: the extension of German economic — that is, political — influence in Eastern Europe. But in seeking to enlist the Western powers as accessories, indeed underwriters, to the adventure of their former enemy, German thinking had arrived at a new creative level. At the same time, moreover — and this was perhaps the most significant dimension of that thinking — in the consortium

14. H. Pogge von Strandmann, 'Großindustrie und Rapallopolitik. Deutsch-sowjetische Handelsbeziehungen in der Weimarer Republik', *HZ* 222 (1976), p. 269.
15. Ibid., p. 262.
16. Rathenau to Bethmann, 30 August 1915, in Walther Rathenau, *Politische Briefe* (Dresden, 1929), pp. 45ff.
17. Ibid., p. 272.
18. Ibid., p. 282.

Germany intended first to establish equal status with her Western partners (*Gleichberechtigung*) and aimed eventually to come to a position of dominance. In this way, the Eastern-oriented members of the government hoped, Germany could win revision of the Treaty of Versailles, not by way of Paris or London, but through Moscow.

The cooperative effort of Germany and her Western partners in the consortium would 'open' the Soviet economy to Western commercial and industrial investment. German activity in Russia, Berlin hoped, would stabilize the economy, allowing an eventual expansion to its full potential with the recovery of Germany's prewar industrial domination of Europe. Thus, the liberal-imperialist war aim — an economic *Mitteleuropa* dominated by Germany — would be implemented, even enlarged, by means of the economic *Ostreich*, which, being achieved by peaceful means, promised to be far more durable than any wartime creation. Under the aegis of the partnership between Berlin, Washington, London and Paris, in opening the Soviet economy to Western development, Germany's ability to pay reparations — and this was the lure — would not only be secured, it would even be augmented.

Thus, in the final analysis, the consortium would further Germany's 'fulfilment' of the Treaty of Versailles, a fulfilment which, in German terms, was aimed at the ultimate revision of the Treaty itself and the recovery, indeed enhancement, of Germany's former Great Power status. In pursuit of this goal, Rathenau, in concert with other leading German industrialists, continued to refine his advances to the Soviets. The Germans, particularly the industrialists, Himmer maintains, ' . . . regarded Russia as their economic colony. In short, they meant to pick Russia clean'.[19] Rathenau was an enthusiastic confederate, arguing that 'an organization must be created in Russia which may purchase and export all available wealth . . .' and continuing 'everything which Russia can no longer afford is to come out . . .', words echoed by Stinnes, Wirth and others.[20]

Yet Germany's plans were not realized. The Soviets rejected her offer of 'international assistance',[21] countering by the demand of an

19. Himmer, 'Rathenau', p. 171.
20. Ibid.
21. Ibid., p. 181: 'The strategy advanced by Rathenau for Germany in the three-cornered struggle with Russia and the Entente in which he believed [Germany] was engaged, and which led to Rapallo, was a blend of rationalization and delusion. It was not without reason that he believed the Entente was waging economic warfare against Germany. The seemingly logical requirements of survival in this struggle, however, contributed to the perpetuation of German imperialist designs on Russia — designs which had been rendered utopian by the German collapse in 1918 and by the victory of the Red Army in the period of the civil war and foreign intervention in Russia. Rathenau and his colleagues were forced to recognize the limitation of German capabilities — that they could not alone impose their will on Russia — but their frustration bred, instead of abandonment of the unrealistic goal, rationalizations for its continued pursuit.'

Allied guarantee backed by loans for repayment of the outstanding prewar Czarist debts. In response, the British Prime Minister Lloyd George and his French colleague, Premier Aristide Briand, suggested an international economic conference, perhaps in Genoa in 1922, to seek a comprehensive solution to various urgent European economic problems.[22] One of its most important goals would be the economic reconstruction of Central and Eastern Europe. Lloyd George in particular was attracted to the idea of closer commercial and economic relations between Britain and the Soviet Union as a means of reconstructing the U.K. economy.

Although German–Soviet economic negotiations bore no fruit in 1921, each partner was intent on preventing the other from reaching an understanding with the Western powers.[23] To this end, Gregory Chicherin, Soviet Commissar for Foreign Affairs, halted in Berlin in early April 1922 while on his way to the Genoa Conference on international economic reconstruction. Chicherin, who had been preceded by Karl Radek in January, sought to strengthen German–Soviet relations by defining a common basis. Within days, his efforts were rewarded, for the German and the Soviet delegations left Berlin for Genoa, each carrying a draft agreement which, in fact, became the Rapallo accord.

Neither Wirth nor Rathenau were willing to commit Germany before the Genoa Conference, and therefore refused to sign an agreement with the Soviets in Berlin. Reichspresident Ebert, moreover, opposed any treaty, then or later.[24] In waiting until the conference, Germany hoped to exploit the proposed agreement as leverage in dealing with the West. At the international conference on economic reconstruction, held in Genoa from 10 April to 19 May 1922, however, it immediately became evident that there was little hope of a comprehensive economic settlement. In fact, the German delegation became increasingly concerned lest the Western powers court the Soviet delegation with promises of a share in the reparations settlement

---

22. Taylor, *English History*, p. 189. The background and details of the Genoa Conference are described in great detail and with equally great clarity by Carole Fink, *The Genoa Conference. European Diplomacy, 1921–22* (Chapel Hill, 1984).

23. Nicholls, p. 79: 'Lloyd George, in particular, became very interested in the expansion of Anglo-Russian trade. The British Prime Minister had promised Britain's soldiers a "world fit for heroes to live in" when they returned from the war. Instead they found a stagnating economy and large-scale unemployment. Favorable terms of trade with Russia would brighten the prospect. For their part the French were eager to obtain compensation from Russia for Tsarist loans repudiated by the Bolshevik government. As a lever to obtain Soviet compliance on both trade and debt questions the Western Allies might hope to use Article 116 of the Versailles Treaty, which reserved Russia the right to make reparations demands against Germany for damage done during the war.'

24. Erdmann, 'Weimarer Republik', p. 232.

(according to Article 116 of the Versailles Treaty) in exchange for Soviet payment of Czarist debts. Capitalizing on mutual anxieties, the German and Russian delegations withdrew early on the morning of Sunday, 16 April, to the neighboring resort of Rapallo. The preliminary groundwork having been completed during the Berlin talks, the two sides quickly came to an understanding which resulted in the Treaty of Rapallo. Official diplomatic relations were resumed, and, under the terms of the treaty, both parties agreed to drop any and all reciprocal claims arising from the war. Thus, Article 116 of the Treaty of Versailles, which had cancelled the Treaty of Brest-Litovsk and left open the possibility of Russian reparations claims against Germany, no longer constituted an obstacle to further relations. In addition, the German government relinquished any existing claims following Soviet nationalization of German property. Both parties extended most-favored-nation status to the other. Finally, mutual needs were acknowledged in the declaration by Germany of her willingness to underwrite private investment — that is, the extension of credit — in Russia. Although it was generally suspected in Western capitals that the Treaty contained secret military or commercial clauses, this was not the case.

The Rapallo Treaty had a profound effect on German foreign policy. Although the threat was far more apparent than real, German diplomats congratulated themselves on preventing Soviet association with the Western powers. At the same time, a common suspicion of the West produced renewed cooperation between the signatories. And even though the treaty of Rapallo contained no formal provisions for secret economic or military cooperation, it greatly enhanced the possibilities for subsequent agreement. No later than the next decade, cooperation of this kind would be in progress between Russia and Germany.[25]

The impact of Rapallo on the Genoa Conference was that of an unexpected bombshell; the German–Soviet *rapprochement* stunned and amazed the other participants. Suspicion as to possible secret articles and concern over the effects of the treaty overshadowed the remaining sessions.[26] To this day, controversy surrounds the meaning of the Rapallo Treaty. In one view, the treaty was the diplomatic

---

25. E. H. Carr, *German–Soviet Relations Between the Two World Wars, 1919–1939* (New York, 1966), p. 64: 'The fact of signature was more important than the formal contents of the treaty.' See also Carr, *Bolshevik Revolution*, v. 3, pp. 374f.

26. Nicholls, p. 81: 'There was no secret military protocol attached to the Rapallo Treaty, but its conclusion meant that collaboration between the Red Army and the Reichswehr was likely to be intensified, and this was in fact the case.'

turning-point of the Twenties.[27] Others accord it little or no significance, maintaining that it produced no change in the European political climate.[28] Perhaps the most interesting perspective on the Treaty of
Rapallo, though, is offered by von Riekhoff, who believes that it
produced very important strategic advantages for Germany against
Poland. Evidence of this, he avers, was Poland's neutrality during the
Ruhr crisis: though it might seem that this was dictated rather by the
backward state of Polish military preparedness than by Soviet
pressure.[29]

Although the Rapallo Treaty was a purely diplomatic agreement
governing specific legal and financial aspects of German–Soviet relations, it was greeted with particular pleasure by the military establish-
ments of both countries. Both the *Reichswehr* and the Red Army
believed that it provided the basis for broadening their mutual contacts
which antedated the treaty by over a year and which would eventually
enable the two outcasts from Versailles to pursue an active revisionist
policy. Parallel to the German–Soviet economic negotiations, in early
1921, contacts between the *Reichswehr* and the Red Army had also
developed. Both sides believed that they could benefit from such talks.
The result of these early contacts was an exchange of matériel and
subsequent testing of new military hardware. Since the *Reichswehr*
was denied offensive weapons, the use of Red Army facilities for
development and testing of new weapons proved extremely valuable.
Not long after the inauguration of clandestine tests, there began a kind
of military love affair, which included the exchange of officers and
joint maneuvers. Ultimately the *Reichswehr* believed closer military

27. See in this connection Carr, *Bolshevik Revolution*, v. 3., pp. 339–80 and in
particular J. Korbel, *Poland between East and West. Soviet and German Diplomacy
toward Poland, 1919–1933* (Princeton, 1963), *passim*, as well as Nicholls, p. 82: 'Rapallo
was the first real attempt by the Germans to take the initiative in foreign affairs and
overcome their isolation. In many ways it was successful — the Russian-German
contacts forged by the treaty continued and were the basis for more important economic
cooperation later on. The fact that Germany had a link with Moscow gave her diplomatic advantages three years afterwards when she came to bargain with the West in a
more favorable atmosphere.'
28. Representative of those who see little significance in Rapallo is T.H. von Laue,
'Soviet Diplomacy: G.V. Chicherin, Peoples Commissar for Foreign Affairs,
1918–1930', in G.A. Craig and F. Gilbert, eds., *The Diplomats* (New York, 1974), pp.
234–81. On the various interpretations of Rapallo and the historical literature surrounding the diplomacy of Rapallo, see H. Graml, 'Die Rapallo-Politik im Urteil der
westdeutschen Forschung', *VZG* 18 (1970), pp. 130–2. Although somewhat more
temperate, Krüger nevertheless sees little gain in Rapallo. 'Russia was doubtless the
winner', but even this signified little since she was still completely isolated. The
tremendous problems of Western Europe — finances, reparations, security — still
overshadowed all else. Krüger, *Außenpolitik*, pp. 175–83.
29. v. Riekhoff, *German–Polish Relations*, *passim*; also Graml, 'Rapallo-Politik', pp.
241, 249–50, 260. Clearly, Poland was unprepared for military operations: Korbel, pp.
130–2.

cooperation would enable Germany to revise her Eastern frontiers in concert with the Soviet Union. Many German officers had never given up their central goal, 'by means of power politics to restore the German Reich to its former position as a world power in Continental Europe, and, if necessary or possible, even by force of arms'.[30] Toward attainment of this goal, supported by the broad spectrum of German military officers, a variety of foreign policy alternatives were developed in the Bendlerstrasse. To varying degrees and at different times, these ideas would influence foreign policy throughout the lifetime of the republic. The discussion fluctuated between two extremes, which can only be briefly sketched here.

The most radical suggestion, and the one which represented an uninterrupted extrusion of Wilhelmine-imperialist policy into republican foreign policy, was that of General Hans von Seeckt, *Chef der Heeresleitung* from 1920 to 1926.[31] Seeckt's vision was of an isolated Germany combining with an equally isolated Russia to crush the infant Poland; then, with Russia covering the rear, Germany would be free to wage a 'war of liberation' against France.[32] By this means, Germany and Soviet Russia could re-create the frontiers of 1914. Seeckt exaggerated ostensible differences between France and Britain, which he believed portended the imminent collapse of the Entente — a misconception shared by many of his contemporaries in Weimar politics. When the split occurred, Seeckt maintained, Germany would naturally side with Britain in order to ensure British neutrality if not actual help against France. Seeckt's wildly optimistic evaluation of Britain's probable reaction to such a radical alteration in the continental balance of power can be taken as symptomatic of the 'continuity of error' in Prussian-German foreign policy.

Following on this, Seeckt developed a kind of graduated plan (*Stufenplan*), already revealed in German policy during the war. Firstly, in the spirit of 'a turn to the East', he proposed that, with help from Soviet Russia, Germany could destroy Poland. The second step, viewed by Seeckt as 'necessary' for Britain, was an Anglo-German alliance, the prerequisite for Germany's war of retribution against France. The choice of friendship with London rather than Paris was a foregone conclusion, given French hostility toward Germany. However, there remained the far-reaching traditional question of the choice between East and West.[33] Seeckt's vision re-echoed the traditional

30. H.-A. Jacobsen and W. v. Bredow, eds., *Mißtrauische Nachbarn. Deutsche Außenpolitik, 1919 bis 1970. Dokumentation und Analyse* (Düsseldorf, 1970), p. 9.
31. Carr, *Bolshevik Revolution*, v. 3, pp. 309f.
32. Hillgruber, *Kontinuität*, p. 17.
33. Seeckt, in Jacobsen and Bredow, *Mißtrauische Nachbarn*, p. 32.

German military goal: backed by an Anglo-German alliance and after a victorious campaign in France (both unfulfilled in 1917), the 'march East' would begin; in short, an *Ostpolitik* already successfully initiated in 1917–1918 could be revived and continued. Although this concept, enjoyed broad support within the *Reichswehr* and generally by a wide cross-section of the German population, it could not officially influence Weimar policy. Yet it did not remain pure theory. With the assiduously cultivated secret German-Soviet military contacts, the Wilhelmstrasse endeavored to keep the *Ostpolitik* idea alive.[34] In so doing, German diplomats and military leaders fashioned an alternative[35] to official foreign policy, an alternative typical of the Weimar Republic's characteristic dualism between political and military influences.

Diametrically opposed to von Seeckt's conception was that of Kurt von Schleicher, even though it similarly ignored power-political realities in the radically altered postwar environment. In 1918 Colonel von Schleicher, later *Reichswehr* Chief of Staff and fleetingly *Reichskanzler*, had already developed a foreign policy alternative founded on the propositions of General Joachim von Stulpnagel. Schleicher, correctly assessing both the altered political situation following the German collapse and the nation's immediate needs, urged that in the first instance Germany put her economic house in order. Having thereby re-established the necessary social and political order, Schleicher maintained, only then would it be possible to consider a deliberately paced reconstruction of Germany's power-political situation. Hillgruber points out:

> In other words, Germany could not immediately undertake — as Seeckt demanded — an old-style cabinet policy, in the sense of the traditional *Primat der Außenpolitik* — which Schleicher felt was hopeless — in an attempt to become active once more in the international political arena, but rather, to establish a long-term comprehensive policy: to consolidate and secure a domestic political basis for a vigorous pursuit of German foreign interests, then subsequently to introduce an 'active' foreign policy, with the goal of re-establishing Germany's Great Power position in Europe.[36]

Such a strategy for the recovery of Germany's former Great Power status at once differentiated and graduated, with its shifting accent on domestic and international policy, contains future German foreign policy in outline, as it was pursued, for example, by Gustav Stresemann. Schleicher, like successive German statesmen in the Twenties,

---

34. See F. L. Carsten, *Reichswehr und Politik*, 1918–1933 (Cologne, 1964), pp. 18ff. and *passim*.
35. Carr, *Bolshevik Revolution*, v. 3, p. 310.
36. Hillgruber, *Kontinuität*, p. 17.

saw that the new Polish state, created at the expense of territorial losses by Germany and Russia, provided a focus for the enmity of both countries. Meeting on this common ground, German and Soviet officials could begin to overcome their own mutual hostility resulting from the annexationist Treaty of Brest-Litovsk.

In the Wilhelmstraße, the foremost representatives of an Eastern orientation in German foreign policy were Count Ulrich von Brockdorff-Rantzau and Ago von Maltzan, head of the German Foreign Ministry's Eastern Section. Both men saw Soviet–German cooperation as a valuable counter to the West, one which would, in the blunt words of Brockdorff-Rantzau (15 August 1922), prevent their country being 'delivered up to the mercy of the Entente Powers'.[37] Yet both of them, together with their followers in the Wilhelmstraße, felt no doubt that the relationship constituted a 'shotgun marriage' rather than a 'love match'. In 1922, the idea that Germany and the Russian *'roten Kameraden'*, would one day together defeat France, struck the Maltzan-Rantzau camp as completely absurd. It is not surprising, then, that the foreign policy alternatives of the Foreign Ministry differed markedly from the *Reichswehr's* demand for the use of military force to realize German interests, a policy based on a military alliance with the Soviet Union, with whose help Germany would reassert her former authority.

Though sharing the military leaders' goal, the Foreign Ministry saw the means to that end quite differently. German–Soviet cooperation was considered critical, since it offered the only way for Germany to pursue a successful policy aimed primarily at revising the German–Polish border by leverage on the West. Such a concept was virtually a constant factor in the formulation of post-Versailles German foreign policy. As such, it forms a continuum, along which to measure the foreign policy goals defined by a significant group within the Foreign Ministry, including future State Secretary Bernhard von Bülow and future Foreign Minister Konstantin von Neurath. Despite the differences between Reichswehr and Foreign Ministry policies, and even clearer in the light of hindsight, the alternatives originally seemed complementary. When the Treaty of Rapallo gave substantial support to the proponents of *Ostorientierung* (reiterated by the 1926 Treaty of Berlin), both generals and diplomats hailed it as a victory for their position. Despite the apparent connection between Rapallo and Berlin, the concept of *Ostorientierung* shared by the diplomats and representatives of commerce and industry differed markedly from the military

---

37. Brockdorff-Rantzau, in M. Walsdorff, *Westorientierung und Ostpolitik. Stresemann's Rußlandpolitik in der Locarno–Ära* (Bremen, 1971), p. 12

view. Martin Waldsdorff, having made the comparison, points out that 'the representatives of the Foreign Ministry adamantly rejected the use of force for the realization of their aims, not only out of tactical considerations, but on principle as well'.[38] Although the Wilhelmstraße continued to work closely with the *Reichswehr*, Edward W. Bennett shows that the reaction of the diplomats, notably Neurath's and Bülow's, to the clearly aggressive designs of the generals during the Geneva Disarmament Conference of 1932 was distinctly hostile.[39]

Let us return to the Genoa Conference and the Treaty of Rapallo. The German–Soviet agreement cast a long shadow over the Conference, and the economic negotiations dragged on inconclusively. Although the reparations question was not formally part of the Conference agenda, its longed-for solution still eluded the delegates. Not Rapallo, however, but rather the absence of the United States prevented a general reparations settlement and proved the cause for the failure of the conference.[40] The actual effect of Rapallo was thus only evident months later. France, of course, immediately suspected the anti-Polish, and to some degree anti-French, nature of the treaty. Even in the absence of concrete evidence, the Quai d'Orsay could only assume the existence of secret military articles attached to the Rapallo agreements. Moreover, French policy was profoundly affected by the threat of German–Soviet military cooperation. Poland, next to Great Britain undoubtedly France's most important ally, now appeared openly challenged, indeed, perhaps even jeopardized. To make matters worse, since the London Ultimatum Wirth's policy of fulfilment had, as intended, produced more frequent interruptions in German shipments of strategic materials to France, as well as increasing deficits in cash transfers. Finally, British policy, which aimed at stabilizing continental Europe, revealed a certain sympathy toward Wirth's policy of fulfilment. Thus isolated and fearing the collapse of France's security system, Premier Poincaré saw as his only alternative vigorous steps to enforce the London reparations schedule and to shore up his sagging security system.

In the spring of 1922, despite rising domestic economic crisis, the hegemonic position of France in continental Europe appeared still unchallenged. Nevertheless, the center of gravity in Europe had begun to shift inexorably away from Paris, indeed even away from London, across the Atlantic to Washington. The inevitable shift of power in the direction of Washington, which from this distance seems increasingly

38. Ibid., p. 13.
39. Bennett, *Rearmament*, pp. 237, 255–7.
40. W. Link, *Die amerikanische Stabilisierungspolitik in Deutschland, 1921–1932* (Düsseldorf, 1970), p. 122.

clear, was scarcely apprehended at the time. Without US help, however, the reparations complex could never be permanently settled, and despite her refusal to participate in the Genoa Conference, America's re-entry into European affairs was just a matter of time. France, observing developments with mounting anxiety, would have to react quickly if she meant to salvage her victory won at such expense between 1914 and 1918 and institutionalized with such care from 1919 to 1922. Rapallo offered Poincaré relief: an energetic French response would quieten domestic cacophony whilst reasserting French security. Weariness with German arrears and public suspicion about Rapallo created a domestic climate in which Poincaré could act against Germany in an area where France had long taken an interest: the Rhineland and the Ruhr.[41] The Franco-Belgian occupation of the Ruhr put an end both to the German policy of fulfilment, and also to German efforts at an 'active' policy of revision. At the same time, however, it spelled the demise of the French policy of 'productive guarantees'. Thus, as will be seen, the Ruhr conflict simultaneously demonstrated with absolute clarity the limits of both French and German foreign policy.

New Perspectives in German Foreign Policy: American Stabilization Policy in Europe

In this section we will reconsider the French occupation of the Ruhr in yet another context: that of the opportunities thus presented to Berlin for German-American financial cooperation.

The French policy of 'productive guarantees', culminating in January 1923 in the Ruhr occupation, brought the disparate elements of German foreign policy into stark relief. First, an 'active' policy of revision was seen to be impossible, in the sense propounded by General von Seeckt and his circle: collaboration with Soviet Russia in order to force Poland back to her 'ethnographic' frontiers — in other words, to the borders of 1914. With the Treaty of Rapallo German–Soviet relations, until now restricted to informal economic contacts and clandestine military cooperation, could rise to a political plane and thus to substantial improvement. But more active relations with Russia were as detrimental for a German revisionist policy as they were helpful. Given France's leading military position, Poland could at best be neutralized but not 'smashed'. France, for her part, viewed Rapallo as a provocation. Domestic opposition was silenced at last and, brushing

41. Graml, 'Rapallo-Politik', pp. 260f.

aside British temporizing, Poincaré now contemplated aggressive intervention. The French goal of politicizing reparations demands and achieving them by force appeared attainable — ironically enough, with German assistance.

Second, German attempts at revision by a calculated 'policy of fulfilment' thus far lacked concrete results. For one thing, right-wing domestic opposition was insurmountable. Wirth's opponents accused the government of willing submission to Allied domination without extracting any concessions from the Treaty of Versailles and therefore needlessly abandoning German territories. Right-wing politicians in particular labeled this 'the policy of abandonment and sell-out', striking a responsive chord among their fellow Germans. Added to domestic political limits, the policy of fulfilment was also limited in economic terms. Whether or not there was any intention ever to pay, the prerequisite for regular, exact reparations payments was a stable economy relatively free from crisis. But, as contemporaries and later scholars all agree, rising inflation made fulfilment impossible.[1] Nevertheless, the German policy had a profound effect on European affairs: for, as Werner Link contends, to demonstrate the impossibility of meeting the Versailles terms by the very attempt to fulfil them to the letter, 'constituted a vicious circle of default, [and] threatened sanctions, both military and non-military, with catastrophic political and economic consequences'.[2] The Ruhr crisis demonstrated the bankruptcy of that tactic, pursued in one form or another since the Fehrenbach Cabinet (mid-1920s), which linked revision to short-term, meticulous fulfilment.

Lastly, a third possibility for German revisionist policy had existed immediately after the war in the tentative contacts between German and French industrialists, who hoped to cooperate in the development of French ore and German coal. This plan, conceived well before the Armistice as a German war aim, died in the Franco-German industrial talks of 1919–1920. From the German perspective, French dependence on German coal should have led to a community of interests in cooperative industrial development: the intention, of course, was to fetter France's economy by degrees. French dependence would have provided a suitable instrument for forcing revisions of the Treaty of

---

1. Hiden, *Germany and Europe*, p. 29. See also Maier, *Recasting Bourgeois Europe*, p. 243: 'Still there was bitter debate between the advocates of "fulfilment" and those nationalists who, as Georg Bernhard said, "thoroughly share the view, even if they state the contrary, that we can achieve the luxury of simply shoving the Versailles Treaty aside and not fulfilling it".'

2. Link, 'Die Beziehungen zwischen der Weimarer Republik und den USA', in M. Knapp, et al, *Die USA und Deutschland, 1918–1975. Deutsch-amerikanische Beziehungen zwischen Rivalität und Partnerschaft* (Munich, 1978), p. 66f.

Versailles. It should also be noted that, in this context, additional motives can be adduced, not the least of which was personal profit. Nevertheless, while seeking to extract political power and advantage from the penetration of French industry by German concerns, the policy produced no notable success before 1923. Yet it offered an alternative to the idea of fulfilment and more especially, to the 'active' revisionism proclaimed by the Right and the *Reichswehr*. In time, under Gustav Stresemann and later under Franz von Papen, the use of private German industrial contacts would become an important tool of German foreign policy.

Thus far, Germany had failed to achieve a revision of the Versailles settlement. Despite *Ostorientierung*, and the hope of an alliance in the East; despite *Westorientierung* and efforts at 'fulfilment'; and despite the help of German private industry, she failed to recover her former position as a Great Power. The Franco-Belgian occupation of the Ruhr hastened the failure of these policies. The way lay open for new choices.

The impetus for a reorientation in German foreign policy came not from Berlin but from London. As early as the Paris Peace Conference, German observers noted differences between France and Britain over questions of Germany and postwar European reconstruction. Great Britain's staggering wartime debt, economic crisis, unemployment and the restive members of the Empire, all made the stabilization of continental Europe an essential goal, allowing British energies to be turned to domestic problems. Rapid and effective reconstruction of the continental economy was vital if Britain's export-oriented economy was to recover from the wartime loss of markets. While the British public might not yet realize the link between European stability and the home economy, influential industrial and financial interests recognized the need for a normalization of relations. The heart of continental economic health was Germany. For Britain she was the traditional trading partner and competitor — and also the key to future economic well-being. On Wall Street, too, a stable Germany was at the center of long-range commercial and financial plans. Germany was also the linchpin of any hope for a stable Eastern Europe, and would remain so throughout the interwar years.[3]

As the British economic situation worsened, the desire to reintegrate Germany in European economic, and hence political, affairs became ever more acute. Accordingly, London's first priority was to clarify the interrelationship between German financial stability and reparations payments. As Graml remarks, 'it was self-evident that such

3. Krüger, *Außenpolitik* p. 215.

regulation would require the recognition of equality of treatment [*Gleichberechtigung*] for Germany'.[4] Lloyd George, hard-pressed by domestic interests, developed numerous proposals for European economic stabilization and the consequent reconstruction of the British economy. Germany always played a key role in his plans. German strategists found in this justification of the hope for closer Anglo-German relations which would eventually split the already wavering coalition of wartime victors.

It will be remembered that one of Lloyd George's favorite schemes was an international consortium to underwrite the Soviet economy, by which means he hoped to develop both Soviet raw material potentiality and the possibility of a new export market there, at the same time checking the danger of Bolshevism. But this was not the full extent of his vision, for he also intended to promote greater American investment in Europe, simultaneously bringing Germany into the renegotiation of reparations. This would establish *Gleichberechtigung*, compel rational handling of reparations questions and ultimately lead to normalization of German–French relations.

The German Foreign Minister Walther Rathenau recognized that by participating in Lloyd George's scheme, Germany had a real chance of breaking out of her diplomatic isolation and, above all, might achieve economic and political *Gleichberechtigung*. Since the plans for a consortium to open up the Soviet economy bore extensive similarities to plans developed by German industrialists and politicians during and after the war, participation in the British plan could give Germany the opportunity for an 'active' policy of revision. H.G. Linke points out: 'Rathenau, unlike his colleague Maltzan, held fast to the consortium; less as an aspect of German-Soviet policy than as a chance for developing a relationship of greater trust with the West and a possible relief from some of the onerous reparations obligations.'[5]

The opposition of those who favored bilateral ties with Moscow, the Maltzan group in the *Auswärtiges Amt* and the *Reichswehr*, prevented Rathenau from immediately accepting Lloyd George's proposal. But the stiffest opposition came from Moscow itself. Although a trade agreement with Britain had been signed on 16 March 1921, the Soviets took great care to guard against what they viewed as a capitalist 'takeover'. Rapallo finally put a stop to Lloyd George's plan.

Yet this did not dampen the spirits of the Prime Minister. A new project was required to reduce tensions in Europe and bolster British policy. In an attempt to meet at least part of France's exaggerated

4. Graml, *Europa*, pp. 126f.
5. H. G. Linke, *Deutsch-sowjetische Beziehungen bis Rapallo* (Cologne, 1970), p. 170.

demands for security and, most importantly, to avoid French intervention in Germany, Lloyd George proposed that Germany enter the League of Nations. He intended to put Germany in a position of having to support the *status quo*, since that was in fact the political result of League membership. The Prime Minister reasoned, too, that a Germany attached to the League would appear far less threatening to Paris. One primary advantage of German membership was that it would permit France to seek immediate assistance in the event of a German violation of the treaty. But at the same time, her response would be limited, since any sanctions she contemplated would have to be consistent with the League Covenant. From the German point of view, membership of the League would virtually eliminate the possibility of unilateral French action as in the Ruhr.[6]

Though falling short of rejection, German response to the idea was cool and reserved. This was, as it happened, a tactical error. The German government was in a very delicate position, in terms both of domestic politics and of foreign affairs. The various factions opposing 'fulfilment' were equally resistant to entry into the League, seeing it as nothing more than another 'sell-out'. In the end, the Germans used the convenient excuse of domestic opposition to conceal deeper reservations, and advanced conditions for German entry which from the outset were sure to be unacceptable to the Allies:

> In reality [the Germans] sought to avoid that recognition of the *status quo* inherent in entry, and to avoid the resentment of their only recently-won Russian friends, who would no doubt have viewed German entry as the beginning of a Western orientation in German foreign policy in direct contradiction to Rapallo: it would therefore have caused great distress [in this new partnership]. Already, therefore, signs had appeared that a joint Soviet-German venture at revision, without immediate benefits or adequate protection against French retaliation, drastically limited German diplomatic freedom of action.[7]

Clearly, the time was not yet at hand when the League would offer a possible means of justifying and realizing German revisionist aims.

Another British proposal, however, struck a responsive chord in Germany, but despite initial appearances this project broke on the rock of American opposition. Following the collapse of the Genoa Conference, during the latter half of 1922, in an attempt to find a way out of the reparations impasse, the British government once again seized the initiative with an engagingly simple suggestion: in one 'great

6. Graml, *Europa*, p. 154.
7. Ibid., p. 156.

transaction' to cancel all inter-allied debts, with the result that reparations could be liquidated. At a single stroke, political and economic crisis could be averted on a global scale. To no-one's surprise, the United States and France flatly rejected such a scheme. American investors grasped immediately that with such a plan they would in fact wind up shouldering the reparations burden in the form of cancelled debts. The obvious failure of this one last great gesture compelled a reluctant Britain to look to the payment and collection of her own war debts. In part forced by American insistence on repayment, the British government indirectly dunned its wartime debtors in the Balfour Note of 1 August 1922: this stated that unless the US cancelled European war debts, Britain would be forced to collect the amounts owed her in order to meet her own obligations to American creditors. To Poincaré America's veto of a general cancellation confirmed the value of his politicization of reparations. By the late summer of 1922 he had no further room for maneuver. The Anglo-French conflict over reparations payments became increasingly bitter during the waning months of 1922.[8]

Encouraged by the latest British reparations activity, Germany approached the Reparations Commission on 12 July 1922 to request cancellation of the remainder of her obligation in 1922 and a moratorium on payments for 1923. First Wirth and later Cuno pleaded that German finances were in such disarray that further payment would bankrupt the country and so lead to domestic chaos. Playing what he

---

8. Schuker, p. 178: 'Probably no French government in mid-1922 could have agreed to reduce reparations further and yet hope to survive. Certainly Poincaré, who had made enforcement of reparations the *raison d'être* of his ministry, could hardly acquiesce in the bankers' demands. The German government's failure to halt the inflation and to take measures for the rehabilitation of Reich finances might be attributed to weakness or intentional policy. The documentary evidence now available points to a measure of truth in both explanations, but at the time the French felt strongly that the Germans were deliberately ruining their own currency to give a fraudulent impression of national bankruptcy. It appeared virtually incontrovertible to official Paris that, even allowing for domestic political difficulties, Germany had made no more than a perfunctory effort to fulfill the London Schedule.' While the attitude of France was inclined toward discipline when dealing with Germany, Britain, for different reasons, was inclined to show more understanding for Germany. This led to considerable tension in Anglo-French relations. W. N. Medlicott, *British Foreign Policy since Versailles, 1919–1963* (London, 1968), pp. 45f.: 'Ostensibly the essential difference between the British and French theses on the reparations issue concerned Germany's inability to pay... but in practice more was involved in the Anglo-French difference than the fixing of a figure and the devising of inducements to pay it. Incompatibility of political aim and national temperament prevented the rational assessment of Germany's "ability to pay". British ministers admitted their failure to sympathize or make friends with Poincaré. Great Britain with her dependence on external markets and a flourishing state of world trade had reason to doubt whether even a large sum in reparations was worth collecting by means of coercion which would once more throw international politics into turmoil. France's economy was so constituted as not to be particularly sensitive to this kind of shock; she felt, too, a grievance on account of her own indebtedness to Great Britain.'

thought to be his trump card, in December 1922 Cuno invited an international commission to Berlin to verify the claims of incapacity to pay. But without awaiting the results of the commission's investigation, Germany demanded additional relief from payments. In Schuker's opinion, 'this proposal amounted in effect to a calculated decision by Germany to force a confrontation'.[9] And indeed, it was too much for France to endure. To Poincaré it was an open provocation; at last he had the opportunity to carry out the policy of 'productive guarantees'.[10] Despite a strong protest, Britain maintained official neutrality as French and Belgian troops occupied the Ruhr. Nor did the League of Nations inhibit France's unilateral action — Belgium's share in the occupation being incidental. In the end, Germany's newfound understanding with Russia failed to deter France from sending in troops. Lacking any support among her continental neighbors, Germany looked to America for help.

American concerns were similar to those of Great Britain. Both Washington and Wall Street proclaimed interest in the reintegration of a liberal, democratic and capitalist Germany into the Western community of nations and Western economic life. It was believed that a harsh, punitive peace worked against that integration, producing instead an uneasy international climate, and would push Germany into the arms of either the Bolsheviks or revanchist nationalists.[11] Although America appeared to withdraw once more from European politics following the war, she carefully constructed an informal economic system in Europe, in the sense of the 'open door policy', which — and this should be emphasized — placed Europe under American economic domination. As Europe's pivotal economy, Germany was the central link in the American system, destined to become the US's continental partner. With this policy, America intended to effect a general application of the 'open door' in Europe, aimed at exerting not only economic, but also political, influence in the Old World. The temporary political withdrawal of the United States from Europe can in no way at all be interpreted as an economic withdrawal.[12]

This policy had concrete results. As early as 1921, America had signed a separate peace with Germany, in order to stabilize and secure

9. Schuker, p. 23.
10. Ibid., pp. 178f: 'The French occupation of the Ruhr represented a desperate attempt to break the pattern of German resistance. Poincaré undertook this hazardous operation only when every alternative method for compelling payment appeared to have failed and when efforts to secure the international banking community's assistance to Germany without revising the reparations schedule had also broken down.'
11. W. Link, 'Der amerikanische Einfluss auf die Weimarer Republic in der Dawesplanphase, Elemente eines "penetrierten Systems",' in: Mommsen, et al, *Industrielles System*, p. 487.
12. On this point, see Link, *Die amerikanische Stabilisierungspolitik, passim.*

the young republic as a market for American exports and investments.[13] This special relationship was evident in the German–
American trade agreement of 1923, which established bilateral trade
between the two partners. German policymakers recognized very
early the potential value of the US as an ally in their effort to break 'the
fetters of Versailles'. Hopes for American support were grounded in
part on German–American negotiations dating back to 1917, as German and American officials prepared for the armistice and the peace
conference, attempting (against Anglo-French opposition) to make
Wilson's peace proposals the basis for the peace talks. Following
Versailles, German leaders remained aware that leading American
politicians were convinced that neither French security nor the stability of Europe could be found in the maintenance of the existing
situation, but that it would be achieved only by taking Germany into
the Allied camp.[14] For Germany, the United States represented not
merely an important source of capital, a fact increasingly apparent to
leading German politicians and industrialists from 1918 to 1924, but
(as Link points out) also offered a political counterweight to the
guarantors of the Versailles settlement:

> As she struggled against the commercial restrictions of the Treaty of
> Versailles, Germany's efforts coincided with those of the US, in attempting
> to construct a liberal non-discriminatory global system of trade. For the US,
> global policy meant global economic policy and for Germany, global
> economics offered the means to resume a more active role in world affairs.
> [*Die USA betrieben Weltpolitik als Weltwirtschaftspolitik, und Deutschland
> wollte über die Weltwirtschaft in die Weltpolitik zurückkehren.*][15]

From the beginning, then, Germany hoped for American intervention
and mediation in the reparations question. As viewed from Berlin, it
was necessary to parry any French effort to overwhelm or capture the
German economy. Equally, it was imperative that Germany not fall
into a kind of semi-colonial dependence upon Britain. To counter
Anglo–French influence, Berlin accepted as the lesser of two evils a
certain subordination to American financial and economic policy.
There would be a period, limited and transitional, during which
American commercial and financial efforts to penetrate the German
economy and markets would be tolerated. During this phase, German
productivity would rise and a politically valuable interdependence
would develop as the result of increasingly coincident material inter-

13. Link, 'Die Beziehungen', p. 64.
14. Ibid., pp. 64f.
15. Ibid., p. 65.

ests. This strategy never anticipated a formal alliance between Germany and the United States, but, as we shall see, by the end of the decade it had borne fruit. As Link tells us, from the outset it was embraced by parties across the German political spectrum:

> Resting on a relatively broad concensus, from the SPD to the *Deutschnationalen*, the official foreign policy of the republic, therefore, was from the beginning aimed at winning the support of the United States for German recovery. Given the situation, [German foreign policy] could not aim at an alliance, but rather hoped to secure American mediation in European affairs, which would result in a nexus of German–American interests [*deutschamerikanische Interessenverflechtung* for the immediate and foreseeable future.[16]

American politicians, however, seemed extremely reluctant to allow their country to become involved in reparations questions, for fear of compromising American 'neutrality'. Officially, Washington maintained a neutral stance on the matter, in order to preserve the fiction of separation between war debts and reparations. There was a stern rejection of:

> . . . any connection between reparations payments and the settlement of debts contracted by the Western allies during the war, since in that event [the US] would have immediately become a participant in the reparations conflict and would run the risk, in the last analysis, of being the only party capable of funding reparations.[17]

America's absolute insistence on the distinction between war debts and reparations gradually gave way, however, to a certain informal status as a 'third party' in this international financial dilemma.

Until the end of 1922, American policy was confined to efforts at convincing Germany that she must pay reparations, while simultaneously attempting to persuade France that only an economically healthy Germany, secure in territorial integrity, could fulfil the reparations obligations.[18] Washington wanted to dispatch an 'independent' committee of bankers and economists to evaluate Germany's ability — or lack of it — to pay, with the intent of rescheduling the annual remittances. The investigation would also give the information needed for deciding the amount of a contemplated international loan to Germany. The worsening crisis of late 1922, which led ultimately to the Ruhr crisis, offered American policymakers their first opportunity

16. Ibid., p. 66.
17. Ibid., p. 69.
18. See ibid., p. 70.

since Versailles for direct initiative in European affairs. Following several fruitless attempts at mediation, France's occupation of the Ruhr created a situation in which America could no longer avoid an active role. As the German authorities met French occupation with passive resistance and the French responded with increased force, American policy was influenced in two ways. In an immediate sense, unrest in Germany threatened burgeoning American investments there. Meanwhile, worldwide exports of US goods gradually increased to fill the void left by the withdrawal of German exporters from the world market as the crisis worsened. In the end, however, whatever apparent advantages the situation offered to American businessmen were outweighed by the 'solution' contemplated in Paris. Seeing that passive resistance was in the long run hopeless, on 26 September Germany's new Chancellor and Foreign Minister Gustav Stresemann declared an end to it. Despite rising opposition, however, he accepted the agreement for resumption of reparations payments made between French government and private industry in the Ruhr. The MICUM (*Mission interallié de contrôle des usines et mines*) agreements, signed on 23 November 1923, under which reparations payments would have resumed early in 1924, France's resultant industrial domination of the Ruhr and her intended separation of the Rhineland from Germany — all these combined were too much for either British or American authorities to accept,[19] and they rapidly decided on summoning two expert committees for a far-reaching review and general solution of the reparations question.

The eventual result of this was the Dawes Plan, which entailed a complete reform under foreign direction of the German financial economy, with fundamental tax reforms, massive foreign support of German national finances and, finally, the installation of an international regulatory agency.[20] Under severe pressure from American financial and political interests, France was forced in return to back down from her aggressive unilateral policy of 'productive guarantees'.

The resignation of Poincaré as Prime Minister on 1 June 1923 symbolized the passing of French power as the most important el-

---

19. Ibid., p. 73.
20. See Schuker, pp. 181–86: 'Sidestepping the issue of Germany's total liability, the committee put forward only a schedule of annual payments. . . In practice the Dawes Plan marked another sharp reduction of the German debt. Its 1924 value was roughly equivalent to a capital sum of 39 to 40 milliard gold marks — assuming that it continued in operation without emendation for the maximum period of sixty-four years. . . The Dawes Plan called for German payments beginning with 1 milliard gold marks in 1924–1925 and rising gradually to a standard annuity of 2.5 milliards, a rate to be reached in 1929–1930. . . The Dawes Plan, in short, mixed concrete and well-conceived proposals for German financial rehabilitation with purposeful obscurity in issues where opposing positions appeared irreconcilable.'

ement in Continental politics.[21] But much more, the defeat of France's Ruhr policy ushered in a new phase of German foreign policy marked by increased mutual understanding with the United States. Unwilling to allow either a French take-over of German heavy industry or the collapse of the German economy, America intervened on the side of Germany to regulate the reparations problem. Her readiness to play a direct and formal role in the reparations negotiations was demonstrated by the Dawes Plan, the result of the London Reparations Conference in July–August 1924. Through forceful arbitration, Washington succeeded in the immediate regulation of the reparations question.

German–American financial cooperation therefore produced direct beneficial results for German foreign policy.[22] Krüger has pointed out the latter's new maneuverability after the end of passive resistance on 26 September 1923. While it was clear that Germany had lost her struggle with France in a military sense, the differences between 1918/1919 and 1923 were dramatic: '. . . there was no victorious coalition [against Germany] nor was Germany completely isolated this time'.[23] But according to Erdmann, it also led to a change of policy: 'Stresemann found the actual support for stabilization which he sought, insofar as by liquidating the Ruhr conflict he secured American credits.'[24] The American financial expert became the ubiquitous figure at every international financial conference. The Dawes Plan put an end to what Poidevin and Bariéty call the 'Cold War' between Germany and France. It ended the Ruhr conflict and was, likewise, the first step on the road to Locarno, the League and an end to German diplomatic isolation.

21. See Schuker, p. 231: 'At the time [of Poincaré's resignation on 1 June 1924], his resignation was widely interpreted abroad as marking symbolically the end of France's unilateral determination to enforce Germany's strict conformity to obligations under the Treaty of Versailles.' See also, Poidevin and Bariéty, *Frankreich und Deutschland* (Munich, 1982), pp. 332–40.
22. Stresemann to Maltzan, 7 April 1925, quoted in Link, 'Die Beziehungen', p. 77: '. . . dass die Entscheidungen über Europas Zukunft im wesentlichen in den Händen der Vereinigten Staaten liegen.' See also Schuker, p. 265: 'Stresemann believed that the German interest lay in encouraging investment of American capital in the Reich over the long as well as the short term. Some people might not approve of capitalism's decisive role in world affairs, he reflected, but 'if American capitalism had not been against us, then we certainly would not have lost the war'. Once international capital acquired a material interest in German prosperity, he held, the major powers would take quite a different view of things.'
23. Krüger, *Außenpolitik*, pp. 218–19.
24. Erdmann, 'Weimarer Republik', p. 260.

3

The Primacy of Revision, 1924–1929

Toward Locarno and Geneva: Stresemann's *Entspannungspolitik*

When he assumed the dual burden of the Chancellorship and the portfolio of Foreign Minister on 13 August 1923, Gustav Stresemann inherited a situation grave and dangerous indeed. Since January of the same year, German passive resistance to the occupation of the Ruhr had resulted in complete economic and financial chaos, which threatened to bring about political disaster as well. During his 'hundred days' as Chancellor, as he skilfully balanced two successive coalition governments, Stresemann succeeded in bringing Germany out of the depths of despair. On 26 September he declared an end to passive resistance. Shortly thereafter, supported by Reichsbank President Hjalmar Schacht, he began to stabilize the virtually hopeless financial condition. Stresemann and Schacht hoped to avoid further sanctions against Germany by relying on continued diplomatic negotiations to reduce reparations.

At the same time, however, Stresemann's Chancellorship was deeply imperilled both from the Right (with the Bavarian separatist uprisings and the Hitler *Putsch* of 8–11 November) and from the Left (the Socialist and communist uprisings in Saxony and Thuringia). Parallel to these outbreaks, Stresemann had to contend with what his government viewed as very serious attempts by the French government to stimulate Rhenish separatism.[1] The Rhenish separatist movement, apparently centered on the person of Konrad Adenauer, had received sporadic French support and encouragement since the final days of the war. During the Ruhr crisis, more direct overtures were made to the separatists, which to Germany seemed to threaten the very integrity of

1. McDougall, *France's Rhineland Diplomacy, passim*. For additional remarks on Rhineland separatism and especially on the role of Adenauer, see H. Köhler, *Autonomiebewegung oder Separatismus? Die Politik der 'Kölnischen Volkszeitung' 1918/19* (Berlin, 1974).

the national state.[2] Despite such disturbances, however, in mid-November Stresemann announced a plan for the stabilization of the financial economy, in concert with his Minister of Finance, Dr. Hans Luther, and Reichsbank President Schacht. This plan created a new currency system and formed the basis for a period of expansion and prosperity. Even with such efforts, however, the German economy was still at the mercy of foreign credit. What economic expansion was possible would only occur on a base of foreign investment and when that dried up, reparations payments would be among the first of the government's obligations to be abandoned.[3]

Despite his plan for stabilization, Stresemann could not weather the intense political storm of his term as Chancellor. On 23 November 1923 his second and final cabinet fell. Although no longer Chancellor, he nevertheless retained the post of Foreign Minister, an appointment he was to hold until his death on 3 October 1929. During the next six years, therefore, German foreign policy came to be closely identified with the name of Gustav Stresemann.[4] What were his characteristics as Foreign Minister and how did he seek to implement his foreign policy goals?

The outlines of Stresemann's foreign policy were already visible even before 1914. In view of Germany's relatively limited supply of raw materials and her strategically disadvantageous geographic position in Central Europe, on the eve of the great war Stresemann advocated among his liberal–imperialist colleagues (who thought less in military or power-political terms than in those of economics) a large-scale central European economy, dominated by Germany. When measured against Russia, the United States and above all the British Empire, this would provide the Reich with guaranteed import and export opportunities safe from foreign influence. Beyond *Mitteleuropa*, Germany's overseas possessions would yield valuable raw materials and provide essential markets for the home industrial economy. Stresemann considered it self-evident that German economic well-being depended on the development of such a continental

2. See in this connection Erdmann, 'Weimarer Republik', p. 243.
3. A. Rosenberg, 'Außenpolitik in der Stabilisierungsphase', in G. Ziebura, ed., *Grundfragen der deutschen Außenpolitik seit 1871* (Darmstadt, 1975), p. 270.
4. Ibid., p. 275: 'Stresemann war der erste deutsche Staatsmann seit Bismarck, der einen wirklichen, umfassenden Plan der Außenpolitik hatte und ihn im wesentlichen konsequent durchführte.' See also J. Bariéty, 'Der Versuch einer europäischen Befriedigung: Von Locarno bis Thoiry', in H. Rössler, ed., *Locarno und die Weltpolitik 1924–1932* (Göttingen, 1969), pp. 32f: 'In der Erörterung der deutschen Locarnopolitik nimmt die Figur Stresemanns natürlich einen eminenten Platz ein, handelte es sich doch um dessen Außenpolitik.' For the most recent treatments of Stresemann, see Wolfgang Michalka and Marshall Lee, eds., *Gustav Stresemann* (Darmstadt, 1982); and Krüger, *Außenpolitik*, especially pp. 207–18.

scheme, supported by overseas possessions. Correspondingly, an imperialist *Weltpolitik*, if properly pursued, could overcome weakness on the one hand by stimulating the German economy, whilst on the other it could preclude armed conflict as far too damaging to trade. In Stresemann's view, the World War was not only a struggle against France, but ultimately against the British Empire, Germany's global commercial rival and the greatest enemy of his 'liberal–commercial', imperialist *Weltpolitik*.

The war, unexpected and unwanted by Stresemann, nevertheless was an opportunity for Germany to establish once and for all her absolute claim to Great Power status. This could be accomplished by defeating France and erecting a Central European *Grossraum*, thus making Germany an effective rival to the British Empire. Michael-Olaf Maxelon has demonstrated that the concept of a Central European economic empire controlled by Germany became a permanent aspect of Stresemann's wartime thinking, which also envisaged that France would (be compelled to?) belong to this German economic domain:

> That Stresemann was willing to force France against her national interests to enter a German industrial superiority, reflects the degree to which the need for security dominated Stresemann's thinking on economic imperialism... Stresemann the annexationist and vocal advocate of a 'victorious peace' was in fact far more concerned over the economic future of the German Reich than with any pan-German imperialist drive for conquest; his '*Mitteleuropa-Konzeption*' was more defensive than offensive.[5]

The collapse of the German Reich in 1918 put an abrupt end to such dreams. Nevertheless, there is a clear continuity in the views of Stresemann before and after the war, evidenced by the fact that, following the defeat, his foreign policy conceptions were aimed at returning Germany to her former position as a Great Power.[6] Stresemann steadfastly insisted of Germany's right as a Great Power to claim her place among the community of nations. But again, as before, he rejected the use of military force, emphasizing rather Germany's peaceful economic and political recovery. Following the war, then, Stresemann's central aim was the restoration of a sovereign and equal Germany: this could only be achieved by making use of the German economy. Stresemann attached himself to those liberals on the periph-

5. M.–O. Maxelon, *Stresemann und Frankreich. Deutsche Politik der Ost-West-Balance* (Düsseldorf, 1972), pp. 277f.

6. Ibid., p. 281. See also W. Weidenfeld, 'Gustav Stresemann — der Mythos vom engagierten Europäer', *GWU* 24 (1973), p. 745: 'Ich glaube, die Benutzung weltwirtschaftlicher Zusammenhänge, um mit dem Einzigen, womit wir noch Großmacht sind, mit unserer Wirtschaftsmacht, Außenpolitik zu machen, ist die Aufgabe, die heute jeder Außenminister zu lösen hätte.'

ery of the Wilhelmine political spectrum who viewed economics as the most powerful force for political action, and who thoroughly rejected the use of armed force, either in the East or West, on realistic rather than on ideological grounds. This set him on a collision course with a large part of the *Reichswehr*, particularly the group around General von Seeckt; their rigid thinking went no farther than the concept of Germany as a continental Prussian state whose power would always rest on military calculations. Hildebrand says:

> Still [Stresemann] did not consider allowing [Germany] thereby to become dependent upon the Entent Powers in order eventually to undertake military operations in the East with Western backing. Nevertheless, he vigorously opposed those in the Foreign Ministry, the Reichswehr and in industry who called for an alliance with the Soviet Union which threatened to pay the West back in kind [for their defeat of Germany].[7]

It would only be possible for Germany to overcome the diplomatic isolation imposed on her by the Treaty of Versailles by taking great care not to threaten the interests of France. Any attempt to moderate the conditions of the treaty was likely to be interpreted in Paris as a challenge to French security. The essential elements and objectives of Stresemann's policy toward France were already apparent as early as 1920–1921: (1) resistance to any French initiatives which threatened the security, territorial integrity or national unity of the Reich; (2) economic agreements compatible with both Germany's reparations obligations and her industrial capacity; (3) Franco-German economic pledges on the basis of complete equality; (4) the revision of that dishonorable act, the Treaty of Versailles; (5) the reduction of outstanding political tensions between Germany and France and their eventual settlement by treaty. Only after achieving these goals, Stresemann asserted, could Germany recover her position as a sovereign and equal Great Power.[8]

Stresemann's policy with regard to France was in no way an isolated element of his foreign policy, but conceived within a far more complex system of international relations. Apart from direct Franco–German relations, certain other factors entered into his political calculations, such as the apparently rejuvenated British concept of 'balance of power' on the European continent and America's increasingly obvious interest in a stable continental economy capable of absorbing US

7. Thus Hildebrand in a review of Weidenfeld's book on Stresemann's policy toward Britain: 'Stresemanns Bemühung um England — Taktik, Ziel und Hindernisse', *FAZ*, 22 September 1972.
8. Maxelon, *Stresemann und Frankreich*, p. 283.

exports.[9] Stresemann was among a bare handful of major Western politicians fully to comprehend the political and diplomatic changes wrought by the First World War, and one of an even more exclusive number who realized that the only victor of that conflict was the United States, transformed by the war into the leading world power. Accordingly, it would be to Germany's economic and political advantage to develop the closest possible ties to the United States, while simultaneously working to undermine French economic and military power. Finally, Stresemann understood how valuable were latent Western fears of the Bolshevization of Eastern and Central Europe. In view of this appreciation of the varying influences on German foreign policy, therefore, it can hardly be claimed that Stresemann's foreign policy was aimed exclusively at France, although that country necessarily played a central role in his considerations.[10] The nature of the relationship with France was not merely governed by such factors as the Treaty of Versailles and reparations, but was also affected by Germany's relations with the other victors. To quote Rosenberg: 'Stresemann remained unshaken in his conviction that without Anglo-American intervention, direct Franco-German cooperation was highly unlikely. It is not surprising that Stresemann's ideas were greeted warmly in England.[11]

Thus, given the obstacles to Franco-German understanding, next to the United States, Great Britain occupied the most important position in the foreign policy of the long-serving Foreign Minister. Why? In the first place, Stresemann felt that, although the war had driven France and Britain together, the closeness of this relationship was tempered by old-established British interests, which led her to resist any other Power's hegemonic domination of the continent. British policy on the Ruhr crisis seemed in some quarters to indicate a return to a more traditional foreign policy and the search for a 'balance of power'. Britain would therefore be inclined to play the part of arbiter in

9. See above all Link's study, *Amerikanische Stabilisierungspolitik*.
10. Graml, *Europa*, p. 174: 'Das politische Chaos, in das Europa in 1923 vor allem durch Frankreich gestürzt worden war, erwies sich mithin insofern als fruchtbar, als sich im Laufe des Jahres die Erkenntnis durchsetzte, dass die europäische Politik, wenn sich der Kontinent die Möglichkeit einer Serie kleiner Kriege oder gar eines neuen allgemeinen Kreiges ersparen wolle, zwei konkrete Aufgaben bewältigen müsse: die deutsch-französische Verständigung und eine Reform des Völkerbundes. Gelang eine Annäherung zwischen Paris und Berlin, so mochte das französische Sicherheitsbedürfnis seine hysterische Aggressivität und das französische Hegemonialsystem seine jede vernünftige Außenpolitik ausschliessende Präponderanz im Denken des Quai d'Orsay verlieren. . . .' In acknowledgement of this, Stresemann was forced to accord France priority in German foreign policy, for he recognized as the most urgent task of German policy 'ohne Zweifel die Beendigung des "Kriegszustandes" zwischen Frankreich und Deutschland'. Ibid., p. 175.
11. Rosenberg, 'Stabilisierungsphase', p. 272.

continental affairs, a fact on which Stresemann was to count in his efforts to overcome the Versailles system. In addition, British commercial and economic interest in a stable German economy within a stable continental economy constituted an important factor in Stresemann's veiled policy of revision, the intricacy of which Werner Weidenfeld aptly described:

> To the degree that Stresemann gave the highest priority to Anglo-German cooperation he also pursued the goal of hindering any renewal of Anglo-French cooperation from which Germany was excluded. At the same time, in his demands for British mediation he saw possible leverage for a relaxation in Franco-German tensions. Throughout, he hoped that, out of self-interest, Britain would use her influence to prevent a Franco-Russian combination, a thought which made German flesh crawl.[12]

Thus, Anglo–German relations occupied a special place in Stresemann's foreign policy, and this is indeed true for German foreign policy in the post-war years in general. On precisely this point — the German analysis of Britain's continental interests — the question must arise whether the German leadership was being realistic in their appraisal of British intentions, or whether in fact the evaluation represented wishful thinking rather than *Realpolitik*. Hildebrand has indicated that neither Stresemann nor the contemporary German leadership in general accurately perceived the British 'balance of power' policy:

> Great Britain was by no means ready to support Germany merely out of anxiety over the need to create a counterweight to an ambitious and hegemonic France. Rather, London clung to Anglo-French cooperation in order to preserve Britain's continental influence, while at the same time attempting a gradual normalization in British relations with the defeated Germany. The German 'continuity of error' with respect to Britain, that is, the serious misjudgment of the actions and reactions of British global policy which had been the *Leitmotiv* of the Bismarck and Wilhelmine eras, can scarcely be overlooked in the diplomatic considerations and initiatives of the [Weimar] period.[13]

Nevertheless, and this must be emphasized, Stresemann's estimation of British continental policy differed markedly from right-wing estimates. The Right, in particular Hitler (and to some degree the Left as well), interpreted the lack of British support for France's policy of 'productive guarantees' and the Ruhr occupation in 1923 not only as a sign of cooling Franco-British relations, but even as a reorientation

12. Weidenfeld, 'Mythos', p. 748.
13. Hildebrand, 'Stresemanns Bemühungen um England'.

away from France and in favor of Germany. Indeed, within military circles, particularly that of von Seeckt, there was widespread acceptance of an 'inevitable' clash of French and British arms. Even while cabinet-level officials in the Foreign Ministry and the leadership of the moderate center parties bemoaned the lack of British support, at the same time they cherished hopes of an Anglo-German alliance.[14] In the light of conservatives' misapprehension and moderates' dreams, Stresemann had to tread a very narrow line indeed between support and condemnation for his policy on Britain.

Mindful of his critics on the Right, Stresemann took great care to pursue what appeared as the traditional Wilhelmine goal of Great Power status, a position characterized by complete freedom of maneuver in foreign policy. But while his Wilhelmine predecessors, above all Grand Admiral von Tirpitz, had sought to achieve European hegemony through a policy of 'calculated risk' directed at a decisive confrontation with the global naval power of Great Britain, Stresemann rejected such an idea.[15] Moreover, he sought to avoid at all costs anything which might limit Germany's diplomatic options, and in particular one-sided alliance systems. This leads Walsdorff to question Stresemann's mainly Western orientation, even though the latter made little secret of his preference for Western culture.[16] Rather, Walsdorff emphasizes that Stresemann's Western policy must be interpreted in the first instance as the key to his *Ostpolitik*. Only after the settlement of immediate problems in the West could Germany turn to the solution of more fundamental Eastern questions, in particular the revision of the German–Polish frontier. 'In a shrewd appreciation of the possible', Stresemann wanted to avoid the trap into which his nationalist opponents had fallen; the simultaneous pursuit of both Western and Eastern foreign policy goals. Germany's only immediate concern, then was to avoid the *status quo* along her Eastern frontier hardening to prevent future territorial revision. Meanwhile, a settlement of Franco-German differences could serve not only to stabilize Germany's Western defences, but also 'to encourage a lack of interest of France in power politics and alliance in the East'.[17]

The wisdom of Stresemann's tactics seemed confirmed by the gradually cooling relations between France and Poland during the mid-twenties. His foreign policy had avoided a compromising 'either–or' choice between West and East. 'Rather', concludes Weidenfeld, '[it invoked] a coolly calculated, constant struggle, a permanent confron-

14. Graml, *Europa* p. 177 and *passim*.
15. Weidenfeld, *Englandpolitik*, p. 294.
16. Waldsdorff, *Westorientierung*, p. 12.
17. Ibid., p. 23.

tation with all the forces of the international political system'.[18] By 'permanent confrontation', Weidenfeld clearly means that the Foreign Minister never lost sight of the various factors influencing German foreign policy, with its alternate cooperation and confrontation, of fulfilment and revision. Correspondingly, within the logic of his system, Stresemann's goals crystallized in order of priority.[19] Following the settlement of reparations questions, he could move for an end to occupation: first the Ruhr and eventually the remainder of the territory occupied under the Versailles Treaty. The return of the Saar and an end to military control were closely related questions. Next came revision of the Eastern frontiers. The Western security pact and German entry into the League represented tactical measures to be undertaken as revision in the East approached. For Stresemann, Eastern revision and the recovery of territory lost to Poland had very real value, while the recovery of Germany's former colonies or a possible *Anschluß* with Austria played no serious role in his foreign policy.

The achievement of Stresemann's interlocking hierarchy of goals required a delicately balanced approach toward France, aimed at reducing, and if possible eliminating, French diplomatic alternatives. As the strongest continental power, France could not be challenged directly. Germany must seek, rather, on the one hand to forge economic links with the Anglo-Saxon powers, while on the other strengthening relations with the Soviet Union through intensified trade and diplomatic ties. It was intended that France, left ultimately without diplomatic alternatives, would 'for financial, economic and security reasons turn to Germany. . . [thus creating] the only compelling and logical basis for a revision of the Treaty of Versailles. In fact, exactly that was the essence of the German-French *Verständigungspolitik* in correspondance to Stresemann's thinking'.[20] Without French assent neither the peaceful revision of the Versailles Treaty nor the resultant return of Germany to future Great Power status were possible. Thus Stresemann correctly gauged political realities; his *Verständigungspolitik* with France was not only calculated on the basis of the relative strengths and weaknesses of both countries, but was clearly tactical in nature.

It may here be asked whether Stresemann was able to realize either his short-term or his long-term goals and if his policy was one of *Realpolitik*? The Dawes Plan, and with it the beginning of American stabilization policy in Europe, provided the necessary impetus for the

18. Weidenfeld, 'Mythos', p. 746.
19. Ibid., p. 747.
20. Maxelon, *Stresemann und Frankreich*, p. 288.

solution of the most difficult and potentially dangerous postwar problem: reparations. While none doubted that this most recent international financial settlement was only a temporary solution,[21] it soon became clear that reparations were no longer merely an instrument of French power politics, but had become serious international financial business and, more importantly, an element of American global finance.[22] Accordingly, the Dawes Plan represented a severe blow to France.

It should not be forgotten that reparations were instrumental to French security, since their burdening of German national finances and economy would reinforce the Versailles settlement clause requiring German disarmament. In this fashion France intended to perpetuate Allied victory over Germany or, in other words, French continental hegemony. Deprived of reparations as one means of achieving security, the French leaders were gripped by rising anxiety over possible future confrontation with a resurgent Germany. In this climate, however, Britain appeared ready to make concessions to French security demands, and her government renewed efforts to strengthen League of Nations powers in respect of collective security. The Geneva Protocol of 2 October 1924 proposed expansion of the League Covenant to include provisions for mutual assistance in the event of aggression. But it was not approved by the British Dominions, who refused additional obligations which might draw them into European affairs. According to a later observer, 'that had the same meaning for French security demands as the Anglo-American failure to ratify the guarantee treaties at Versailles'.[23]

In response to the failure of collective security, London and Paris opened negotiations aimed at a possible bilateral security pact. In late 1924, the prospect of such an Anglo-French pact, together with new and well-founded IMCC charges concerning incomplete and dilatory German disarmament, combined to weaken considerably Germany's relatively strong diplomatic position following the Dawes Plan. In view of the IMCC report, evacuation of the Cologne zone in the occupied Rhineland, scheduled to take place on 10 January 1925, was postponed by the Allies until evidence could be given as to satisfactory progress toward German disarmament. Before evacuation, Germany must first prove her true intent by disarming in compliance with the

---

21. Schuker, *French Predominance*, p. 386: ' . . . when the Germans accepted the Dawes Plan, they fully intended to ask for another reduction in reparations within three or four years. The outcome at London, by tying France's hands in the event of default, made it virtually certain that the next German bid for revision would meet with success.'
22. Rosenberg, 'Stabilisierungsphase', p. 269.
23. Erdmann, 'Weimarer Republik', pp. 261f.

letter of the treaty. 'As seen from Berlin', concludes Jon Jacobson, 'the events of December 1924 — the non-evacuation of Cologne and the rumors of an impending Anglo-French alliance — appeared to indicate an abrupt change in the course of German relations with the West and to forecast a reverse for Germany'.[24] The situation called for prompt and effective countermeasures.

In January 1925, Stresemann proposed to the British Foreign Secretary Sir Austen Chamberlain a Western European security pact. The plan already had a certain history. As early as December 1922, German Chancellor Cuno had offered a security pact as a means of avoiding the occupation of the Ruhr and providing France with additional security guarantees.[25] During the Ruhr crisis, the offer had been repeated to the Western powers. Although nothing came of it at that time, the idea never dropped completely out of sight. Almost from the minute he became foreign minister, Stresemann was encouraged by the British ambassador — later his close associate — Lord d'Abernon to consider the plan once again.[26] Finally, various factors made the scheme attractive to all sides. For Germany, a security pact offered a real possibility of achieving evacuation of the occupied territories without further disarmament.[27] Furthermore, it would once and for all guarantee her Western frontiers against French armed intervention, and so impose very definite limits on France's diplomatic and military freedom of action.[28]

For France, a Western security pact was an alluring alternative to the unsuccessful Geneva Protocol and the equally unsuccessful Anglo-American guarantee declarations. It would offer a British guarantee of the German–French–Belgian frontier, and also promised security against German attack.

In British eyes, such a pact seemed to offer a return to the 'balance of power' in Western Europe. It promised to stabilize the Rhineland and thereby fulfil much of the French demand for security. A particular attraction was the fact that all this could be accomplished with minimal British commitment to the continent. Although conservative imperialists like Churchill, Balfour and Lord Curzon rejected European involvement, a Rhineland pact offered Austen Chamberlain an ideal means of supporting France without the far more restrictive obliga-

---

24. See Jon Jacobson, *Locarno Diplomacy. Germany and the West, 1925–1929* (Princeton, 1972), pp. 10f.
25. Schuker, *French Predominance*, pp. 24, 346.
26. F. G. Stambrook, '"Das Kind" — Lord D'Abernon and the Origins of the Locarno Pact', *CEH* 1 (1968), pp. 233–63.
27. Marks, *Illusion*, pp. 62f.
28. Jacobson, *Locarno*, p. 38.

tions of a bilateral treaty.[29] Throughout, he was convinced that a Rhineland pact was the best way of advancing the principle of collective security, since it would greatly reduce the chances of Europe slipping back into the pattern of hostile alliance systems.[30]

On 16 October 1925, after long and difficult negotiations, a series of treaties were signed in the Swiss lakeside resort of Locarno. The agreements, known collectively as the Locarno Treaties or the Rhineland Pact, consisted of a series of arbitration treaties between Germany, France, Belgium, Poland and Czechoslovakia, aimed at the peaceful settlement of disputes among the signatories. The guarantee pact between Germany, France and Belgium was specifically designed to project the signatories against aggressive attack. Additionally, the treaties offered guarantees by Great Britain, France, Belgium, Germany and Italy for maintenance of the existing frontiers and demilitarization of the Rhineland. Finally, should one party be attacked, it would receive military support from the other signatories.

What was the long-term effect (not apparent in 1925) of the Locarno Treaties on international policies? Jacobson, whose interpretation of the Locarno Treaties is perhaps the most lucid, emphasizes several results. A possible Anglo-French alliance was avoided, but insofar as British military assistance to France was guaranteed in the event of German aggression, the pacts enhanced the changes for an early evacuation of the Rhineland. The Locarno Treaties ruled out the use of military sanctions against Germany, *under certain circumstances*: so that, barring violations of the treaties by Germany, they assured her territorial integrity. Such security was necessary if Germany was to be attractive as a financial and trading partner to American investors, and to this extent, she therefore viewed the Rhineland Pact as a defensive necessity. Moreover, Locarno opened new perspectives, exactly as Stresemann had foreseen. In the long run, by settling Franco-German matters in the west the Rhineland Pact opened the door to a negotiated revision of the Eastern frontiers, since Stresemann was able to avoid an *Ostlocarno*[31] which would have guaranteed the German–Polish frontier. The Franco-Polish alliance system could therefore be undermined. Strategically, the Locarno Treaties represented a considerable

29. Ibid., p. 21: 'Chamberlain accepted the Rhineland Pact not because he preferred it but because it was the only form in which the cabinet would accept a British guarantee of French security.'

30. See ibid., p. 23: Chamberlain was captivated by the idea, since it avoided ' . . . the disadvantageous consequence of an Anglo-French alliance — the division of Europe into two alliance systems, perpetuating the situation which existed before, during, and following the war, i.e., a continent separated into two hostile camps'.

31. On the question of an 'Eastern Locarno', see the still useful Christian Holtje, *Die Weimarer Republik und das Ostlocarno-Problem 1919–1934* (Würzburg, 1958).

improvement in Germany's diplomatic situation, for the danger of a two-front war was greatly reduced.[32]

Although the Locarno Treaties materially improved Germany's position in Europe, they were bitterly attacked at home. Stresemann was accused of having willingly accepted the conditions of Versailles, thereby recognizing Germany's territorial reduction.[33] He was, however, in a very delicate position, unable to make the most of the advantages accruing to Germany from the treaties. 'Stresemann could not enunciate the extent of his triumph to the German electorate without creating acute political difficulties for the other men of Locarno, especially Briand [by now Foreign Minister], whom he wished to keep at the Quai d'Orsay',[34] points out Sally Marks. She concludes that this turned out to be a great advantage to Stresemann, who 'consequently. . . used his own political difficulties to extract further concessions as the price of German ratification'.

In October, the Locarno treaties were initialled by their architects, Stresemann, Briand and Chamberlain, as well as Mussolini, who attempted to upstage colleagues by his dramatically late arrival in Locarno at the wheel of his own open roadster. Formal signature took place in London in early December 1925. Even before the October meeting Stresemann had begun to lay the foundation for domestic support of a Western security pact. In numerous speeches, articles and letters — as, for example, the famous Crown Prince letter of 9 September 1925[35] — he attempted to allay the critics' fears. Again and again he reassured his audience that the central goal of German foreign policy was and would remain the re-establishment of Great Power status within the frontiers of 1914 and that the Locarno Treaties were an essential contribution to that goal. He was, however, careful not to mention the touchy question of the evacuation of the occupied territories, not wishing to influence adversely the talks on this subject which ran parallel to his campaign for ratification of Locarno.

The strategy worked. By mid-November the Allies announced that,

32. Jacobson, *Locarno*, pp. 40f.
33. Marks, *Illusion*, pp. 72f.
34. Ibid.
35. G. Stresemann, *Vermächtnis: Der Nachlaß in drei Bänden* (Berlin, 1932), II, p. 553. In this connection, see also the article by R. Grathwohl, in which he offers an interpretation of the Crown Prince Letter as a thoroughly nationalistic document: 'Gustav Stresemann: Reflections on His Foreign Policy', *JMH* XLV, 1 (1973), pp. 52–70, reprinted in Michalka and Lee, *Stresemann*, pp. 224–43. Krüger is critical of the heavy reliance of scholars on a handful of "key documents" (*Schlüsseldokumente*) in interpreting Stresemann's foreign policy. The Crown Prince Letter is one such piece, although Krüger acknowledges that Grathwohl's interpretation places the right emphasis on the letter, within the correct domestic political context: Krüger, *Außenpolitik*, pp. 207–8, n.1.

having regard to the Locarno agreements, evacuation of the Cologne zone would take place on 1 December 1925. At the same time, there would be a reduction in the number of occupation troops in the two remaining zones. In an additional concession, the authority of the IMCC would be cut back to a purely symbolic function. Little more than a year later, on 31 January 1927, the Interallied Military Control Commission withdrew completely from Germany.

The two successes — evacuation together with curtailment of IMCC powers and its eventual withdrawal — were the immediate benefits. Stresemann insisted all along that such benefits were the corollaries (*Rückwirkungen*) of the Locarno treaties. He hinted broadly that Germany could expect additional advantages.[36] Although between October and December 1925 this had met with Allied resistance, Stresemann soon turned the *Rückwirkungen* to his domestic advantage. Despite objection from the DNVP, whose cabinet representative had already resigned in protest on 26 October, the Reichstag ratified the Locarno Treaties, *par raison et contre coeur*. The way was now open for the eventual entry by Germany into the League of Nations.

Between Cooperation and Confrontation: German Minorities Policy

Integral to Locarno was the entry of Germany into the League of Nations, for not until she took her place at Geneva did the Treaties take effect. Her entry was essential to the Western security pact, since it afforded the only way in which the mechanism of the League Covenant could be applied directly to Franco-German affairs.[1] One of Stresemann's central foreign policy goals was the eventual transformation of the League into an instrument suited to German revisionist aims.[2] In pursuit of this goal he was not alone. Von Bülow, at that time Head of the League of Nations Section of the German Foreign Ministry and later State Secretary, originally doubted that such use could be made of the League. By the end of 1925, however, he had modified his views and for a time came to share his Foreign Minister's conviction that the League might be of value in Germany's revisionist endeavors.[3]

36. Jacobson, *Locarno*, pp. 60–67.

1. Rosenberg, 'Stabilisierungsphase', pp. 272f. On German League of Nations policy in general, see K. M. Kimmich, *Germany and the League of Nations* (Chicago, 1976).
2. Kochan, *Struggle*, pp. 43ff.
3. B.v. Bülow, *Der Versailler Völkerbund* (Berlin, 1923), pp. 525–71; Poensgen to Schubert, 12 December 1925, in *ADAP*, I, 1, pp. 64–76. Outside Germany, Bülow's

Within the Foreign Ministry there was general agreement that German membership could reduce the League's effective resistance to changes in the *status quo*, consequently leaving Germany free to pursue a more 'active' policy of revision. In fact, German strategy of undermining the peace-keeping capacity of the League had already begun during the Locarno negotiations. In the preliminary talks about possible entry, Stresemann had repeatedly emphasized the vulnerable geographic position of the German Reich, accentuated by her advanced state of disarmament, as dictated by the Treaty of Versailles. His intent was to show German passivity, and he went on to argue that it was this, combined with geographic vulnerability, which made it impossible for Germany to take part as a member of the League in possible future sanctions. After considerable negotiation, the Allies relieved Germany both of the obligation to participate in sanctions according to Article 16 of the Covenant, and also of the obligation to allow the transit of other League members' troops across Germany in the application of sanctions.[4] This concession was included in the famous Annex F of the Locarno Treaties.

By demanding the waiver of Article 16 in Germany's case, Stresemann hoped to achieve more than one aim. Firstly, he sought to reduce the effectiveness of the League as an organism for collective security.[5] Secondly, he succeeded in weakening its sanctions system. Since as far as Germany was concerned, Locarno would settle matters in the West, to weaken the League's sanctions system would have predominantly Eastern implications. Indeed, the special status conferred on Germany by Annex F had a very real impact on Poland. In any Russo-Polish conflict, Poland would be isolated, since Germany could stand on her privilege of refusing League forces transit. This raised the question 'whether any sanctions could be taken against Russia once Germany was a member of the League'.[6] Thus, even before Locarno, the first

---

hostility to the League was gradually acknowledged. Finally, in 1931 he was described by the British ambassador as 'almost purely obstructionist'. Rumbold to Simon, 'List of Leading Personalities in Germany', Berlin, 2 April. 1932 (PRO: Political, Central Germany 1931, 3028); E. v. Weizsäcker, 'Die Deutsche Völkerbundspolitik nach Räumung des Rheinlandes und nach Abschluß der Reparationsfrage', Berlin, 16 April 1930 (AA: Referat Völkerbund, Deutschland/B. 16 L532633–641).

4. J. Spenz, *Die diplomatische Vorgeschichte des Beitritts Deutschlands zum Völkerbund, 1924–1926. Ein Beitrag zur Außenpolitik der Weimarer Republik* (Göttingen, 1966), pp. 96ff. See also: Krüger, *Außenpolitik*, pp. 291–301.

5. H.W. Gatzke, *Stresemann and the Rearmament of Germany* (New York, 1969), pp. 39f. Although Krüger is something of an apologist for German foreign policy during the Weimar Republic, even he raises the question '. . . ob die Aussage der Anlage F. nicht einen Trend zur Verwässerung des Art. 16 fortsetzte'. Krüger, *Außenpolitik*, p. 300.

6. Erdmann, 'Weimarer Republik', p. 263.

step was taken toward weakening the Franco-Polish alliance and the eventual demotion of French continental hegemony.

There was yet a further motive behind the Foreign Minister's efforts and this had to do with Russia. At no point was Stresemann prepared to allow Locarno or Germany's subsequent entry into the League of Nations to jeopardize German–Soviet relations. Over and over again he emphasized to Moscow that Germany had no intention of supporting an anti-Soviet policy in the League, offering as proof the concessions which he had wrested from the Allies on Article 16 and on sanctions. The Foreign Minister's solicitude for good relations with the Soviets in part reflected domestic political reality. At this stage, even if he had wanted to (which he did not), Stresemann would have had great difficulty in liquidating Germany's Rapallo policy. Had he entered into the Western security pact, which guaranteed Germany's western frontiers at the sacrifice of friendship with Russia, this would have been interpreted by every German as a voluntary surrender of revisionist aims and an open acceptance of the Treaty of Versailles. This, Graml remarks drily, 'would have cost the Foreign Minister his political existence, perhaps even his life'.[7]

To the same extent that Stresemann avoided a decline in German–Russian relations, so did he strengthen his bargaining position *vis-à-vis* the West. Thus, from the outset he demanded a permanent seat for Germany on the League Council, along with the other Great Powers, Great Britain, France, Italy and Japan. Both Stresemann and his colleagues in the Wilhelmstrasse viewed fulfilment of this request as a material advance toward resumption of Great Power status and equal treatment (*Gleichberechtigung*).[8]

Prior to German entry, the composition of the Council had remained unchanged. Permanent membership was limited to Great Powers and it was understood that should the United States or the Soviet Union enter the League, a permanent place awaited them on the Council. Although the tenure of non-permanent members was limited to three years, non-permanent membership of the Council had remained constant since the birth of the League in 1920. Among these members, a certain political–geographic distribution was represented: former Allies, former neutral powers and a representative from the American Hemisphere. The German demand for a permanent Council seat reopened for the first time since 1920 the complex issue of Council representation. It served as a convenient excuse for those powers who,

---

7. Graml, *Europa*, p. 197.
8. Köpke, 'Stichworte für den Auswärtigen Ausschuß', Berlin, 22 March 1926 (AA: Referat Völkerbund, Ratssitz Allg./Bd. 3, L466239–245); Zechlin, *Aufzeichnung*, Berlin, 26 March 1926 (Ibid., L466305–308).

whatever their motivation, sought permanent representation in the Council: Brazil, Spain and Poland. German entry, originally planned for March 1926, had to be postponed until September and German anger and resentment mounted during the intervening months as the League re-examined the Council and its makeup. Consequently, both quantitative and qualitative changes resulted from what was called the 'Council Crisis of 1926'. These arose from attempts to fit into the Council not only Germany, but also representatives from other blocs, now deemed necessary by the Allies. The membership grew from ten to fourteen. In addition, an intermediate status of 'semi-permanence' was created, enabling a non-permanent member to renew membership. Semi-permanence was accorded to Poland, in response to her demands for a permanent seat. Brazil received neither permanent nor semi-permanent status and petulantly withdrew from the League. The Council underwent a significant quantitative change in 1926 with the entry of Germany and six other new members. Between 1926 and 1933, the period of German membership, no less than 25 states occupied non-permanent Council seats. This instability, initiated by the reform compromise of 1926, can to some degree be ascribed to subsequent German policy in the League, with the objective of maintaining within the Council 'a controlled state of flux'.[9]

German demands for a permanent Council seat dominated foreign affairs during the spring and summer of 1926. Both Brazil and Poland made identical demands, forcing Stresemann to refocus German energies to prevent Poland from receiving a permanent seat. He skilfully changed tactics, alternating between concession and threat. At the March Council session, as his demand for a permanent seat was not immediately accepted, the Foreign Minister demonstratively left Geneva. Within days he increased the pressure on the Western powers with an even more expressive gesture. On 24 April 1926, Stresemann played his trump card by reaffirming the spirit of Rapallo in a new German–Soviet agreement known as the Treaty of Berlin. Poland had to be content with a semi-permanent seat on the Council, as the best that France could achieve. So, on 8 September 1926, Germany entered the League as a permanent Council member. Her Great Power status was officially recognized.

Due to the political retreat of the United States from Europe after the war and the absence of the USSR from political events in Central and Western Europe, the League of Nations assumed an almost

9. For a more comprehensive analysis of Germany's policy with respect to the Council, see M. Lee, 'Disarmament and Security: The German Security Proposals in the League of Nations, 1926–1930. A Study in Revisionist Aims in an International Organisation', *MGM*, I (1979), pp. 35–45.

entirely European character. Strongly influenced, if not indeed controlled, by Britain and France,[10] the League appeared to be less a means of collective security than an instrument of Anglo-French policy: the aim here was the security and perpetuation of the continental *status quo* as established by the Treaty of Versailles and only slightly altered by Locarno. This Anglo-French axis and its influence on League policy was clearly visible in the constitution of the Leage Covenant, whose intention was declared to be the preservation of peace. In addition, the League served to confirm the political status of members, particularly in the case of the handful of Great Powers with permanent membership in the League Council: Great Britain, France, Italy, Japan, and since 1926 Germany as well. The United States and the Soviet Union had only to signal their readiness to take their vacant places in this 'club'. Supplementing the permanent members were non-permanent members, elected from the Assembly for five-year terms. The Council, the League's most august body and court of last resort, would take the chief place in any action against security violations. But the political reality was quite distinct from principle. In practice, the Council's response to such violations reflected less the principles of the Covenant than the national interests of its members, and this provoked much of the criticism levelled at the League during the interwar era. The charge that the League simply extended prewar political antagonisms into the postwar era is not entirely unjustified.[11]

In view of such strong Anglo-French influence in the League, membership promised few immediate advantages for German revisionist policy. In its structure, moreover, the League was scarcely flexible enough to respond quickly to the subtle shift in continental power politics which since 1924 had gradually tipped the balance in Germany's favor. Finally, neither the League itself nor German membership in it could overcome the growing contradiction between a general policy of revision of the Versailles system, taking place outside the League and independent of its influence, and its own dedication to conserving the very treaty system under revision.

The question arises, then, whether within such an unreceptive and basically static assemblage German policy could reasonably be ex-

---

10. It was the conviction of the German Foreign Ministry that the League was the tool of Anglo–French policy. See M. Lee, 'The German Attempt to Reform the League. The Failure of German League of Nations Policy, 1930–1932', in Deutsches Historiche Institut Paris, ed., *Francia. Forschung zur westeuropäischen Geschichte* (Munich, 1978), v. 5 (1977), pp. 473–90.

11. On the history and structure of the League of Nations, see F. P. Walters, *A History of the League of Nations* (London, 1960); and A. Pfeil, *Der Völkerbund. Literaturbericht und kritische Darstellung seiner Geschichte* (Darmstadt, 1976).

pected to achieve its revisionist goals. Apparently not. Thus, for example, Albert Dufour-Feronce, the highest German official in the Secretariat (the League's administrative branch) asked his Foreign Minister fully two years after Germany's entry into the League: 'Have we any League policy at all? And if so, what is it?'[12] Sadly, it is far easier to answer this question with hindsight than it was at the time, for not even Stresemann himself ever set out clearly and precisely Germany's policy in the League.

Such a policy would naturally depend upon two fundamental factors: on the one hand, the structure of the League of Nations as described above, and on the other, Stresemann's own ambivalent attitude toward it. It was never certain whether he intended the League to play a central role in German foreign policy or whether German participation was merely the consequence of his Locarno policy and a convenient opportunity for periodical duplication of Locarno's summitry.[13] Perhaps most revealing was the uncertainty among German policymakers themselves as to Germany's status within the League: should she consider herself the weakest of the Great Powers, or the strongest of the lesser powers? Vacillation between both opinions depended upon changes of the situation. As a permanent member of the Council, Germany sought at all times to protect her Great Power status, in particular opposing Council reform involving an increased number of permanent members. At the same time, however, Germany courted secondary and lesser states and hoped to become their spokesman, in an effort to create broad support for the eventual attempt to overturn what was described in Berlin as Anglo–French domination of the League. Nowhere is this ambivalent posture more evident in retrospect than in Stresemann's policy within the League Council. He was determined, on the one hand, to undermine its ability to respond vigorously to aggression, yet at the same time he sought to preserve the Council as the bastion of Germany's Great Power status and to give it the central role in Germany's security proposals. The implication of this policy will become apparent presently.

As part of his domestic campaign to win ratification of Locarno and acceptance of German entry into the League, Stresemann sketched out the gains to be won from German participation in what was considered a tool of the Allies. Thus, many Germans overcame their hostility to the thought of participation at Geneva by harboring grandiose hopes for their government's League policy. Although the public continued

12. Dufour to Stresemann, Geneva, 4 December 1928 (AA: Nachlaß Stresemann/Bd. 74, H168675–682).

13. M. Lee, 'Gustav Stresemann und die deutsche Völkerbundspolitik', in Michalka and Lee, *Stresemann*, pp. 350–74.

to nurture these overblown expectations, within a few months of entry Wilhelmstraße officials became aware that considerable patience would be required if Germany were to benefit from her membership. But domestic political pressures made patience an untenable policy. Stresemann and his successors, therefore, preferred to extract short-term gains from German League membership, rather than labor over long-term policy, and, because of this, a consistent League policy is difficult to discern. The improvisational and opportunistic nature of German League diplomacy clearly reveals itself in the policy toward the minorities question.

The great events of 1924 in the West, the London Reparations Conference and the Dawes Plan, had a profound effect on Eastern Europe. As capital began once more to flow into Germany, her policy in Eastern Europe ceased to be merely a series of reactions to events; the Wilhelmstraße now began to chart a much more comprehensive and long-range course in the East. Part of the Dawes capital quickly found its way into Eastern Europe, as the Germans, emulating their American patrons, attempted to set up a 'penetrating system' of financial investment in the weak and impressionable infant economies of the newly-liberated Eastern states.[14] From 1924 on, German–Polish tensions, present since 1919, worsened. In 1925, Germany, in an attempt to batter the Polish economy into submission and eventual dependence, proclaimed an economic boycott of Poland. What Poincaré had looked for in occupying the Ruhr in 1923, Stresemann hoped to accomplish by commercial and economic means against his eastern neighbor. However, his first attempt to deploy Germany's economy as the engine of territorial revision failed. With the Pilsudski coup of May 1926, it became obvious in Germany that economic pressure had failed, so that in the winter of 1926/7 Stresemann lifted the boycott.[15] The thaw in German–Polish relations was accompanied by improved relations with Czechoslovakia.[16]

In contrast to the gradually improving relations between Germany and her two immediate neighbors to the east, relations with the Soviet

---

14. Link, 'Der amerikanische Einfluß', p. 486. Compare this with Campbell, *Confrontation*, pp. 186f: '. . . [the Germans'] plan consisted primarily in waiting until the international political climate and the economic recovery of Germany would make possible a gradual reassertion of German influence in Central and Eastern Europe. This process would certainly have been at least initially economic; indeed the Czechs already complained in 1927 that the Germans were taking capital in loans from America and Britain and reinvesting it in Eastern Europe.'

15. v. Riekhoff, *German–Polish Relations*, p. 131: 'The general trend in policies and attitudes became more conciliatory. This positive development was less a reflection of Locarno than the result of the considerably improved economic situation and a favorable domestic political constellation in both countries.'

16. Campbell, *Confrontation*, pp. 198f.

Union began to cool. Though not entirely unforeseen, the deterioration in Russo-German relations caused some concern in the Wilhelmstraße. Nevertheless, the tumultuous domestic events in the Soviet Union and the stronger Western orientation of recent German foreign policy multiplied misunderstanding and suspicion between the two countries. Despite the 1926 Treaty of Berlin, German–Soviet relations were at their lowest point since the assassination of Count Mirbach. Matters did not improve in 1927 as Britain severed relations with Russia, for Stresemann was forced to walk a very fine line between London and Moscow. Whatever the cost, he could not afford to sacrifice the East–West balance which had characterized German foreign policy since Rapallo.[17]

Similarly, the Foreign Minister attempted to maintain a balance between the shrill cries of German conservatives for an active minorities policy, on the one hand, and the demands of a more calculated Western policy on the other. Furthermore, in 1927, all Wilhelmstrasse officials unanimously agreed that the time for a minorities initiative was not yet at hand: 'As long as Germany failed to enact her own liberal legislation protecting minorities and could therefore expect [continued] unfavorable foreign reaction, it appeared to the Reich government more prudent to keep clear of minorities questions in the League.'[18] In place of an active minorities policy, during the first years of League membership the *Auswärtiges Amt* restricted itself to a series of informal contacts with various minorities groups.[19] Germany provided extensive financial support to numerous minorities groups in Eastern and Southeastern Europe, but the bewildering array of informal groups pursuing their own particular interests in Germany and abroad made an official minorities policy next to impossible.[20]

Much the same policy was pursued in the League of Nations.

17. H. L. Dyck, *Weimar Germany and Soviet Russia, 1926–1933. A Study in Diplomatic Instability* (New York, 1966), pp. 67–139. Indeed, Krüger goes so far as to say that, following the Locarno Treaties, Weimar foreign policy was based almost entirely on a Western orientation. Krüger, *Außenpolitik*, p. 297.

18. Pieper, *Minderheitenfrage* p. 147; compare the contrasting C. Fink, 'Defender of Minorities: Germany in the League of Nations, 1926–1933'. *CEH* V, 4 (1972), pp. 330–57; and the more recent and more balanced treatment by Fink, 'Stresemann's Minority Policies, 1924–29', *JCH* 14 (1979), pp. 403–22, reproduced in Michalka and Lee, *Stresemann*, pp. 375–99. Fink still portrays Stresemann as a tireless defender of minority rights, leaving the impression of a much more active policy than is presented here. Krüger, on the other hand, plays down German minority policy to such a degree that it barely comes up in his treatment of Weimar foreign policy: Krüger, *Außenpolitik* pp. 470–3.

19. N. Krekeler, *Revisionsanspruch und geheime Ostpolitik der Weimarer Republik. Die Subventionierung der deutschen Minderheit in Polen, 1919–1933* (Stuttgart, 1974), *passim*; J. Hiden, 'The Weimar Republic and the Problem of the Auslandsdeutsche', *JCH*, 12 (1977), pp. 273–289.

20. Hiden, *Germany and Europe*, p. 279.

Although the protests and petitions of German minorities found support from other Council members in the League as well as Germany herself, she regularly tried to prevent minorities questions coming before the Council, since, as an interested party, she would have been barred from taking part in adjudication. The aim of German minorities policy, therefore, was to insure that German minorities remained a cohesive force in their countries of residence and retained their sense of German identity. They must remain national enclaves, indeed political stepping-stones for the 'large scale' revision contemplated one day for the East.[21] German minorities policy thus constituted a parallel or flanking aspect of the 'penetrating system' of economic investment in Eastern Europe, with the simultaneous objective of increasing political influence in East and Southeast Europe. It was in the German interest, therefore, to avoid a permanent minorities settlement, and indeed to keep the German minorities question as active, as acute, as possible.[22] This inflamed problem would, above all, cripple Polish foreign and domestic policy: 'The issue was territory, not people. In an important sense, then, the Germans in Poland were in reality the hostages of Berlin, not Warsaw.'[23]

Stresemann had hoped to avoid an open struggle in the League over minorities questions, but by the latter half of 1928 this was no longer possible. In Germany, demands for a more active minorities policy grew more strident until at last they could no longer be ignored. In September 1928, as representative of the Reich in place of Stresemann, who was recovering from illness, Chancellor Hermann Müller forcefully called for the settlement of minorities questions in a speech to the League Assembly. Throughout the fall, pressure on the Wilhelmstrasse mounted as more and more parties demanded forthright action following a rising number of petitions to the League by German minorities in Poland, specifically in Upper Silesia. Finally, the storm broke in a bitter shouting match between Stresemann and Polish Foreign Minister August Zaleski in Lugano at the Council session of December 1928. Stresemann's dramatic performance had precisely the effect he desired: he became the spokesman for German outrage on the min-

---

21. Pieper, *Minderheitenfrage*, pp. 95f.
22. Ibid, pp. 337f. See also Lee, 'Völkerbundspolitik', p. 360: '. . . wie die deutsche Minderheitenpolitik zeigt, war die Regierung zu keinem Zeitpunkt bereit, eine endgültige Minderheitenregelung zu akzeptieren. Weder mit einer Umsiedlung noch mit einer Assimilation wollte man sich abfinden. Deshalb war der oberste Grundsatz Berlins, unter der deutschen Minderheit in Polen einen Zustand der gesteuerten Unruhe aufrechtzuerhalten. Eine derartige Unruhe würde nicht nur die Minderheitenfrage im Völkerbund am Kochen halten, sondern auch ein ständiger Pfahl im Fleische Polens sein, der die Mittel des Landes aufzehren und seinen Widerstand gegen eine schließliche Gebietsrevision schwächen würde.'
23. Ibid.

orities problem; his domestic opponents lined up behind him to support a foreign policy they had formerly attacked.[24]

Stresemann's minorities initiative, although he and the Wilhelmstraße had been forced into making it, had real tactical value. In seeking to deflect domestic criticism of his efforts to negotiate an early evacuation of the Rhineland and a further reduction in reparations, he had discovered in the minorities issue an almost perfect lightning rod. No other question could so capture public attention. Originally, far from contemplating a minorities offensive, Stresemann appears to have been prepared to sacrifice this aspect of foreign policy for the sake of immediate achievement of revisionist goals in the west. For this reason the paper setting out Germany's official attitude as to the League's process for dealing with minority petitions was thrown together in great haste; it reached the Council in time for its March 1929 session, but, conceived as it was under great strain, it ran counter to League principle. Philosophically and institutionally the League was set up to protect the rights of minorities but at the same time to ease their transition or assimilation into their country of residence. This emphasis on assimilation contrasted sharply with German minorities policy in Poland. Accordingly, the proposal of March 1929 sought to reverse League policy, calling for a study-committee to examine the possibility of the creation of a permanent minorities commission, which would have more nearly fit the long-term aims of German minorities policy in the east. This proposal, Germany hoped, would provide short-term relief from an otherwise difficult situation, since she was really not prepared for a full-scale minorities offensive. Furthermore, the government wanted to preserve the German minority in Poland intact, as a mine, so to speak, planted deep beneath enemy lines. But at its June session in Madrid the Council rejected Germany's proposal and, in direct contrast, vigorously supported the principle of assimilation.

The restrained German response to the Madrid Council decision was a clear sign that the minorities initiative had been purely tactical and undertaken for its value in showing Stresemann's domestic detractors that his foreign policy was indeed aggressive and revisionist. Completely engrossed with reparations negotiations, Stresemann expressed himself well satisfied with the outcome. Privately, however, the Wilhelmstraße was bitterly disappointed. State Secretary Carl von Schubert, who had grave misgivings about the minorities policy,

---

24. Rumbold to Chamberlain, Berlin, 24 December 1928 (PRO: Political, Central/Germany 969, 12907): 'Since Herr Stresemann's return from Lugano, criticisms of his foreign policy have died down and public opinion seems to be concentrating its attention on the forthcoming meeting of the experts [of the Young Committee in Paris in February) and the possibility of a settlement of the reparations question.'

resentfully reported to the Reich Chancellery that there was nothing more which could be achieved in this field.[25] With similar resignation, Gerhard Köpke, Head of the Western Section in the Foreign Ministry, admitted to the British ambassador Sir Horace Rumbold that Germany had timed her moved very badly:

> Dr. Köpke . . . expressed the interesting view that the minorities question should not have been raised just yet. It was too soon after the war. I inferred that had it not been for the passage of arms at Lugano between Dr. Stresemann and M. Zaleski, the question would, as far as the Germans are concerned, have been allowed to simmer.[26]

Although Köpke no doubt appreciated the domestic tactical gain extracted from the minorities offensive of 1929, the Council's decision to support assimilation certainly appeared to be a severe blow to long-term German objectives. Stresemann's Eastern policy, however, was more complex than it appeared. Germany's minorities policy was a central element in a more comprehensive strategy designed to secure the earliest possible territorial revision of the Eastern frontiers. Although the presence of German minorities in Eastern and Southeastern Europe complemented German economic penetration there, the agitation by these minorities ran counter to the generally peaceful and continuous nature of German *Ostpolitik*. For this reason, Stresemann was in the end prepared to sacrifice his minorities policy to domestic political considerations, a tactically daring political decision which he hoped would free him to undertake the delicate negotiations surrounding the Young Plan and the Hague Conference with relatively broad domestic support. As the bitter struggle surrounding ratification of the Young Plan in Germany suggests, the Foreign Minister was not entirely successful in deflecting domestic opposition. Since the minorities policy was held by the German public as virtually synonymous with the League of Nations policy, the failure of the German minorities offensive of 1929 was inevitably interpreted to mean the general failure of Germany's League policy.

German minorities policy clearly reflected the fundamentally Western orientation of German foreign policy under Stresemann. By means of his *Verständigungspolitik*, which had reached its high point with Locarno, and German entry into the League, Stresemann accomplished a definite change in the political climate of postwar Europe, and so brought Germany out of her diplomatic isolation. The key

---

25. Plank, *Aufzeichnung*, Berlin ND (June) 1929 (BA: Nachlaß Punder, #74).
26. Rumbold to Henderson, Berlin, 17 June 1929 (PRO: Political, Western/LoN 185, 14125).

to his success was Germany's improved relations with France, thereby increasing her diplomatic maneuverability and achieving a very real rise in prestige among her European partners, both within the League and outside it.[27]

In Locarno, however — and Walsdorff's examination of the limits of Stresemann's foreign policy is particularly illuminating — the central motives of *Verständigungspolitik* remained only partially fulfilled.[28] For Stresemann, Locarno had both a tactical and a strategic function. Tactically, Germany could expect to effect an evacuation of the Rhineland, the return of Eupen-Malmedy and an early plebiscite in the Saar, all signifying the recovery of German sovereignty and with it an autonomous foreign policy. Strategically, the policy of understanding and cooperation between Germany and France, symbolized by Locarno, was aimed at the eventual separation of Western from Eastern questions, so that if Western security was guaranteed by a security pact, this did not preclude the future possibility of Eastern territorial revision.[29] Clearly, then, the abundant promise of Locarno remained for Stresemann only partially fulfilled, since within his lifetime only the tactical goal of an evacuation of the Rhineland was achieved. Strategically, however, Locarno and his *Verständigungspolitik* represent ostensible success, since Eastern questions were in fact separated from Western. In approaching Stresemann's Eastern policy, however, some caution must be exercised. Following Pilsudski's coup of mid-1926, Poland's economic and financial recovery put an end to German efforts to manipulate her economic affairs.[30] Once efforts to capture Poland's economy fell through, argues Maxelon, any chance of revision by means of economic leverage faded. Thus, he maintains, from 1927 on the Reich government had the opportunity to drop its claims to revision or at least to redefine them as long-range aims.[31] But no political party in Germany would hear of such a thing. Ironically, it remained for Hitler to drop the claims to Polish territory in the German–Polish non-aggression pact of January 1934. Hitler's motives, however, were totally cynical and his peace with Poland only temporary.

Despite his strategic success at Locarno in separating Eastern from Western questions, however, Stresemann's concept of peaceful revision of the German–Polish frontier was at the time unworkable.

27. Graml, 'Präsidialsystem', p. 135.
28. Walsdorff, *passim*
29. Ibid., pp. 289–91.
30. On the subject of German economic manipulation in the East as a tactic aimed at Eastern revision, see ibid., pp. 199–200.
31. Maxelon, *Stresemann und Frankreich, passim*.

Maxelon accordingly characterizes the paradox in his foreign policy as the conflict between pre-1914 diplomatic goals and post-1918 diplomatic strategy.[32] Stresemann was fixed in an impossible dilemma, for, while political reality demanded that he seek to reconstitute Germany as a Great Power, that same political reality dictated his strategic methods, and foredoomed his efforts at Eastern revision. At the root of Stresemann's predicament was Germany's economic power, for him the decisive factor in his policy of peaceful revision. The economy could not yet fulfil such a demanding role, however, since its strength — its capital — was only borrowed. It was not merely that reparations tied the German financial economy to that of America: any effort to deploy the German economy as a vehicle for revision would only strengthen the nation's dependence on American capital.[33] This therefore excluded from Stresemann's tactical arsenal confrontation, particularly with the United States:

> Stresemann, who saw in good German–American relations the second focus [besides France] in his 'elliptical' conception, was in any event resolved, in fact compelled, to avoid at all costs a collision course with the United States. . . . The actual basis of Stresemann's foreign policy, namely the economic power of the Reich, revealed itself in the event of a conflict as chimera, since to a decisive degree it was only borrowed.[34]

Germany Demands Equality: The Disarmament–Rearmament Question

Looking back on the events of Locarno, Lord d'Abernon enthusiastically concluded: 'In 1925, in the course of a few weeks the European

32. Ibid., p. 297.
33. A good recent treatment of American capital export to Germany can be found in C. – L. Holtfrerich, 'Amerikanischer Kapitalexport und Wiederaufbau der deutschen Wirtschaft 1919–23 im Vergleich zu 1924–29', *Vierteljahrsschrift für Sozial – und Wirtschaftsgeschichte*, 64, 4 (1977), pp. 497–529.
34. Ibid., p. 294; compare with the similar analysis of Rosenberg, 'Stabilisierungsphase', p. 276: 'Wesentliche Einwendungen lassen sich nicht gegen diesen politischen Gedanken Stresemanns im engeren Sinne machen, sondern nur gegen die weltwirtschaftlichen Zusammenhänge, in die Stresemanns Politik hineingehörte. Stresemann konnte alle seine Erfolge nur erzielen, indem er Deutschland an das westliche Finanzkapital und ganz besonders an die New Yorker Börse anhängte. Daraus ergaben sich nicht nur die peinlichen Einzelheiten der fremden Gläubigerkontrolle über Deutschland, sondern das Geschick Deutschlands im Ganzen war von jeder Schwankung der amerikanischen Prosperität abhängig. Auf den Auslandsanleihen beruhte die Fähigkeit Deutschlands, Reparationen zu zahlen. Wenn Deutschland einmal nicht zahlen konnte, brach sein internationaler Kredit zusammen, und dann war das ganze politische System gescheitert, daß Stresemann so mühsam errichtet hatte.'

barometer passed from "Storm" to "Fair". . . ."[1] The sudden change in the European diplomatic climate which began at Locarno and continued with Germany's entry into the League of Nations a year later was hailed as the beginning of a new era in European affairs, the 'Locarno Era'. Among the immediate and most important results of this climatic change was the confirmation of *de jure* equality to Germany among her Western partners. *De-facto* equality, however, was not a product of Locarno, for that was interpreted by both sides to mean German equality of armaments, something very definitely outside the conditions of the Treaty of Versailles. Yet Locarno and the League seemed to offer Germany a new diplomatic platform from which to pursue her aim of 'equality of treatment', or *Gleichberechtigung*. From 1926 on, German foreign policy was no longer merely a series of defensive reactions to Western initiatives, as it had been up to the end of the Ruhr crisis, but rather an active, even offensive, series of diplomatic moves. Following Locarno, it became a carefully calibrated series of diplomatic steps calculated to achieve detailed and related goals which in their sum would gradually dismantle the Treaty of Versailles. Stresemann's ultimate goal and hence that of German foreign policy itself went considerably beyond simple revision of the Versailles system: he intended on the ruins of Versailles to reconstruct and even to expand the prewar Great Power position of the German Reich. This was a goal with which all Reich citizens could identify; the means of accomplishing it, however, was a question of such incendiary provocation that in an important sense it was close to the heart of Weimar domestic political unrest. Nowhere were the problems of Germany's 'active' foreign policy of revision more apparent than in the question of disarmament and security which came before the League of Nations between 1926 and 1929/30.[2]

A central foreign policy aim, reinforced by armed French intervention in the Ruhr during 1923, was the end of Western military hegemony over Germany. A particularly appropriate means to achieve this end appeared to be Article 8 of the League Covenant, by which all signatories pledged themselves to disarm to a level consonant with their own national security. Since Germany had already reached an

---

1. Lord E. D'Abernon, *An Ambassador of Peace. Lord D'Abernon's Diary* (London, 1930), v. III (*The Years of Recovery, January 1924–October 1926*), p. 18.
2. Krüger chooses to depict Stresemann's foreign policy during the period 1927–1930 as subtle and differentiated, more overtly cooperative, with the goal of attracting foreign — American — capital and consolidating Germany's commercial position, especially in Eastern Europe. Although he depicts the serious internal differences within the Wilhelmstrasse about security and arbitration, he does not examine the detailed effect of German security proposals on the League, which leads him to conclude that German policy appeared more cooperative than perhaps it was. Krüger, *Außenpolitik*, pp. 386–96.

advanced level of disarmament, as dictated by the Treaty of Versailles, she intended to turn this apparent weakness to advantage by demanding that others disarm to the same level. From the German perspective, the great discrepancy with the unabated high armament of her neighbors, meaning France, meant that the interests of security were not served at all; Germany was completely vulnerable, France outrageously over-insured. Berlin demanded, therefore, that disarmament under Article 8 begin at once.[3]

Germany's calls for general disarmament were most threatening to France, whose foreign policy demanded the establishment of absolute security guarantees before any consideration could be given to disarmament.[4] Only after her eastern frontiers were secure from German attack and the Western powers — including Germany — had recognized and guaranteed the *status quo* established by Versailles would France feel secure. In the face of this uncompromising insistence on security before disarmament, the Wilhelmstrasse concentrated on developing a strategy to isolate France and overcome her opposition to German armament equality by urging general disarmament to Germany's level. As an obstacle to European peace, France should be forced either to disarm (which the Germans realized would never happen) or, better yet, to accept German rearmament in the name of balanced armament levels in the West.[5]

The first opportunity to confront France directly over the disarmament question came in May 1926, when Germany officially took her seat at the meeting in Geneva of the Preparatory Commission on Disarmament. Within the *Auswärtiges Amt*, however, on the very eve of the meeting there was no consensus on the position to be taken in the talks. Just how realistic were their own demands for general disarmament or German rearmament? The only point of common agreement was that somehow *Gleichberechtigung* must be achieved. But how? Some optimistically believed that the Allies could be persuaded to disarm to Germany's level.[6] But a far larger number doubted

---

3. W. Deist, 'Internationale und nationale Aspekte der Abrüstungsfrage, 1924–1932', in Rössler, *Locarno und die Weltpolitik*, p. 67. See ibid., p. 80: 'Diese Rechtsthese — Deutschland habe ein Anrecht auf die Abrüstung andere Staaten nach dem Versailler Muster — war zwar Gemeingut aller politischen Parteien des Reichstags und fand, durch die sehr rege deutsche Publizistik in dieser Frage, auch im Ausland Anhänger, aber in der diplomatischen Auseinandersetzung blieb sie im ganzen doch eine stumpfe Waffe.' On the disarmament question in general with respect to Germany, see M. Salewski, *Entwaffnung und Militärkontrolle in Deutschland, 1919–1927* (Bonn, 1966).
4. Deist, 'Aspekte der Abrüstungsfrage', pp. 73f.
5. Unsigned, undated memorandum, Berlin (14 May 1925), *ADAP*, Series B, I, 1, pp. 520–23.
6. Unsigned, undated memorandum, Berlin (January 1925), pp. 120–25.

whether Germany could succeed in any disarmament initiative.[7]

The skeptics appeared vindicated, for during the following twelve months little progress was observed in the Preparatory Commission. In April 1927, von Bülow, reviewing the previous year's negotiations, concluded that the best chance for general disarmament lay outside the League in bilateral pacts such as the Washington Naval Agreement.[8] Nevertheless, the disarmament talks had some value, 'since they gave Germany the opportunity for the first time since Versailles to put her views before the international community'.[9]

After a year of negotiations it appeared that the unbridgeable gap between France and Germany over the primacy of security or disarmament threatened to bring the talks to an end. But by early fall 1927 conditions suddenly improved. At the September Assembly the French Foreign Minister, Aristide Briand, accepted for the present that an Eastern Locarno was out of the question and that additional security guarantees must be sought elsewhere. At the same moment, his German counterpart seemed eager to cooperate in moving disarmament security talks away from the existing standstill.[10] Stresemann hastened to sign the Optional Clauses of the Permanent Court of International Justice at the Hague; these pledged Germany to submit international disputes to binding arbitration by the Court. His motives were purely tactical, as his legal experts had told him that 'the actual legal significance [of the Optional Clauses] is extremely limited', but that their propaganda value was consequently all the greater.[11] As the first signatory to the clauses, Stresemann won for Germany a bloodless victory. The Foreign Minister intended not only to out-maneuver

7. Hoesch to Berlin, Paris, 15 December 1925, ibid., pp. 76–78.

8. v. Bülow to Dufour, Berlin, 4 April 1927, in Lee, 'Disarmament and Security', p. 38.

9. Deist, 'Aspekte der Abrüstungsfrage, p. 79.

10. H. Lippelt, '"Politische Sanierung" — Zur deutschen Politik gegenüber Polen, 1925–25', *VZG*, 19 (1971), p. 328: 'Die beharrliche Weigerung, die Ostgrenze zu akzeptieren, blieb eine Maxime der deutschen Außenpolitik.' Compare with Jacobson, *Locarno*, p. 156; 'In Paris, Briand made no consistent attempt, either before or after Zaleski's statements, to make the evacuation of the Rhineland dependent on a new guarantee for Poland. Characterizing the arrangements for Eastern Europe made at Locarno as "final and satisfactory", he had told Hoesch in 1926 that to make evacuation dependent on Eastern Locarno was "absurd" and would "only impede or prevent a Franco-German settlement". In 1927 Briand, along with Chamberlain, had privately and informally approved Stresemann's right to seek territorial revision prior to any multilateral guarantee of Eastern European security, and he had joined with Chamberlain to aid Stresemann in thwarting a Polish scheme for what Berlin regarded as an Eastern Locarno in disguise. Although one statement made by Berthelot in February 1928 led Hoesch to report that Paris intended to insist that Poland and Czechoslovakia participate in any discussions of evacuation, in fact the French did not respond to Zaleski's statements with an attempt to link evacuation with an Eastern Locarno. Berthelot himself reacted to Zaleski's declarations with impatience, telling Chamberlain that Zaleski "talked a great deal too much".'

11. Lee, 'Disarmament and Security', p. 38.

France, particularly in the light of the disarmament deadlock, but also to demonstrate Germany's willingness to undertake international obligations in the service of peace. It was France's move.

The response was a proposal from Paris that a special committee of the Assembly examine the interlocking questions of disarmament and security. Such a committee offered the very real procedural advantage of being able to examine each aspect as a separate issue.[12] The Assembly accepted the French suggestion, and on 24 September 1927 created the *Comité d'arbitrage et de sécurité*, its initial session to be held in December of the same year. The initiative had swiftly changed hands and now Germany was forced to respond. Under pressure from both the *Comité d'arbitrage* and the Council, the Reich government strained every nerve to prepare a statement of Germany's position on security, which was finally submitted to the committee on 26 January 1928 under the innocuous title 'Remarks by the German Government on the Work Program of the Security Committee'.[13] It was short and to the point. Demands for security were skilfully linked to revision; it was expressly stated that Germany could neither accept her frontiers in their present form, nor could she support treaties which would not permit the eventual revision of her borders. The urgent necessity to achieve comprehensive measures for European security was bound up in the German perception with the need to provide for the future alteration of the *status quo*. Here could be detected not only the framework of the German disarmament policy, but also its goal.

Surprisingly the arbitration committee accepted the German suggestions as the basis for discussion. Several treaties were developed which together were to form a comprehensive security system.[14] These fell into three groups. The first called for peaceful settlement of disputes by means of arbitration or mediation. The second group pledged support for the victim(s) of aggression. Lastly, a third batch of treaties called for bilateral pacts pledging abstention from war and peaceful settlement of disputes.

The *Austwärtiges Amt* could be well satisfied with this development, since none of the treaties contemplated the use of sanctions nor, more importantly from its perspective, did they seek to guarantee or maintain the *status quo*.[15] Combined under one cover, the treaties were called the 'General Act for the Pacific Settlement of International

---

12. Ibid., p. 39.
13. 'Bemerkungen der deutschen Regierung zu dem Arbeitsprogramm des Sicherheitskommitees' (AA: Referat Völkerbund, Comité d'Arbitrage/Bd. 3, K665903–910).
14. *The General Act. Pacific Settlement of International Disputes*, Geneva, 15 October 1928 (LoN: C.537.M.164.1928.X.)
15. Lee, 'Disarmament and Security', p. 41.

Disputes'. In an attempt to get to the heart of the security question, Germany submitted an additional seventh treaty, aimed at 'strengthening the means of preventing war'. Treated separately by the committee but attached to the General Act, it pledged all signatories to work with the League Council in seeking a peaceful settlement of disputes and to adhere to the Council's decision. The security committee recommended the 'General Act' and the 'Model Treaty to Strengthen the Means of Preventing War' to the Assembly in September 1928. After several years of negotiation and revision, the 'Model Treaty' came to include additional features favored by Berlin: demilitarized zones, demarcation lines and mandatory troop withdrawals. The Reich government could take satisfaction in the fact that its security proposals had in fact been adopted by the security committee and the Assembly.

With respect to disarmament, however, the Wilhelmstraße had little to show for its efforts during the late 1920s. The persistent connection between security and disarmament in the minds of many of her adversaries prevented a solution satisfactory to Germany. France in particular was still wedded to security guarantees, so much so, in fact, that she could scarcely conceive of disarming herself or of permitting Germany to rearm to her level. The Preparatory Commission held out no possibility for a disarmament settlement; rather, by its inability to settle vexatious but ultimately unimportant details, it heightened the urgency of the long-awaited general disarmament conference. When in fact the Council did set the date for the opening of the disarmament conference for February 1932,

> ... [it] was reacting more to the pressures of the [League Assembly] and world public opinion, not, however out of a conviction that conditions favored a successful outcome by the conference. The opposite was the case; the opposing sides had not softened but hardened. Both Germany and France felt themselves isolated, Germany in her demands for equality of treament [*Gleichberechtigung*], France in her insistence on comprehensive security guarantees. Neither Great Britain nor the United States were prepared to commit their prestige or power toward the negotiations of a settlement of the problem; neither had a clear enough concept of European policy to permit any constructive Anglo-American initiative in the foreseeable future.[16]

Ironically, where once it had claimed that security and disarmament were separable issues, the Reich government now resolutely, if somewhat unrealistically, insisted that disarmament and security were indeed closely bound together and that both would naturally result once

16. Deist, 'Aspekte der Abrüstungsfrage', pp. 82f.

Germany received *Gleichberechtigung*. General security, the Wilhelmstraße had always argued, would be the logical and immediate consequence of general disarmament. For the Germans, however, 'disarmament' meant equality of armaments, regardless of whether that state of affairs resulted from general disarmament to their level or from German rearmament to the level of neighboring states. Thus, both security and disarmament always meant *Gleichberechtigung*. In addition, security had political as well as military connotations, since in German eyes it implied the right to seek revision of the *status quo*. Here, cast in terms of disarmament and security, was the central goal of German foreign policy: the revision of the Treaty of Versailles. In this respect, then, revision became a *sine qua non* to any security guarantee: no German government could contemplate such an agreement without simultaneous assurance that it would facilitate Eastern revision.

How, then, were revision and the League incorporated in German foreign policy? What were the implications of the disarmament security policy for German plans within the League of Nations? Economic policy was one effective means for achieving revision; Germany saw her League of Nations policy as another particularly promising approach. Well before Germany's entry it was clear that Anglo–French influence would prevent her from transforming the League into a vehicle for European revision. The Wilhelmstraße nevertheless deliberately undertook so to weaken the League that in the end revisionist aims might be pursued more or less undisturbed, without fear of League sanctions. This is the context in which German security proposals must be viewed, for any security system based on the League rested on the Council. Germany's strategy was to destabilize the League Council; the tactics used were to support frequent rotation of non-permanent Council members, so promoting the election of weak or ineffective nations, and thereby sapping the Council's power to act in the face of threatened aggression.

Germany did not have to wait long for confirmation that this policy was effective. The Manchurian Incident of 1931 and Japan's eventual withdrawal from the League in 1932 conclusively demonstrated the Council's inability to play a forceful and effective role in maintaining peace.[17] German League policy, therefore, from the outset was less than wholehearted, her membership an interlude. The withdrawal from the League implemented by Hitler in 1933 was in fact prepared long before the advent of the *Führer*.

17. C. Thorne, *The Limits of Foreign Policy. The West, the League and the Far Eastern Crisis of 1931–1933* (New York, 1973).

Evacuation of the Rhineland, the Young Plan and Continued American Stabilization in Germany

With the ink barely dry on the Locarno Treaties, Stresemann turned to the next step in his comprehensive diplomatic strategy: an early evacuation of the Rhineland and a general settlement of reparations. As a more immediate advantage, it would also serve to quell domestic political opposition to Locarno. The first promising opportunity to raise both issues presented itself directly after Germany's entry into the League.

On 17 September 1926, Stresemann and Briand slipped unnoticed into the little French town of Thoiry, not far from Geneva. Over a leisurely lunch, Stresemann offered a financial settlement in exchange for early evacuation of the Rhineland.[1] German railway bonds would be recapitalized, and the proceeds applied to paying off a substantial portion of the reparations obligation, in exchange for which France would evacuate the Rhineland and allow Germany to ransom the Saar. Stresemann's wide-reaching scheme had an added economic dimension, since part of the income from the sale of railway bonds would go toward stabilizing the French and Belgian francs, and the Polish zloty. Scarcely concealed in the Thoiry scheme was Stresemann's intention to capture not only the French, but also the Belgian and Polish economies, and through these countries' economic dependency on Germany to prise revision out of reluctant adversaries.[2] Although daring and large-scale, Stresemann's scheme, according to Link, was hardly surprising:

> Thoiry was revisionist only with respect to evacuation and the Saar, not in respect to reparations [in the sense of establishing a new total]. In terms of reparations policy it concerned the fulfilment of the Dawes Plan, that is, the exploration of all its possibilities. That at all stages of the negotiations Stresemann took great care not to appear anti-American has since been well substantiated.[3]

Bariéty, on the other hand, believes that it was Briand who seized the initiative at Thoiry, attempting through closer Franco-German cooperation to force Germany away from America and at the same time gradually wean her from dependence on American capital.[4] Krüger, for his part, views Thoiry as a limited success for the Reich govern-

---

1. J. Jacobson and J. T. Walker, 'The Impulse for a Franco-German Entente: The Origins of the Thoiry Conference, 1926', *JCH* 10, 1 (1975), pp. 157–81.
2. Marks, *Illusion*, p. 83; Jacobson, *Locarno*, pp. 83–90.
3. Link, *Amerikanische Stabilisierungspolitik*, p. 403.
4. Bariéty, 'Europäische Befriedigung', p. 43.

ment, 'for France had allowed herself to enter into negotiations on a variety of crucial questions — evacuation of the Rhineland, the Saar, Eupen-Malmedy — and these talks had taken place on the level of diplomatic negotiations.[5]

The conversations at Thoiry were sincere and friendly in tone; yet they remain controversial. They produced no political results, however, since both parties faced withering domestic criticism upon returning from Geneva. Perhaps in an attempt to overcome that criticism, perhaps to exert pressure on France, once back in Berlin Stresemann impetuously announced that 1927 was the year in which the Allies would finally and completely evacuate the Rhineland. Reaction in France, however, was scarcely what he had anticipated. Poincaré, once again Prime Minister, forced Briand to distance himself from the Thoiry suggestions. The French Premier felt fully capable of stabilizing the franc without German subvention, and so it proved, for by the end of that fall the franc had staged a remarkable recovery. Flimsy as they were, the bridges built at Thoiry collapsed.[6]

For German foreign policy, therefore, 1927 was a year of unfulfilled expectations. Faced by mounting domestic criticism of his 'sell-out' to the Allies, in the winter of 1927/28 Stresemann renewed in earnest his efforts to obtain an early evacuation of the Rhineland. The weightiest argument for this was his contention that since Germany was effectively disarmed, French security already existed. Equally telling was the fact that since the Dawes Plan Germany had met her reparations obligations to the letter. To Stresemann, France no longer had any cause to view the Rhineland in the same light as the Ruhr in 1923 — namely, as a guarantee against German default. Having met the treaty obligations, Germany had the right, according to Article 431 of the Versailles Treaty, to prompt evacuation of occupied territories.[7]

It may be asked why German pressure for an end to the Rhineland occupation met with less opposition than might have been expected. On 27 August 1928, the Kellogg–Briand Pact, which formally outlawed war 'as an instrument of national policy', was formally signed in Paris. Attending these ceremonies, Stresemann talked with Poincaré and renewed his demands for evacuation, saying that it seemed appropriate now that the Kellogg Pact had been signed, even more so than after Locarno. Poincaré countered that a general reparations settlement must precede any evacuation of the Rhineland. Stresemann had finally received the signal he sought: France accepted the need for revision, in

---

5. Krüger, *Außenpolitik*, pp. 360–1.
6. Marks, *Illusion*, p. 83; Jacobson, *Locarno*, pp. 83ff; Kimmich, *Germany and League*, pp. 109ff.
7. Jacobson, *Locarno*, p. 146.

fact was resigned to further revision of reparations.[8] Her Foreign Minister hoped to achieve long-term stabilization of her vulnerable economy by more precise regulation of the reparations question, in no way settled by the Dawes Plan. A final reparations schedule would bring about the possibility of long-range economic planning in France, and the occupied German territories seemed to provide an ideal means of reaching a conclusive long-term settlement.[9] For tactical reasons, then, the Quai d'Orsay linked reparations and evacuation closely together in order to extract the greatest possible economic and political compensation for evacuation.[10] Thus, by late summer 1928, French interest in evacuation had become apparent to Stresemann.

On 16 December 1928 the principals announced in Geneva that a solution was necessary to the two problems of reparations and evacuation. This, in the words of contemporaries, was the decision for a 'final liquidation of the war in the west'. Germany successfully solicited American help in the regulation of the reparations question, and between January and June of 1929 a commission of financial experts chaired by the American banker Owen D. Young deliberated in Paris.

What were German hopes for the Young negotiations? Most apparent was the problem of the final reparations total, left undetermined by the Dawes Plan of January 1924, whose schedule could therefore only be temporary. Throughout the mid-twenties Berlin had worked for just this moment: 'The German "policy of fulfilment" during the Dawes era depended not so much on a "purely objective economic resolution [of the reparations question]" as on private-capitalist interests, particularly those of the United States.'[11] In consequence, German policy since the Dawes Plan had worked to bring the German and American economies closer together, so that with American help Germany could cast off her role as nothing more than the object of the Versailles system. Link points out that in his efforts to bring the two nations into economic partnership Stresemann viewed their individual interests as perfectly 'consonant':

> In armament reduction, security and guarantees of peace, official [German] policy ran parallel to American policy. Until achievement of a satisfactory reparations settlement, armaments equality and evacuation of the Rhine-

8. Ibid., pp. 161f.: '. . . even Poincaré decided that the best way to insure the payment of reparations was not by continuing or extending occupation but by ending it.'
9. Erdmann, 'Weimarer Republic', p. 267.
10. Marks, 'Myths', p. 250: 'French leaders, badly scared by the severe financial crisis which France had suffered in 1926 and aware that the bargaining value of an early Rhineland evacuation was declining as the treaty date for withdrawal drew closer, decided to trade early evacuation for French military and financial security.'
11. Link, *Amerikanische Stabilisierungspolitik*, p. 400.

land, [German foreign policy] would have to acknowledge the absolute connection between regulation of reparations and establishment of peace as strategically necessary for German recovery. The parallel course of American and German policies was virtually guaranteed by their 'consonant interest' (Stresemann) in Germany's incorporation into global economics and that interdependence of debtor and creditor in the private sector which was the hallmark of German-American relations and which presaged both the nature and the termination of the policy of revision.[12]

With the coveted American financial and political assistance, Germany could obtain a far-reaching revision of reparations. With payments established on a 59-year schedule, under the Young Plan the annual amount was reduced to a level substantially below that of the Dawes schedule, easily maintained by Germany since 1924. In addition, the REPKO and its supervisory agencies were replaced by the Bank for International Settlement, to be situated in Basel, Switzerland. With the dissolution of the Reparations Commission, Germany's finances were no longer subject to Allied regulation and she accepted the burden of transferring reparations funds to the beneficiaries through the Bank for International Settlement. In the event of default on these considerably reduced obligations, Germany could appeal for assistance to an international committee of experts. In the end, what mattered was her total debt, assessed under the London Ultimatum of 1921 at 132 milliard gold marks. Now, after two successive revisions, Germany's final debt was put at 40 milliard gold marks.

Despite the evidence of a very real improvement compared with the conditions of the Dawes Plan, the Reich government was not satisfied. It worked feverishly to ensure ratification of the Young Plan, since failure to ratify would have meant the continuation of the Dawes schedule, and threatened a return to diplomatic isolation, carrying with it a reversal in German-American relations. Yet ratification was a highly divisive domestic issue, since the political opposition saw it as a sign of final submission to the treaty and as precluding further renegotiation of reparations. In fact, Stresemann had gained a substantial victory in the field of reparations: yet to quell his opponents he still had to present some visible gain in return for acceptance of the Young Plan. He accordingly pressed for additional concessions as the price of German agreement: immediate evacuation of the Rhineland and the return of the Saar.[13]

While the German government was not altogether pleased with the

12. Link, 'Die Beziehungen', p. 82.

13. Jacobson, *Locarno*, pp. 267f; Marks, *Illusion*, pp. 102f; Link, *Amerikanische Stabilisierungspolitik*, pp. 474; Link, 'Die Beziehungen', pp. 89f.

Young Plan, neither was its French counterpart. But any sign of resistance from France was quickly suppressed by the combined pressure of Britain, America and Belgium. At the Hague Conference on 21 August 1929, the principals agreed to accept the Young Plan, accompanied by the immediate evacuation of the two remaining occupied zones of the Rhineland. On 30 November 1929 the last troops left the second zone; on 30 January 1930 the third and final zone was cleared. Stresemann had thus accomplished complete evacuation of the Rhineland five years prior to the date set by the Treaty of Versailles.

Gustav Stresemann based his foreign policy concept on the essential recognition that the economy was the driving force of German foreign policy.[14] Necessarily, given this emphasis on economic affairs, one nation was critical to German calculations: the United States. Following the Ruhr crisis, the German economy, assisted by American capital, was stabilized according to the Dawes Plan regulation of reparations, so enabling Germany to become a significant factor in European politics. As Link notes: 'Thanks to German-American cooperation, Germany became within a relatively short time . . . an astonishingly potent force in international affairs.'[15] This close cooperation became a means of extracting step-by-step revisionist concessions from the treaty powers. Both parties, the same author indicates, stood to gain:

> Beyond the material justification for German-American cooperation was justification in ideal terms, oriented toward the goal of cooperative peace guarantees. Under American influence the French concept of collective security in Europe would gradually give way to the American concept of 'peaceful change' . . . American policy of 'peaceful change' and German policy of revision were never entirely identical, but during the Stresemann era they converged.[16]

Stresemann took pains to encourage close German-American cooperation, not only for the immediate value to German diplomacy and economics, but for the equally important indirect effect of impeding bilateral cooperation between the USA and France. The acid test of German-American relations was always whether they benefited Germany's policy of revision as against France's policy of maintaining the

---

14. See the speech of Stresemann to the DVP central committee, 22 November 1925: 'Rede Stresemann vom 22.11.1925 vor dem DVP–Zentralvorstand', *VZG* 15 (1967), p. 434. See on this subject K. H. Pohl, 'Deutsche "Wirtschaftsaußenpolitik" 1925/26. Zu einigen Aspekten der Stresemannschen Europa–Politik', in Michalka and Lee, *Stresemann*, pp. 426–40.
15. Link, 'Die Beziehungen', p. 82.
16. Ibid., pp. 102f.

status quo.[17] For example, the Kellogg Pact offered the opportunity for Germany to demonstrate commitment to peace, and at the same time conveniently served as a basis for German demands for armament equality. US influence, moreover, was instrumental in further revision of reparations for it was 'the American goal ... to "depoliticize" reparations by their systematic transformation into private debts'.[18]

That policy was very much in harmony with German reparations policy. With American help the 'politicization' of reparations, as seen for example in Poincaré's policy of 'productive guarantees' in 1922–23, could be prevented after 1924. Finally, the Wilhelmstraße believed, commercial and economic cooperation with America promised the chance of further reparations reduction, perhaps even eventual annulment of remaining sums payable. The reparations negotiations of 1928–1929 bore out this confident assessment of the benefits of German-American relations. In fact it was America and not Germany who reopened the reparations question in 1928.

Although it was a 'small step' toward 'depoliticization' of reparations, the Young Plan was greeted by German and American financiers alike as an improvement on the Dawes Plan, because it enabled a significant amount of Germany's obligations to be converted to private debts by means of a generous rediscount rate.[19] But this favorable outcome was not achieved without considerable diplomatic maneuvering.

During the Young Plan negotiations, Finance Minister Schacht failed to link a reparations settlement with a political settlement entailing the return of the Polish Corridor and German colonies. Washington wanted none of it. American pressure was, however, instrumental in helping the Germans overcome Anglo-French resistance concerning debt reduction, elimination of control agencies in Germany and the revised schedule of annual payments. Indirectly, US pressure also contributed to the relative ease with which Stresemann was able to combine a reparations settlement and early evacuation of the Rhineland. Although the inflated expectations of the Reich government and the nationalist Right were not entirely fulfilled by the Young Plan and evacuation, the successes of 1929 brought Germany materially closer to the goal of a revision of the Versailles settlement and an end to reparations. But far more important, the events of 1929 marked a success for German policy in its aim of drawing the United States ever closer and away from the former Allies. 'In reality through her

17. Ibid., p. 80.
18. Ibid., p. 98.
19. Ibid., pp. 98f.

leading role in the Young Loan and through parallel transactions of a private nature, the United States was tied even more closely to Germany than under the Dawes Plan and became even more dependent upon the functions of the international credit system'.[20] Under Stresemann, therefore, German foreign policy achieved what had earlier seemed impossible: to attract the United States out of its original course of mediation so that ultimately American stabilization policy and German revisionist policy ran virtually parallel.[21]

Stresemann was not alone in pursuing his policy of simultaneous cooperation and confrontation, nor were his ideas free from the influence of others. His greatest supporter was von Schubert. Schubert, whose career as State Secretary in the Wilhelmstraße from 1924 to 1930 closely paralleled that of his Foreign Minister, gave Stresemann enthusiastic and often decisive support. With shrewd understanding of the subtleties of Germany's postwar situation, he advocated a policy of understanding and involvement with the other Great Powers. In contrast to nationalist, Rightist and militarist demands for the unilateral implementation of German aims by force if necessary, Schubert called for compromise and conciliation in the peaceful pursuit of revisionist goals.[22] That policy, conceived and in part practiced by these two men, constituted a new approach to Germany's postwar diplomatic problems and has been described as 'the start of a new conception of international security and peace'.[23] Nevertheless, their statecraft, even though it bore first fruit in the years 1924 to 1929, attracted vehement criticism and opposition not only within the *Auswärtiges Amt* itself, but much more broadly within Stresemann's own party, the DVP, and the nation. But by late 1930 much of Stresemann's policy lay in ruins.[24] Spiralling economic crisis and the legions of the

20. Ibid., p. 100.
21. M. Vogt, 'Letzter Erfolg? Stresemann in den Jahren 1928 und 1929', in Michalka and Lee, *Stresemann*, pp. 441–65. Vogt concludes that Stresemann's successes in 1928–1929 were politically limited, but despite contemporary political criticism, he became a symbol for postwar reconciliation and therefore a 'moral sucess'.
22. P. Krüger, 'Friedenssicherung und deutsche Revisionspolitik. Die deutsche Außenpolitik und die Verhandlungen über den Kellogg-Pakt', *VZG*, 22(1974), pp. 227–57.
23. Ibid., pp. 256f.
24. P. Krüger, 'Beneš und die europäische Wirtschaftskonzeption des deutschen Staatssekretärs Carl von Schubert', in *Bohemia. Jahrbuch des Collegium Carolinum* (1973), p. 339: 'Nach den aufreibenden Kämpfen um die Rheinlandräumung und nach dem Tod Stresemanns kam die innenpolitische Wende in Deutschland, der Sturz des sozialdemokratischen Reichskanzlers Hermann Müller und der Regierungsantritt Brünings. Schubert konnte seine Pläne nicht verwirklichen — es gab 1930 überhaupt keine Debatte mehr darüber, dass er gehen musste. . . .' See also R. Berndt, 'Wirtschaftliche Mitteleuropapläne des deutschen Imperialismus (1926–1931)', in Ziebura, p. 316: 'Vom Mai/Juli 1930 ab liess sich eine eindeutige Temposteigerung in der Revisionspolitik des deutschen Imperialismus verzeichnen.'

unemployed polarized German politics. No longer would German politics support a temperate foreign policy and modest — if steady — gains. Under extreme crisis foreign policy was pressed ever more openly into the service of domestic politics. Yet death intervened to spare Stresemann this final indignity. On the very eve of Germany's descent into chaos the Foreign Minister, whose last diplomatic victories cost him his health, died on 3 October 1929.

4

Between Revision and Expansion: Weimar Foreign Policy and the Pressures of Domestic Crisis, 1930–1933

Calculated Crisis as a Means to Further Revision

The events of the fall of 1929 were rich in symbolic value as well as material consequence. At the League Assembly in September, Briand shared with the world his Plan for European Union, to which Stresemann replied with hearty approbation. By their warm and eloquent exchange the two statesmen set the tone for further cooperation and progress toward peace, relegating the war forever to the past. For Stresemann, this was the crowning moment of his illustrious career; he had led his country from diplomatic isolation to its rightful place on the council of nations. Although he faced great and powerful obstacles to his foreign policy, in the end he had overcome domestic political opposition. Since the fall of 1923, when he put an end to passive resistance in the Ruhr, Stresemann skilfully balanced his foreign policy between cooperation and confrontation, never moving too far in either direction, and never revealing completely the degree to which his diplomacy was purely tactical or genuinely a 'policy of understanding'.

It is doubtful if scholars will ever reach complete consensus on the nature of Stresemann's foreign policy. We have, however, seen both sides. For Stresemann, the value of security and disarmament talks, minorities policy, relations with Russia, indeed the entire *Ostpolitik* question, was almost surely tactical. On the other hand, in his close association with Briand and in the attention he gave to improving relations with France and Britain, Stresemann was in pursuit of genuine understanding. Yet it must be remembered that Stresemann's ultimate goal was the revision of the Versailles system and the advancement of Germany's international position — the recovery of her Great Power status. In the end, therefore, any genuine understanding between Germany and her Western neighbors was for Stresemann also of

112

tactical value. The road to complete recovery led through Paris, London and Washington. The more cordial her relations with the three, the easier it would be for Germany to overturn the treaty. Indeed, if relations were cordial enough, Germany's former adversaries would initiate much of the revision themselves.

The warmth radiated by Briand and Stresemann at Geneva in September 1929 was a clear sign of Stresemann's success in achieving that understanding with France. Thus, his death on 3 October 1929 was all the more tragic. Within the days of his passing, the spirit of confidence and optimism pervading Germany at the end of the summer of 1929 dimmed with the waning sun. On 29 October 1929, the New York stock market collapsed and with it the German economy. The Wall Street Crash marked not only the end of the Stresemann era, but also the beginning of the end of Weimar parliamentarism.

In German foreign policy, the turning point was evident in the changing of the guard: Heinrich Brüning became Reich Chancellor on 30 March 1930; Julius Curtius succeeded Stresemann as Foreign Minister on 4 October 1929; and von Bülow assumed the State Secretaryship on 2 June 1930 as successor to von Schubert, who was appointed Ambassador to the Quirinal in Rome. These three men, urged on by rising pressure for diplomatic success, became the central personalities of German foreign policy in the early 1930s. Their reign would be characterized by a certain lack of *visible* signs of continuity.[1]

Like Gustav Stresemann, Reich Chancellor Heinrich Brüning found the German economy to be the propulsive force of German foreign policy.[2] And yet under him the economy assumed a new quality. Any attempt to place Brüning within the larger scope of Weimar diplomacy or to compare his foreign policy with that of Stresemann raises

---

1. Campbell, p. 212.
2. In recent years questions on Brüning's economic policies and their function in German foreign policy have sparked off a lively scholarly debate between Knut Borchardt and Carl-Ludwig Holtfrerich. Borchardt claims that while Brüning may have made options on paper, economic reality forced him to pursue his actual deflationary policy. Holtfrerich, on the other hand, shows that Brüning not only had options, but ranked them in priority and then set about accomplishing them, especially winning Germany freedom from reparations. Knut Borchardt, 'Zwangslagen und Handlungsspielräume in der grossen Wirtschaftskrise der frühen dreißiger Jahre. Zur Revision des überlieferten Geschichtsbildes', *Jahrbuch der Bayerischen Akademie der Wissenschaften*, 1979, pp. 85–132, reproduced in M. Stürmer, ed., *Die Weimarer Republik* (Königstein/Ts.,1980), pp. 318–39; C. L. Holtfrerich, 'Alternativen zu Brünings Wirtschaftspolitik in der Weltwirtschaftskrise?', *HZ* 235 (1982), pp. 605–31; K. Borchardt, 'Noch einmal: Alternativen zu Brünings Wirtschaftspolitik?', *HZ* 237 (1983), pp. 67–83. Krüger, on the other hand, sees Brüning limited less by economic factors than by the changes in the Wilhelmstraße, which elevated men disinclined to compromise with the West — Bülow and Weizsäcker — to positions of great influence by 1930. Krüger, *Außenpolitik*, pp. 511–23. See also M. Grübler, *Die Spitzenverbände der Wirtschaft und das erste Kabinett Brüning* (Düsseldorf, 1982), pp. 434–46.

important questions. On what logical premises did Brüning base his foreign policy? What were his goals and methods? His foreign policy may here be considered against the background of global economic crisis and German political unrest.

Stresemann's foreign policy, based largely on confrontation and cooperation, bequeathed to Brüning a situation in which for the first time since 1918 Germany enjoyed a significant degree of scope for diplomatic maneuver. The shock waves from the Wall Street Crash set off a series of secondary crashes throughout the financial capitals of the world. The ensuing global crisis was exacerbated by the American policy of protective tariffs aimed at restricting imports, recall of loans, particularly in Europe, and a general flight of American capital from foreign investment. As a consequence, trade wars poisoned relations and exacerbated international tensions.[3] No government could ignore the altered economic, and hence political, situation in the wake of the Wall Street Crash. In Germany the situation was made even more complex by the extreme division between the political Left and the Right, who fought a particularly vituperative and emotional anti–capitalist propaganda war, attempting to mobilize popular discontent. In this bitter struggle the Right singled out the 'Versailles system' as the primary factor in Germany's economic misery, thus making the treaty inseparable from the political crisis.

The success of the Right in provoking domestic political unrest soon became clear. The election results of 14 September 1930, which added greatly to the parliamentary strength of the communists and propelled Hitler and his National Socialists overnight into national prominence, indicated that the two political extremes had struck a responsive chord among most Germans.[4] As Graml explains, the German voter out of pure ignorance associated Germany's economic crisis with the Treaty of Versailles:

The majority of the German people, whom the Depression struck with particular severity — although scarcely less severely than in American —

3. Graml, *Europa*, pp. 239f.: 'So lag es in den Ländern, die unter der Pariser Friedensregelung gelitten hatten oder mit ihr unzufrieden waren, nahe, die Ursprünge der wirtschaftlichen Nöte in den politischen und wirtschaftlichen Bestimmungen der Friedensverträge zu suchen: Revisionismus und faschistischer Neo-Imperialismus, die seit langem mit den Parolen eines zwischenstaatlichen Klassenkampfes operiert hatten (Habenichtse gegen Besitzende), gewannen im wirtschaftlichen Niedergang eine geradezu magnetische Anziehungskraft, die den entsprechended außenpolitischen Forderungen zum ersten Mal seit 1923 eine Massenbasis verschaffte und damit einen unvergleichlich kräftigeren Impetus verlieh.'

4. In contrast to the election of 20 May 1928, the KPD increased their representation in the Reichstag from 54 seats to 77, while the NSDAP rose from 12 to 107. This was accomplished at the expense of the SPD and the moderate parties of the center.

were inadequately or only partially informed of events outside Germany ... the majority of Germans perceived the Depression as a distinctly German event, for which the antagonists of Versailles, and no less the Weimar Republic, creature of that capitulation, where somehow responsible.[5]

Motivated by economic and political conditions, but at the same time rooted in irrational psychological factors, this disposition to connect Germany's economic crisis to her diplomatic situation led to more strident and threatening demands from virtually every political camp for revision of the 'Versailles system'.[6]

It is against this background of economic crisis and political turmoil that Brüning's foreign policy concept must be analyzed. Directly following the great electoral victory of the National Socialists in the early fall of 1930, the Chancellor laid bare his political aims in astonishingly explicit detail in an interview with Hitler on 6 October 1930. Here he clearly illustrated the elements of his foreign policy and its goals,[7] and meticulously sketched a graduated plan for the benefit of the National Socialist *Führer*. In the early stages, which Brüning considered the most dangerous, German national policy would be almost completely subordinated to foreign policy (*Primat der Außenpolitik*). During the preparatory stage the German economy would be mobilized in the service of foreign policy. Deflationary measures, trade restrictions, price controls, wage cuts: all would be used to harden Germany, 'so that she could resist any external pressure and be in a position to exploit the world economic crisis in order to bring pressure to bear on the remaining Powers'.[8] Under such Spartan measures, by which the entire economy would be reorganized, Germany would strive for agricultural autarky, so becoming as independent of imports as possible. This would create the conditions under

5. Graml, *Europa*, pp. 240f.

6. See in this regard particularly the statements of G. Treviranus, who was linked neither to Hitler nor to Hugenberg: 'Nun fordert der Osten Einheit und Einsatz des ganzen deutschen Volkes. Wir gedenken in der Tiefe unserer Seele des zerschnittenen Weichsellandes, der ungeheilten Wunde in der Ostflanke, diesem verkümmerten Lungenflügel des Reiches .... Unsere inneren Augen schweifen über die deutschen Gaue ... im Schmerz um die heute noch verlorenen, einst wieder zu gewinnenden deutschen Lande .... Weg mit dem Gerede von der Katastrophe, her mit dem Mut, alle Nöte zu bannen.' (10 August 1930) Cited in ibid., p. 244. An interesting comparison to Treviranus' remarks can be seen in the situation analysis of the British ambassador in Berlin, Sir Horace Rumbold, in 1930: 'It may now indeed be said that the first electoral campaign which had taken place in Germany without the shadow of the Rhineland occupation had brought out into the open, through one party or another, all that Germany hopes for and intends to strive for in the field of external affairs.' Rumbold, in *DBFP*, Second Series, I, p. 502.

7. H. Brüning, *Memoiren, 1918–1934* (Munich, 1972), v. I, pp. 203ff.

8. Ibid., p. 203.

which she could liquidate the Young Plan and thus cancel her entire reparations obligation. A simultaneous attack on both reparations and disarmament was the principal aim of his government, Brüning later said:

> The initial effort of our foreign policy was the cancellation of reparations with a simultaneously tackling of the disarmament question. In the course of eighteen months or two years, one could hope that the two questions would have toppled [*ins Wanken bringen*] the Versailles Treaty, without even bringing the subject forward.[9]

Brüning called for a domestic political truce [*Burgfrieden*] at the beginning of his diplomatic offensive. Under its terms, however, 'sharper opposition on the part of the NSDAP to foreign policy' could be most productive in promoting the revisions of the universally condemned Treaty of Versailles. Ultimately, foreign policy successes would serve a domestic purpose, for they would form the basis for constitutional reform 'which if I [Brüning] have my way must end with a monarchist restoration'.[10] Since the *Führer*, whom Brüning was seeking to court, was obviously hostile to the prospect of a new monarchy, it is necessary to examine not only the statements made,[11] but their possible tactical value, given that they were addressed to Hitler.[12] Research has clearly revealed the Reich Chancellor as an anti-parliamentarian and staunch monarchist.[13] Apart from that, however, Brüning's foreign policy shows that his statements to Hitler, far from a mere tactic aimed at the National Socialist antagonist, actually encompassed the essence of his foreign policy.[14]

Brüning recognized that the global depression created the ideal conditions for an aggressive policy to achieve the final revision of the

9. Ibid.; see also Link, 'Die Beziehungen', pp. 104f.; Holtfrerich, *passim*.
10. Brüning, *Memoiren*, p. 204.
11. Here it is appropriate to note that Brüning composed his memoirs well after the events he discusses.
12. Hitler was already the leader of Germany's second largest party and Brüning hoped for his support.
13. See on this note E. Carlebach, *Von Brüning zu Hitler. Das Geheimnis der faschistischen Machtergreifung* (Frankfurt a.M., 1971).
14. This analysis is based on the following: Graml, *Europa*; Graml, 'Präsidialsystem', pp. 134–45; W. J. Helbig, *Die Reparationen in der Ära Brüning. Zur Bedeutung des Young-Plans für die deutsche Politik 1930 bis 1932* (Berlin, 1962); idem, 'Die Bedeutung der Reparationsfrage für die Wirtschaftspolitik der Regierung Brüning', in G. Jasper, ed., *Von Weimar zu Hitler 1930–1933* (Cologne, 1968), pp. 72–98; Th. Vogelsang, *Reichswehr, Staat und NSDAP, Beiträge deutschen Geschichte 1930–1932* (Stuttgart, 1962); Zimmerman, *Deutsche Außenpolitik*; W. Conze and H. Raupach, eds., *Die Staats- und Wirtschaftskrise des Deutschen Reiches 1929/33* (Stuttgart, 1967); K. D. Bracher, *Die Auflösung der Weimarer Republik. Eine Studie zum Problem des Machtverfalls in der Demokratie* (Villingen, 1960); Link, *Stabilisierungspolitik*; idem, 'Die Beziehungen'.

treaty system.[15] Stresemann's policy toward Poland, and in part that toward France, failed, in fact had to fail, insofar as they were aimed at the piecemeal revision of the treaty through the promotion of local economic crises in two neighboring states. Brüning, on the other hand, saw in Germany's radically altered domestic and diplomatic condition after 1929 new leverage by which the entire Versailles system could be split apart. Aggressive economic measures on her part, he argued, could heighten the economic crisis among weaker neighbors. If Germany pursued a deflationary policy, reinforced by a massive increase in exports while at the same time drastically restricting imports, in the present climate of economic and monetary crisis, neighboring states who depended upon exports could be maneuvered into more serious economic crisis.

Stresemann's partly successful 'liberal imperialist' tactic of promoting local and limited crises — examples were Belgium and Poland[16] — was now broadened and transformed by Brüning into an 'all-or-nothing' strategy.[17] German foreign policy, though inherited from Stresemann, now took on a new dimension. For Brüning a partial revision of the Versailles system was out of the question; only complete and utter change would satisfy him.[18] However, its achievement presented certain problems, not the least of which, maintains Link, was American opposition to the final revision of reparations:

15. Brüning, p. 431: 'Frankreich verschärft die Weltwirtschaftskrise — für uns gab es nichts Besseres.' (October 1931). On the close relationship between the depression, and the radicalization of German domestic — particularly party — politics and foreign policy, of particular value is Marks, *Illusion*, p. 114: 'After the election [of September 1930] the Brüning government tried to counter the Nazi threat by embarking on a more aggressive foreign policy, particularly in regard to Austria. This set off within eight months a chain reaction of banking crises from Austria to Germany and eventually to Britain. More immediately the reaction of investors to the German election was swift. The Berlin stock exchange plummeted downward and there ensued a massive withdrawal of capital from Germany as the short-term notes were called in. Within three months at least 1.3 milliard marks were withdrawn, over a third of the foreign exchange then invested in Germany and the equivalent of about three-quarters of the 1930–1931 Young annuity . . . . Few new credits appeared to replace the old. While the German economic crisis was of manageable proportions in August 1930, by December the situation had become acute as unemployment soared . . .' See also Bennett, *Rearmament* p. 49.
16. See in this connection particularly Stresemann's speech to the 'Arbeitsgemeinschaft Deutscher Landsmannschaften in Groß-Berlin', 14 December 1925, in *ADAP*, Series B, v. I, 1, pp. 727–53.
17. Brüning, p. 433: 'Aber für die deutsche Außenpolitik handelte sich um Sein oder Nichtsein.'
18. Although, as Bennett points out, 'the resolve to revise the peace treaties affected every aspect of Weimar foreign policy, and much of domestic policy too', Brüning and Wilhelmstraße differed on just how this revision should be achieved. Brüning's blunt frontal assault on reparations and disarmament (rearmament) contrasted sharply with the more subtle and modulated policies advocated by the career diplomats, most notably Bülow, who sought to avoid confrontation and did not wish 'to flout foreign opinion'. Bennett, *Rearmament*, pp. 55, 74–6.

Henceforth German demands concerning reparations swung to the maximal goal of complete cancellation and in the process collided with the American goal, which was to increase the influence of American capital over German industry through mobilizing bonds, thus never entirely releasing Germany from her reparations debts. That the German government could force the American government to such a revisionist course only two years after the Young Plan and despite such a divergence in goals was the result of the immense private capital investment of the USA in Germany.[19]

Such a collision course had been out of the question for Stresemann. He had accepted Germany's dependence on American capital, courting investment as a means of drawing the United States closer to the Reich, while enlisting American support for partial treaty and reparations revision. For Stresemann this had been both unavoidable and prudent; he never had the political or economic freedom to do otherwise. But by encouraging Germany's dependence on American capital he ultimately made America partially dependent on Germany. Insofar as the United States would move to protect investments in Germany, the latter could count on her support up to a point.

Brüning sought to exploit American investment in Germany, realizing, as had his predecessor, that to some degree he was taking a hostage, whose ransom would be US assistance in cancelling reparations. Once free from that yoke, Brüning would set about reducing the same dependence on Wall Street which had enabled him to scrap reparations. Eventually, he believed, having thrown off American financial influence, Germany would be ready to accomplish the hitherto impossible: revision of the eastern frontiers. But how to free Germany from her reparations obligations? Graml argues that Brüning intended to use his deflationary policy to accelerate the depression in Germany; he would then exploit that distortion to force the Americans, as a means of protecting investments in Germany, to favor ending reparations:

> It is no exaggeration to state that to relieve Germany of her reparations obligations, Brüning cold-bloodedly drove her to the brink of complete economic collapse, that is, he did not merely allow the crisis to run its course, but rather, up to a point, sought its intensification, indeed consciously stimulated it with his financial and economic measures.[20]

Brüning was convinced that under the circumstances the need for Germany's survival would itself create the conditions in which an end

19. Link, 'Die Beziehungen', p. 100.
20. Graml, *Europa*, p. 249.

of reparations and the Young Plan could be achieved.[21] Only then could the complete revision of Versailles take place. To produce these conditions Germany must pursue a brutal deflationary policy, under emergency legislation including strict wage and price reductions, in order to create a favorable balance of trade.[22] This would make it possible to meet the Young Plan payments — until the Plan was dismantled — without foreign assistance, something which since the crash had been impossible. In this manner, moreover, the domestic suffering arising out of such vicious deflation would be linked to the Young Plan in the public mind, both at home and abroad. Painfully exact efforts at fulfilment of the Young terms would conclusively demonstrate the devastating effect of reparations, and that they were in fact unfulfillable. Brüning in January 1931 emphasized that:

> At this point it is clear that along with other things . . . the reparations situation can't go on like this [*daß es so mit den Reparationen nicht gehe*] . . . . Either someone has to give us money, so that we can pay it right back — and even that has an end — or we have to have the opportunity to pay reparations with a gigantic export surplus. But the people cannot endure the latter either. Yet someone has to have the courage to take this course, regardless of how unpopular it is at home.[23]

In this way, Brüning, whose brutal economies won him the epithet *Hungerkanzler*, intensified Germany's economic misfortunes, misfortunes which were originally linked to the withdrawal of short-term foreign credit. Having driven to the brink of economic ruin, the Chancellor rejected his colleague's suggestions of reforms providing some immediate relief for his suffering fellow-citizens. Brüning's subordination of the people's welfare to the higher interests of the state had no peacetime precedent.[24] He imposed a mixture of emergency decrees and martial law while exploiting the domestic crisis without regard for individual suffering. No thought of reform entered the Chancellor's mind, for this would have annulled his strategy, which, as early as summer 1931, showed signs of succeeding and which by the fall of 1932 was to produce very real results for his successor Franz von Papen.

In fact, Brüning's strategy carried him so far that eventually he had to rule out aspects of his policy which he had earlier described to Hitler as worthwhile. The momentum of his decisions, moreover, brought the Chancellor into direct conflict with critical elements of his

21. Grübler, *Spitzenverbände*, pp. 434–46.
22. Marks, 'Myths'.
23. Cited in Helbig, 'Die Bedeutung der Reparationsfrage', p. 76.
24. Graml, *Europa*, p. 249.

predecessor's policy, namely Germany's relations with France. By means of an economic policy of autarky, Brüning had insisted, trade with the West should be drastically limited in order to settle the reparations question. This policy would have shifted the main weight of Germany's economic influence eastward. Yet for the time being even Brüning was forced to deviate from this course, very reminiscent of traditional German *Mitteleuropa-Politik*.[25] Despite the apparent enticements of increased influence in Eastern Europe, such a policy did not offer realistic solutions to Germany's import problems and furthermore threatened to bring her into conflict with Anglo–American interests. That was the conflict that Brüning had to avoid at all costs, since both the United States and Britain were instrumental to the solution of the reparations question. But unlike Stresemann, who viewed Franco–German relations as essential to German foreign policy, Brüning allowed relations with Paris to languish while he nurtured Germany's contacts with Washington and London. Nowhere was his departure from Stresemann's foreign policy more evident, as Graml shows, than in his treatment of France:

> Brüning's cabinet sought less an understanding with France based on fulfilment than an unwritten anti-Frech alliance through persistent tactless repetition of Germany's revisionists claims in Eastern and even Southeastern Europe. . . . Under the prevailing circumstances a sharper contrast to the concept and method of Stresemann's foreign policy can scarcely be imagined.[26]

Still, in contrast to Stresemann, Brüning endeavored to drive a wedge between France on the one side and the United States, Britain and Italy on the other, so as to isolate France and split up the guarantors of Versailles. 'If we succeed in winning over America, Britain and Italy and if the government holds out and we survive by our own strength, then victory is ours', as Brüning summed up his policy in July 1931.[27] At the very least with regard to reparations his view was borne out, for France was forced to stand impotently by as her former allies — Great Britain and the United States — released Germany from the reparations bonds which for so long had held her fast. On 6 July 1931, the Hoover Moratorium suspended all intergovernmental debts — including reparations — for one year. Within twelve months reparations had been permanently cancelled by the Laussane Conference (16 June–9 July 1932).

25. Meyer, *Mitteleuropa, passim*.
26. Graml, 'Präsidialsystem', p. 137.
27. Brüning, *Memoiren*, p. 308.

Nevertheless, while significant differences existed between the policies of Stresemann and Brüning, one crucial similarity remained: Brüning intended, with the help of economic pressure — indeed better said, by means of economic extortion — finally to solve the delicate question of revision in Eastern and Southeastern Europe. Like his predecessor, Brüning was persuaded that Germany's economy was her most powerful weapon. This he indicated to his cabinet in the spring of 1931:

> The strongest weapon in Germany's diplomatic arsenal is the fact that we are an importer of agrarian produce. This weapon must be ready. . . . If reparations must be paid from export surplus then the agrarian nations would necessarily be ruined. . . . Due to her high tax and reparations burden, Germany is compelled to pursue a policy which she regrets. In the end, however, the agrarian states will have to pay the reparations.[28]

These statements leave no doubt as to the intention of Brüning's 'stick it out' (*Durchhalte-*) strategy. In view of the worsening global depression this *Durchhaltepolitik* constituted nothing less than diplomatic extortion. It was aimed at bringing the long and tedious reparations negotiations and the excessively high (from the German standpoint) reparations demands to an end by facing creditors with the choice between settlement or the threat of impending collapsed of the German economy and utter domestic chaos. That he was aware of the domestic dangers inherent in his 'all-or-nothing' policy was revealed by Brüning in the following situation analysis given in his last speech before the Reichstag on 11 May 1932:

> There is danger, but in that danger hope. For every country in the world it is this: that in the next weeks or months the crisis will make such monstrous strides forward [*so ungeheuer Fortschritt machen wird*] all over the world that to wait even for a few weeks or months might create a situation from which no one could recover. . . . If the German people can keep their nerve, if to the last person we pull together to make the supreme effort in the coming months, then the German people will certainly not be among those who, as the result of the general crisis, succumb. . . . We just must not weaken during the last five minutes![29]

By means of calculated manipulation and intensification of Germany's depression, Brüning aimed to make his country the first of the stricken nations to emerge from the depths of the depression, and particularly to outstrip the less-industrialized nations — meaning the Eastern and

---

28. Cited in Helbig, 'Die Bedeutung der Reparationsfrage', p. 78.
29. Ibid., pp. 79f.

Southeastern European states. The advantage which Germany would enjoy over her neighbors in such a situation was apparent to all.[30]

As well as considering Brüning's diplomatic intensions, it is necessary to turn briefly to the functional value in domestic terms of his foreign policy. Brüning, it can be unequivocally stated, sought to use foreign policy as a means of manipulating domestic politics. In this, maintains Helbig, he toyed with the National Socialists:

> Both a non-fulfilment of the Young Plan, resulting from Germany's own policies, as well as the financial and economic collapse of the Reich, would have surrendered Germany in diplomatic terms to France. The price which the Reich government had to pay to avoid both cases was, as Brüning well knew, greater economic misery and with it the growth in the power of National Socialism.[31]

Thus the Chancellor struck a perilous balance between two extremes: on the one hand, deflationary economies which were bound up with the rise of National Socialist power; on the other hand, submission to French demands which would without fail lead to the fall of his government. Inevitably the policy of calculated risk polarized German politics. The steady intensification of domestic economic crisis produced unbearable strains in society, and radicalized politics at both extremes of the political spectrum. Yet it was that very polarization and heightened crisis which was supposed to provide the catalyst for diplomatic concessions and revision in the form of reparations and disarmament concessions. In the end he was a victim of the very domestic unrest he sought to exploit. As Graml indicates, this reflected the almost completely synchronomous nature of Brüning's foreign and domestic policy:

> It may well be correct to say that Brüning's domestic policy was governed by the requirements of foreign policy, but with equal justification one should not underestimate the degree to which Brüning's foreign policy played an important function in his domestic program.[32]

30. See the works by Borchardt and Holtfrerich quoted in Note 2, Chapter 4.1. See also Krüger, *Außenpolitik*, pp. 512–23.
31. Helbig, 'Die Bedeutung der Reparationsfrage', p. 92.
32. Graml, 'Präsidialsystem', pp. 144ff. Graml views the period of presidial government as a distinct and continuous transition from Weimar to Hitler: 'So bietet sich die Außenpolitik des Präsidialsystems — die Kabinette Papen und Schleicher haben auf außenpolitischen Feldern lediglich als Vollstrecker Brünings fungiert — als Teil eines umfassenden Restaurationsversuches dar, die Tendenz zur innenpolitischen Restauration verstärkend und fixierend, andererseits in gleichem Masse von jeder Tendenz verstärkt und fixiert. Diese Außenpolitik hat zur innenpolitischen Faschisierung Deutschlands, wenn gleich ungewollt, einen kräftigen Beitrag geleistet, die internationalen Voraussetzungen für ein Kabinett Hitler geschaffen und die ersten außenpolitischen

The goal of Brüning's stepped-up policy of revision, with its demand of 'all or nothing' as a virtual ultimatum, was to create a breakthrough to freedom of action for German foreign policy within the context of a rapidly changing European balance of power. This newly autonomous foreign policy, supported by the power of Germany's political, economic and military potential, would enable her to assume the economic and political leadership of Eastern and Southeastern Europe, as rightful heir to the fallen Habsburg Monarchy.

The Origins of 'New' Foreign Policy Goals: Germany and Southeastern Europe

By the end of the 1920s, a shift in the continental balance of power in Europe was well under way. The Dawes Plan, the Locarno Pact, Germany's entry into the League of Nations and the Young Plan were the evident signs of this diplomatic evolution. Gradually, Germany returned to an autonomous position within the European council of nations; gradually, France retreated from her hegemonic aims in Europe. This shift in the balance of power, accelerated by the return of the United States to European affairs after 1923, was only partly due to events within Europe: equally important were changing circumstances overseas; the pressure of decolonization, the rise of indigenous nationalism and the appearance of aggressive non-Western military forces combined to exert an additional and powerful influence. By end of the decade no major power in Europe stood to gain so much from these events as did Germany. As London and Paris struggled to protect their global interests, Berlin could exploit the singular advantage that Germany was the one continental power with no such far-flung commitments. Free to concentrate on the shifting continental balance of power, German foreign policy became more flexible, seeking ways to capitalize on the discomfort of both France and Britain.

With their own foreign policies changed or changing, the two latter countries reacted differently to German handling of the situation. France dropped all pretense at *Verständigungspolitik*, returning to an aggressive defense of Versailles. Her response to disarmament negotiations was to strengthen eastern defenses and to renew her unilateral contacts in Eastern Europe. On the other hand, the British Labour Government was under much greater pressure from non-European

---

Schritte des nationalsozialistischen Deutschland ermöglicht. Manche Elemente nationalsozialistischer Außenpolitik hatten ihre Entsprechung in bestimmten Elementen des Präsidialsystems.'

events and consequently its policy was far more receptive to German claims for revision. Supported by the United States, the Foreign Office sought within the limits to satisfy German demands.[1]

As the 1920s drew to a close, the French Government clearly perceived the change in the European balance of power.[2] Gradually, France's response became more vigorous, as measured by Thoiry, the Kellogg–Briand Pact, Briand's plan for a European Union and finally the Tardieu Plan (see below). Taken together, these diplomatic initiatives were intended to replace the crumbling Treaty of Versailles as the basis for a revitalized security policy. Even as French troops withdrew from the occupied Rhineland, on 5 September 1929 Briand put forward his highly-regarded grand plan for a federated European union at the League Assembly. He saw the proposed federation as a sweeping and comprehensive security system. At its heart would be a general reduction of tariff barriers and a well-coordinated, although not uniform, European economy (vaguely suggestive of the European Economic Community of thirty years later). At the time, Briand was accused of propounding a scheme so grand and impractical as to be meaningless; his motives, however, were in fact far more direct and less idealistic than his critics supposed. In short, not unlike his German counterparts, Briand now viewed economic policy as the key to diplomatic success. European Union and Europe's economic integration would accomplish what had eluded him in an *Ostlocarno*: the preservation of those Eastern and Southeastern European states created at Versailles.[3]

How did the Wilhelmstraße react to Briand's pan-European plan for international peace and security? Some argued that the scheme offered Germany considerable economic and commercial inducements; nevertheless most German policy-makers detected the demands of French security behind Briand's plan, and therefore rejected it out of hand. The plan seemed to them 'to be a blueprint for continued French predominance in European affairs'.[4] Briand's pan-European sentiments were interpreted simply as a cover for efforts to preserve the Versailles system and consequently French domination

1. Zimmermann, *Deutsche Außenpolitik*, p. 395.
2. Bennett, *Rearmament*, pp. 94–97.
3. Marks, *Illusion*, pp. 104ff: 'As the old sanctions were dissolving, Briand attempted to enmesh Germany in a new web of European integration, creating an interdependence which might in time eliminate war as a practical possibility. . . . Briand noted that he was placing political matters before economic as economic union depended upon security which in turn was linked to political union. In brief he was attempting to reinforce the existing *status quo*'.
4. Curtius, *Aufzeichnung*, Berlin 10 June 1930 (AA: Referat Völkerbund, Paneuropa Allg./Bd. 3, L503685–691); 'Niederschrift über die Ministerbesprechung am 5.7.1930 (BA: Alte Reichskanzlei, R Min 2b/Bd. 98, D784238–246).

over the continent.[5] The *Auswärtiges Amt* was particularly wary of politicizing economic relations at the cost of commercial freedom — as a severe limitation on German liberty of action — and thus rejected the primacy of politics over economics. As Sundhausen argues, 'the acceptance of French premises would compel German acceptance of stabilization under the already revised Versailles system. By means of a federated Europe, an *Ostlocarno* was envisaged and an *Anschluß* between Austria and Germany made impossible'.[6] In addition, the Reich government was unwilling to advance French plans by giving up a postwar foreign policy strategy which used American cooperation to progress towards instrumental deployment of the German economy.[7]

Briand's proposal of a European union was countered by Germany's bid for an Austro-German customs union.[8] This idea had a long history and was intended to serve a very special function in German affairs. Since Versailles, *Anschluß* had persistently been discussed in Berlin and Vienna. The dissolution of the multi-national Habsburg Empire meant that a political and economic union of Germany and a German-speaking 'rump' Austria was an attractive idea in both capitals. The Versailles Treaty, however, prohibited this 'natural' union and provided that not only the

5. Von Bülow characterized Briand's European Union scheme and its potential consequences for German foreign policy as follows: 'Das gegenwärtige Europa ist gestaltet durch die Friedensverträge, die die Alliierten einseitig geschaffen haben, und sein Charakter wird zum großen Teil bestimmt von Völkerbund, den ebenfalls die Alliierten nach ihren Wünschen geformt haben und in dem sie noch immer ausschlaggebend sind. Selbstredend wünschen sie ein Pan-Europa nur, wenn sie in diesem ebenfalls die Vorherrschaft besitzen. Mir will scheinen, daß wir für ein Pan-Europa nur dann politisches Interesse haben, wenn es auf einer neuen Basis also nicht in Anlehnung an den Völkerbund und an die Verträge aufgebaut wird und uns völlige Gleichberechtigung . . . sichert. Ferner wenn es uns die Möglichkeit bietet, unsere zentrale geographische Lage auszuwerten und nicht umgekehrt uns hindert, unsere geographische Lage gegen die Alliierten auszuspielen.' Bülow to Eisenloher, 7 August 1929 (AA: SW, Wirtschaft 1–Europa/Bd.1). Cited in H.-J. Schröder, 'Deutsche Südosteuropapolitik, 1929–1936. Zur Kontinuität deutscher außenpolitik in der Weltwirtschaftskrise', in W. Schieder, ed., *Außenwirtschaft und Außenpolitik im 'Dritten Reich'*, publication of *Geschichte und Gesellschaft*, II, 1 (1976), p. 14. On the financial and commercial domination of Eastern Europe by Britain, France and the United States during the interwar era, see: G. Ranki, *Economy and Foreign Policy: The Struggle of the Great Powers for Hegemony in the Danube Valley, 1919–1939* (Boulder, Colorado, 1983), and D. E. Kaiser, *Economic Diplomacy and the Origins of the Second World War* (Princeton, 1980).

6. H. Sundhausen, 'Die Weltwirtschaftskrise im Donau–Balkan–Raum und ihre Bedeutung für den Wandel der deutschen Außenpolitik unter Brüning', in W. Benz and H. Graml, eds., *Aspekte deutscher Außenpolitik im 20. Jahrhundert* (Stuttgart, 1976), p. 126.

7. Schröder, in Schieder, p. 15; contrast to Bülow's attitude (see note 5 above): 'Die Vereinigten Staaten z.B. stehen uns in viele Hinsicht näher und sind uns wichtiger als manche der europäischen Staaten.' On the basis of this close economic relationship between Berlin and Washington — also, one might note, between Berlin and London as well — Bülow argued that Germany must avoid becoming involved in the French plan for a European Union. Kaisers, *Economic Diplomacy*, pp. 29–30.

8. F. G. Stambrook, 'The German–Austrian Customs Union Project of 1931: A Study of German Methods and Motives', *JCEH* XXI (1961).

victorious Allies, but also Germany and Austria, guaranteed the political and economic independence of the new Austrian state. In 1922, in order to receive financial and economic support necessary for her survival, Austria had expressly to reiterate renunciation of the *Anschluß* in principle. Political pressure was a major factor here, for both France and Italy vigorously resisted *Anschluß* as a threat to their security. When asked in 1927, even Stresemann rejected the idea of *Anschluß* in the near future: 'His immediate response was to conclude that German political institutions could not absorb an unstable Austria.'[9] Evidently, for Stresemann domestic considerations were secondary to diplomatic when the conversation turned to *Anschluß*: he did not intend to risk the 'spirit of Locarno' and Germany's improving relations with France and Italy for the dubious gain of union with Austria. Nevertheless, the idea of German–Austrian unification was never completely ruled out. Particularly in economic and commercial affairs such an arrangement offered long-term advantages. In early 1927, the German *Industrie- und Handelstag* and the *Reichsverband der deutschen Industrie* had already opened talks with their Austrian opposite numbers concerning a future economic union between Germany and Austria. Similar discussions took place between other industrial and agrarian organizations of both countries.[10]

On the German side, discussion soon took concrete form. Julius Curtius, at that time Minister of Economics, in 1927 developed detailed plans for a German–Austrian customs union.[11] Curtius, later to become Foreign Minister following Stresemann's death, totally agreed with the Wilhelmstrasse's view that the earliest possible date by which such plans could be broached was 1930, so as not to compromise negotiations in the priority areas of reparations and evacuation.[12] But with the onset of the depression the question of some form of union became increasingly acute.[13] On 21 March 1931, Berlin announced that Germany and Austria had concluded negotiations for a customs union.[14]

9. S. Suval, *The Anschluss Question in the Weimar Era: A Study of Nationalism in Germany and Austria, 1918–1932* (Baltimore, 1974), p. 141.
10. Ibid., p. 108.
11. Ibid., p. 148; Campbell, p. 222.
12. Krüger, *Außenpolitik*, p. 350: 'Für Curtius und Bülow wies der Briand—Plan noch einen besonders störenden Zug auf: Er drohte ihr 1930 sich entwickelndes Zollunions–Projekt mit Österreich zunichte zu machen, das rasch in die Rolle einer deutschen Alternative zu den gesamteuropäischen Vorstellungen hineinwuchs. Curtius hatte schon seit Jahren eine Vorliebe für die Zollunion, und es lässt sich mit Recht feststellen, dass ein dramatischer Wandel von Stresemanns Zurückhaltung zur forcierten Aktion 1930/31 stattfand. Auch Bülow trat seit geraumer Zeit für eine aktivere Politik in allen Revisionsfragen und gegenüber Österreich und Südosteuropa ein, sobald Rheinlandräumung und Reparationsregelung erfolgt seien.'
13. Marks, *Illusion*, p. 116: 'While a customs union was not *Anschluß*, it was universally regarded as a giant step in that direction.'

The Treaty Powers, particularly France (vigorously supported by Poland, Czechoslovakia and Yugoslavia), reacted immediately to what they viewed as an Austro-German attempt to overthrow the Treaties of Versailles and St. Germain. The Laval government saw the customs union proposal as nothing more than a clumsy attempt to accomplish *Anschluß* and lost no time in exerting irresistible force on the Austrian government: by financial manipulation, it brought about the fall of one of Austria's largest banks, the *Creditanstalt*. In the face of such extreme pressure, Vienna capitulated and gave up the idea. Britain, with no objection in principle to the customs union plan, appealed to the League of Nations for mediation. The entire matter was turned over to the International Court at the Hague, which in a split decision ruled that the customs union would violate Austria's pledge of 1922. In this manner France was able to check Germany's economic and political offensive, which itself had been a reply to Briand's plan for a European union. Germany still lacked the strength to see such a plan through; her move had been more tactical than strategic, for she remained too weak to take the initiative.

In an attempt to save face and aver her good faith, Germany portrayed the Austro-German customs union as nothing more than an attempt to realize the aim of Briand's European union project.[15] There was, she protested, no contradiction between the two proposals. In reality, however, the customs union project was a direct answer to the Briand plan and aimed at undermining it. The Wilhelmstraße unsuccessfully tried to fit it into the French rubric, dressing it up, as Bülow cynically remarked, 'in a pan-European cloak'.[16]

Beyond the obvious tactical value of the customs union plan, German proposals for economic cooperation with Austria hinted at something far larger than mere *Anschluß*. In this sense, then, we can see the transition in German foreign policy from its concentration on revision of the Versailles system to a conception of foreign policy goals on a far grander scale. As early as mid-1930 this new dimension was revealed in

---

14. On the question of financial crisis of 1931 and the customs union project, see especially Stambrook, 'The German–Austrian Customs Union Project of 1931' and E. W. Bennett, *Germany and the Diplomacy of the Financial Crisis, 1931* (Cambridge, Mass., 1962).

15. Compare that with the reaction of the German ambassador in Paris, Leopold von Hoesch. Hoesch cynically remarked to Berlin that Briand was scarcely so naive that he could not see right through the German customs union scheme. Cited in E. Geigenmüller, 'Botschafter von Hoesch und der deutsch–österreichische Zollunionsplan von 1931', *HZ* CLXCV (1962), p. 589.

16. Marks, *Illusion*, p. 116: 'Finally, the announcement was timed to coincide with the meeting of the committee considering Briand's plan for European union in order to give the customs union project an aura of respectability. As von Bülow had said, "we will dress the matter up with a pan-European cloak".'

a memorandum prepared by the Wilhelmstraße for Chancellor Brüning, urging an entirely receptive Brüning to think beyond Austria. Because of the rapid developments in Southeastern Europe, the union with Austria should be the highest priority in German policy, since from a German-held Austria events in Southeastern Europe could be influenced in Germany's favor in an entirely different way from that presently possible.[17] Thus, to the Foreign Ministry, *Anschluß* seemed a far more compelling question for the future of the Reich than even the Polish Corridor.

The effects of economic crisis in the Danubian–Balkan region opened vast new vistas for German economic and political influence. Until 1930 German foreign policy, although delicately balanced between East and West, had concentrated on Western developments. The Wall Street Crash and the evacuation of the Rhineland profoundly altered the situation. While Western affairs had enjoyed absolute priority in German foreign policy until now, from this point on the focus fell more and more heavily on Central and Southeastern Europe. Whereas diplomatic initiatives in this region would have been premature before 1929/30, following evacuation of the Rhineland Eastern revision became a realistic goal. Traditional German plans for a *Mitteleuropa* surfaced once more, this time in an economic, that is a commercial, reincarnation.[18]

Within this new constellation of foreign policy goals, the ultimate

17. Memorandum from the AA to Reichskanzler Brüning, 7 July 1930, reproduced in W. Ruge and W. Schumann, 'Die Reaktion des deutschen Imperialismus auf Briands Paneuropaplan 1930', *ZfG* 20, 1 (1972), pp. 64f.; compare this with Schröder, in Schieder, pp. 11f. The intention of this policy was already clear in the remarks by E. Koch-Weser in 1929, who had served as Minister of Justice in 1928–1929: 'Mitteleuropa liegt Deutschland näher als Paneuropa. Ein wachsendes und zukunftsfrohes Volk wie das deutsche ... bedarf ... außerhalb seiner engen Grenzen Lebensraum, in dem es seine Kräfte betätigen kann. Mögen die Verschiebungen des Weltkrieges auch noch so groß gewesen sein, die von Naumann immer betonte Tatsache, daß der Lebensraum Deutschlands in Mitteleuropa liegt und im Südosten zu erweitern ist, ist unverändert geblieben. Wir denken nicht an eine Annexion dieser Völker. Aber hier im Osten und Südosten von Deutschland ist der deutsche Sprache als Verkehrssprache verwürzelt und ist deutsches Wissen und Können berufen, an der Entwicklung führend mitzuarbeiten. Hier sitzen uberall die deutschen Minderheiten, die an Bildung und Besitz ihren Herrenvölkern an manchen Stellen voraus sind und ihre wirtschaftliche, ja auch politische Haltung oft massgebend beeinflussen.' E. Koch-Weser, *Deutschlands Außenpolitik in der Nachkriegszeit 1919–1929* (Berlin, 1929), pp. 121f. As for Brüning, he was convinced of the need for economic initiatives in Southeastern Europe, as he reiterated in his memoirs: '[. . .] sie war für Deutschland außerordentlich wichtig als Hebel für die Ingangbringung wirtschaftspolitischer Lösungen im Donauraum nach unserem Sinne.' H.-J. Schröder, 'Die deutsche Südosteuropapolitik und die Reaktion der angelsächsichen Mächte 1929–1933/34', in J. Becker and K. Hildebrand, eds., *Internationale Beziehungen in der Weltwirtschaftskrise 1929–1933* (Munich, 1980), p. 350.

18. R. Berndt, 'Wirtschaftliche Mitteleuropapläne des deutschen Imperialismus (1926–1931). Zur Rolle des Mitteleuropäischen Wirtschaftstages unter dem Mitteleuropa-Institut in den imperialistischen deutschen Expansionsplänen', *Wissenschaftliche Zeitschrift der Martin-Luther-Universität Halle-Wittenberg*, v. 14 (1965), p. 306.

aim of German diplomacy remained what it always had been since 1918: the recovery of Great Power status. With respect to the other Great Powers, this meant rearmament, demanded with what Bennett calls the 'inspired slogan of "equality of rights" [*Gleichberechtigung*]'.[19] With respect to the secondary and lesser states of Central and Southeastern Europe, it meant superiority. In Sundhausen's words:

> In both cases, the instrument was predominantly — although not exclusively — economic. [The aim was] settlement of the reparations question (with a simultaneous attack on the disarmament problem) and a reinforced economic penetration of Southeastern Europe both for the capture of new markets and, equally important, for the express purpose of weakening the French security system, that is, the anti-revisionist bloc.[20]

Vehicle of this new variation in German foreign policy was once again the Reich economy, particularly the light industrial and export sectors, both of which recognized quite early the increasing importance and significant export opportunities offered by the Southeastern European states in view of the worsening effects of the Depression.[21] The question, as H.-J. Schröder puts it, was: 'How could Germany, *despite* her economic weaknesses in the worldwide depression, tie the agrarian states of Southeastern Europe to herself through economic means?'[22]

As a consequence of the accelerating economic change triggered by the Wall Street Crash in Central and Southeastern Europe, the German Foreign Ministry developed for this region a political strategy which need only perpetuate the traditional goals of the Wilhelmine Reich. Schröder, who in his outstanding work on German Southeast European strategy during the early 1930s has described the Wilhelm-

---

19. Bennett, *Rearmament*, p. 95.

20. Sundhausen, 'Weltwirtschaftskrise' p. 159; compare this with Berndt, p. 309: 'Der deutsche Imperialismus erstrebte in der Zeit der Weimarer Republik zunächst mangels anderer Möglichkeiten seine Vorherrschaft in Europa auf ökonomischen Gebiet. Das änderte sich erst zu Beginn der dreißiger Jahre, als mit Hilfe der USA nicht nur die ökonomischen, sondern auch die politischen Fesseln des Versailler Vertrages vor allem in Bezug auf die "Rüstungsgleichheit" für Deutschland zu durchbrechen begann.'

21. Schröder, in Schieder, p. 11. In this context Schröder quotes the President of the *Mitteleuropäische Wirtschaftstage*, Wilmowsky: 'In den Jahren 1929 und 1930 begannen weiterblickende Kreise der deutschen Industrie, insbesondere der Ruhrinudstrie, der Chemischen und der Elektro-Industrie, ihre Aufmerksamkeit stärker auf die wirtschaftlichen Möglichkeiten zu richten, die eine Intensivierung der Handelsbeziehungen zu Südosteuropa unter Umständen ergeben können.' Wilmowsky felt in 1932, 'dass die wirtschaftliche Entwicklung dieser Länder für die gesamte deutsche Wirtschaft von der allergrößten Bedeutung [sei und] dass sich aus diesem Grunde die deutsche Außen- und Wirtschaftspolitik der Pflege unserer Beziehungen zu diesen Ländern besonders annehmen müssen.' In this connection, compare also the interpretation by Berndt of the plans of German industrialists for *Mitteleuropa*: Berndt, p. 317.

22. Schröder, in Becker and Hildebrand, p. 350.

strasse's efforts in great detail, points out the extensive use made of trade preferences with Romania and Hungary.[23] This was a skilful tactic, since the treaties meant that Romanian and Hungarian agricultural commodities were imported by Germany in exchange for lower tariffs on her own industrial goods exported to Romania and Hungary. These lower duties were not preferences, but most-favored-nation rates extended to Germany, which enabled Berlin to reap a dual benefit:

> The refusal to accept preferences for German exports put the Reich government in a tactically advantageous position, able to depict its preference policy as assistance for the troubled agrarian states, without having to disclose its own political motives, which by this time occupied center stage in domestic political debate.[24]

At the beginning of the 1930s, then, this strategy served a double purpose. First, through intensifying economic hardship in Central and Southeastern Europe by means of her own domestic financial and economic policies, Germany could create a situation of increasing dependency by these states, thus eventually extending not only economic but also political hegemony over Central and Southeastern Europe. Secondly, this increased influence would enable the French ring around Germany to be broken; ultimately, this would spell the end of French domination on the continent. 'The less success French diplomacy had in stabilizing French economic and political influence in Southeastern Europe during the Depression, the easier it would be for Berlin to tie the agrarian states of Southeastern Europe economically, and therefore politically, to Germany.'[25] An intensification of the agrarian crisis in the Balkans was in Germany's interests, since Brüning intended to capitalize on the economic troubles in that quarter to further revisionist aims. In the end, then, these 'new' diplomatic goals emerging after 1930, which simply recast the Wilhelmine Reich's traditional goals, formed an ideal basis from which Hitler could advance the expansionist foreign policy goals of National Socialism.[26]

---

23. The continuity in German policy in Southeastern Europe can be clearly distinguished in the work of Schröder which deals with the early 1930s, and in P. Marguerat, whose work deals with the late 1930s: P. Marguerat, *Le IIIe Reich et la pétrole roumain 1938–1940: Contribution à l'étude de la pénétration économique allemande dans les Balkans à la veille et au début de la Seconde Guerre mondiale* (Leiden, 1977). See also Schröder, in Becker and Hildebrand, *passim*.
24. Schröder, in Becker and Hildebrand, pp. 351–52.
25. Schröder, in Schieder, p. 22.
26. Ibid., pp. 22ff; Marguerat, *passim*.

From Brüning to Hitler: Divergence and Congruity in Foreign Policy Goals Between Traditional *Revisionspolitik* and National Socialist *Expansionspolitik*, 1930–1933

In the wake of the Great Depression Heinrich Brüning aimed to put an end to reparations by means of a calculated and forced policy of crisis. The domestic German economic, social and political crisis was manipulated and intensified to the point where reparations could be shown to be a savage and painful burden on her, directly linked to her misfortunes. Once freed from that obligation, Germany would have a certain degree of diplomatic autonomy. Into the bargain, an end to reparations would materially affect the French security system. The Chancellor understood full well the value of his reparations policy as a 'weapon' against the French, with which he could pressure both France and the Southeastern European states to make concessions to the German export economy. 'With the help of the reparations (and disarmament) problem he hoped in the course of eighteen months or two years that the two questions would have toppled the Versailles Treaty, without even bringing the subject forward.'[1]

These political and economic calculations, quite within the framework of *Primat der Außenpolitik*, produced results. Brüning's successors, Papen and Schleicher, reaped what he had sown: final settlement of the reparations question and the formal recognition of German equality of rights, or *Gleichberechtigung*. Following the Hoover Moratorium, which in 1931 granted Germany a one-year suspension of reparations payments, a complete review of the provisions of the Young Plan became necessary. On 9 July 1932 at the Reparations Conference in Lausanne new and final conditions for reparations were announced: the Young schedule, under which Germany would have paid reparations until 1988, was cancelled in consideration of a once-only German payment of 3 milliard gold marks to be made at the end of a three-year extension of the moratorium. With that, reparations came to an end.[2] But at Lausanne the conferees also touched on disarmament. By April, the Germans had been convinced that both Britain and America supported equality of rights.[3] When at Lausanne Papen failed to win French agreement to that principle, it was all the more serious, Bennett points out, since 'the attempt to win [rearma-

1. Sundhausen, 'Weltwirtschaftskrise' pp. 128f.
2. Bennett argues that an end to reparations foreshadowed no significant change in Germany's financial policy: 'The end of the Lausanne Conference meant that Germany no longer had to make a show of financial conservatism to impress her reparations creditors, but a balanced budget was still a totem at home and inflation a taboo.' Bennett, *Rearmament*, p. 186.
3. Ibid., pp. 154–5.

ment] concessions by agreeing to a final payment had not been kept secret from the German public'.[4] In the end both France and Britain rejected demands for armament equality for fear that a rearmed Germany might seek to redress her territorial grievances through unilateral use of force. On this note, Germany withdrew from the Geneva Disarmament Conference on 21 September 1932. After several months of intense diplomatic activity, on 3 December the Western powers overcame France's resistance,[5] and offered Germany 'equality of rights in a system which would provide security for all nations'.[6] Having secured *Gleichberechtigung*, Germany returned to the Geneva Disarmament Conference.

Germany's peremptory exit from the Disarmament Conference, by way of ultimatum, was the dress rehearsal for her eventual withdrawal from both the League of Nations and the Geneva Disarmament Conference a little over a year later. In retrospect this is the less surprising, for since 1930 the consensus of opinion in both the Wilhelmstraße and the Bendlerstraße had been that the League was perhaps more inhibiting than facilitating to German revisionist aims.[7] In the light of this, then, it can be said that Germany's League of Nations policy had come to an end long before the official withdrawal.[8] Hitler's action in October 1933 was, therefore, anticlimactic. The demands for revision cultivated under Brüning's cunning though heavy-handed foreign policy fell like ripe fruit into the laps of his successors, Papen, Schleicher and Hitler.

In contrast to Brüning, Franz von Papen returned to the courtship of France, since he sought to follow a course closer to that of Stresemann.[9] While Brüning pursued revision via London and

4. Ibid., p. 180.
5. Ibid., p. 209–72
6. Ibid., p. 267; Krüger, *Außenpolitik*, pp. 546–51.
7. The increasingly significant role of the Reichswehr in German politics in the late Weimar period is the subject of work by M. Geyer, *Deutsche Rüstungspolitik 1860–1980* (Frankfurt a/M, 1984), especially pp. 129–43; idem, *Aufrüstung oder Sicherheit. Die Reichswehr in der Krise der Machtpolitik* (Wiesbaden, 1980), *passim*; idem, 'Die Konferenz für die Herabsetzung und Beschränkung der Rüstungen und das Problem der Abrüstung', in Becker and Hildebrand, *Internationale Beziehungen*, pp. 155–202; idem, 'Militär, Rüstung und Außenpolitik — Aspekte militärischer Revisionpolitik in der Zwischenkriegszeit', in M. Funke, ed., *Hitler, Deutschland und die Mächte* (Düsseldorf, 1976), pp. 239–68. Throughout his work, Geyer stresses the growing influence of the military on German politics and foreign policy after 1930. By 1932 economic questions were secondary in the eyes of German diplomats. The Wilhelmstrasse was determined to drive disarmament negotiations to the point at which Germany could rearm, while the Bendelerstrasse already had extensive plans for rearmament; long-service professionals and six-month militia, as well as the reintroduction of an air force. See also A. Seaton, *The German Army, 1933–1945* (New York, 1982) p. 24.
8. Lee, 'The German Effort to Reform the League', *passim*; Eyck, v. 2, p. 482.
9. On the pre-French efforts to von Papen's foreign policy, and German relations with France as the key to the commercial penetration of Southeastern Europe, see U.

Washington, Papen preferred the direct route of reopening bilateral contacts with Paris. In this way he hoped to foster a broad understanding betwen Germany and France to serve as the basis for a general solution of outstanding problems between them. Reichswehr Minister General Kurt von Schleicher shared the belief that this direct approach was best, since France had most to lose in matters of treaty revision. Moreover, both men felt that if Germany could come to terms with her greatest antagonist, France, on matters of *Gleichberechtigung*, then the remaining Powers would be no obstacle. Having married into a wealthy industrial family from the Saar,[10] Papen supported private Franco-German contacts out of personal, as well as national, interest. Since 1918 he had encouraged a variety of informal private meetings aimed at closer Franco-German cooperation in the private industrial sector which might ease the tensions between the two countries.[11]

As Chancellor, Papen continued to support similar contacts and sought to conceal worsening Franco-German relations from the public, in the hope of avoiding further domestic tension which he felt would follow on the heels of any such revelation. In his encouragement of private contacts and confidential relations between Berlin and Paris, Papen resumed the style of Franco–German diplomacy exemplified by the Thoiry meeting between Stresemann and Briand. In so doing, he laid the basis for Hitler's bilateral diplomacy. To observers the change in government from Brüning to Papen, thus seemed to indicate a change in foreign policy; according to Pfeiffer this change was more apparent than real, a variation in form, not content:

In Germany the change in government affected German foreign policy in

Hörster-Philipps, *Konservative Politik in der Endphase der Weimarer Republik* (Cologne, 1982).
   10. J. A. Bach, *Franz von Papen in der Weimarer Republik. Aktivitäten in Politik und Presse, 1918–1932* (Düsseldorf, 1977), pp. 10ff.
   11. Von Papen in his many capacities, as a member of the *Zentrum* Party, on the board of *Germania* (the main publication of the party) and as a member of the *Herrenclub*, repeatedly expressed his inclination toward Franco-German cooperation. An especially important forum for his ideas was the 'Deutsch-französische Studienkommitee, which was founded in May 1926 by a heavy-industrialist from Luxembourg, Emile Mayrisch. See F. L'Hullier, *Dialogues Franco-Allemandes, 1925–1933* (Strasbourg, 1971); R. Pfeiffer, *Der deutsch-britischen Beziehungen unter den Reichskanzlern von Papen und von Schleicher* (Würzburg, 1971), p. 4. Papen's ideas on Franco-German cooperation were similar to those of Arnold Rechberg, the soda magnate from Hersfeld, who held that the interdependence of the West European economies argued in favor of political cooperation. Rechberg viewed political cooperation as the natural consequence of economic cooperation, envisaging a grand anti-Russian coalition in the West. Although von Papen's anti-Bolshevik sentiments were not as aggressive as Rechberg's, he did view Western cooperation as essential for the survival of Western culture. Pfeiffer, *Deutsch-britische Beziehungen* p. 4; on Rechberg, see E. von Vietsch, *Arnold Rechberg und das Problem der politischen West-Orientierung Deutschlands nach dem 1. Weltkrieg* (Koblenz, 1958).

two ways, which did not alter the goals of Brüning's policy but rather the manner in which they were to be accomplished. The first change was the resumption of the Stresemann policy of a direct German–French understanding. In this regard, Papen displayed particular energy at the Lausanne Conference. The second change was the uncompromisingly relentless pursuit of national foreign policy goals based on the *Primat der Innenpolitik* .... In reparations, the most urgent problem facing German foreign policy and the one arousing the greatest public interest, Brüning had already done the heavy work with his demand for complete cancellation.[12]

Here Pfeiffer is perhaps a bit too categorical, for it would seem that Brüning had indeed put foreign policy first, seeing in Germany's international position the solution to her internal troubles. The fact that for both Brüning and for Papen domestic political benefits would flow from a resolution of the reparations question and from granting German equality of treatment in armaments talks seems to indicate that foreign policy continued to appeal to Germany's leaders as the means of solving Germany's domestic ills. Papen thus continued and in fact embellished the policy of his predecessor. His problem was made considerably easier by the fact that, despite opposition to his government, domestic public opinion uniformly supported demands for an end of reparations and equality of rights for Germany.

It was Papen's goal, once Germany secured *Gleichberechtigung*, to press for a security system composed of the four Western Great Powers and aimed at Bolshevik Russia.[13] Papen made various efforts to realize his concept of a Franco-German Entente to circumvent the multilateral system of Geneva. Both in press conferences and in private conversations with the French Prime Minister Eduard Herriot at the disarmament talks in Geneva in 1932, Papen declared his readiness to discuss closer Franco-German relations and his desire to bring about an understanding between the two countries. Any obstacles to closer understanding between these neighbors should be overcome in direct bilateral conversations serving to cement a closer Franco-German rapprochement. In Papen's conception, a customs union and general staff talks would precede an alliance system which would eventually

---

12. Pfeiffer, *Deutsch-britische Beziehungen*, p. 175.
13. In this respect Papen's ideas clearly anticipated Mussolini's Four-Power Pact, which was approximately a year in the future, although with a different emphasis: 'Of course the ideas of the German Reich Chancellor and of the Italian head of state in favor of such an alliance were motivated by entirely different factors, for to Papen it was primarily a question of a continental European bloc in which Franco-German cooperation, including cooperation of the two general staffs, would play the decisive role. The closer association of Germany and France would be made possible by the solution of the corridor problem, a solution so unfavorable to Poland that she would be forced to join the Western bloc.' G. Wollstein, *Vom Weimarer Revisionismus zu Hitler. Das Deutsche Reich und die Großmächte in der Anfangsphase der nationalsozialistischen Herrschaft in Deutschland* (Bonn-Bad Godesberg, 1973), p. 41.

embrace not only Germany and France, but Italy and even Poland. Herriot's response was hardly encouraging. The French Prime Minister ducked the issue of a German–French alliance, which comprised recognition of German equality of rights. Apparently France preferred the multi-lateral system of the League to any bi-lateral negotiations with Germany. Papen, however, did not give up and attempted to foster German–French contacts on another level with the help of the German–French Study Committee, also known as the Mayrisch Committee.[14] This was an important private industrial lobby group headed by one Emile Mayrisch; it was founded in 1926 with ample industrial and banking support in order to further Franco-German industrial contacts and to work for cooperation of the German–French–Luxembourgeois heavy industries. It was through this committee that Papen sought to improve contacts with France:

> The first meeting of leading representatives of the German and French chemical and electro industries at the end of April 1932 in Luxembourg . . .recommended . . .an end of reparations as a vital part of a successful defense against the National Socialist and Communist dangers in Germany. The replacement of American credit with French, the formation of a regional customs union between Germany, France, Belgium and Luxembourg, a possible mutual partition of markets in Southeastern Europe and the question of frontier adjustments in the Corridor and Upper Silesia — these questions were included in the discussion. Although no agreement could be reached, the basic consensus existed on both sides that on the basis of a limitation of economic and political goals a lasting Franco-German reconciliation could be reached.[15]

These semi-official contacts between German and French economic and industrial leaders survived the fall of Papen and lasted until well after the National Socialist *Machtergreifung*. As Vice-Chancellor under Hitler, Papen attempted in numerous memoranda and conversations to win the *Führer* over to his concept of a German–French Entente.[16] Papen, however, soon realized that he faced powerful

14. In addition to Wollstein, see especially J. Bariéty, 'Le rôle d'Emile Mayrisch entre les sidérurgies allemandes et françaises après la première guerre mondiale', *Relations Internationales*, 1 (1974), pp. 123–34; J. Bariéty and C. Bloch, 'Une tentative de réconciliation franco-allemande et son échec (1932–1933)', *Revue d'histoire moderne et contemporaine*, 15 (1968), pp. 433ff.; L'Hullier, *Dialogues*; B. Martin 'Friedens-Planungen der multinationalen Großindustrie (1932 bis 1940) als politische Krisenstrategie', in Schieder, *Außenwirtschaft*, pp. 66–88. See also for the entire question of Franco-German negotiations on a steel cartel U. Nocken 'Das Internationle Stahlkartell und die deutsch-französischen Beziehungen 1924–1932', in: G. Schmidt, ed., *Konstellationen internationaler Politik 1924–1932* (Bochum, 1983), pp. 165–203.
15. Martin, 'Friedens-Planungen', pp. 70f.
16. *DGFP*, Series C, v. I, documents 41, 43, 379, 384, 403, 404; *DBFP*, Second Series, v. V, document 490.

resistance on the part of Foreign Minister Konstantin von Neurath, himself vigorously supported by State Secretary Bernard von Bülow. Neurath and his lieutenant Bülow had as their primary goal improved relations with Great Britain and Italy, viewing France as still symbolic of the hated but now virtually defunct Versailles system.[17] The Foreign Minister bluntly lectured the Vice-Chancellor on the realities of German–Polish relations and the position of France in Germany's diplomatic calculations. German–Polish agreement would never produce the necessary Eastern revision, since the question was not a technical one, but rather a matter of ethnic populations and territory. Consequently, Neurath concluded, the only solution was another partition of Poland, to which France would hardly agree. Since German policy was such an obvious challenge to the interests of both France and Poland, cooperation between Germany and either of these countries was out of the question. In this fashion, asserts Günther Wollstein, Hitler was able to check Papen's efforts at Franco-German understanding without entering the argument himself.[18] One might also point out that the *Führer*'s tactics left him free within a year to reverse his course and complete a non-aggression pact with Poland.

Both Neurath and his State Secretary Bülow advocated intensified and aggressive steps toward territorial revision; such a policy was not in harmony with the multi-national schemes of French and German industrialists. Well before the advent of Hitler the Wilhelmstraße under Neurath had resisted Papen. Once Chancellor von Papen fell in December 1932 the Foreign Minister had little time in which to react to his successor, General von Schleicher, whose tenure was so short that little material exists on which to base a constructive judgment about his foreign policy. Nevertheless, it can be said that he contrasted sharply with Papen and was symbolic of a certain continuing factor in German foreign policy: the influence of the *Reichswehr*, specifically on continued military contacts with other countries. In contrast to Papen, who favored an anti-Bolshevik front comprising the Western powers and anchored on a Franco-German Entente, Schleicher valued the continuation of good relations between the Red Army and the *Reichswehr*. This did not leave out the possibility of improved Franco-German relations, but it did include continued German–Soviet cooperation, effectively precluding an anti-Bolshevik bloc.[19] Schleicher intended to pursue a dual strategy. On the one hand, he hoped that better relations with France would leave him free to enlist the Soviet

17. Wollstein, *Weimarer Revisionismus* pp. 39ff.
18. Ibid., p. 42; *DGFP*, Series C, v. I, document 18.
19. G. Post, Jr., *The Civil-Military Fabric of Weimar Foreign Policy* (Princeton, 1973), pp. 301–09.

Union in putting pressure on Poland for the territorial revision of Germany's eastern frontiers. Simultaneously, Schleicher aimed to improve German–Soviet relations, which since 1930 had noticeably cooled; in particular, he wished for more military contacts between the two nations.[20] Despite the fact that German–Soviet commerce remained most satisfactory,[21] the USSR had in recent years shown increasing interest in Western Europe, coupled with growing concern about its economic crisis and political instability. This was evident in the series of non-aggression pacts between the Soviet Union signed with neighboring states and others to the west: Poland, Finland, Lithuania, Estonia, France and Italy. More and more in the early 1930s, Kremlin foreign policy resembled collective security as advocated by the League of Nations; to many observers it seemed simply a question of time before the Soviet government would petition the League for membership. General von Schleicher accordingly intended that closer cooperation should halt the deterioration in Russo-German relations which had begun in 1930, and somehow to reverse course.[22]

The brief period during which von Schleicher occupied the Reich Chancellory produced no visible improvement in German–Soviet relations. It remained for his successor, Hitler, to introduce a radical alteration by allowing relations between the two countries to cool almost to freezing point, while skilfully maintaining a very active and mutually beneficial trading association.

Neither Papen nor Schleicher succeeded in substantially altering the course or character of German foreign policy, nor in fact did either remain in office long enough to make his mark. In domestic policy neither man offered an effective alternative to National Socialism. Hitler waited at the gates. Initially, January 1933 represented no radical break with German foreign policy of the immediate past.[23]

---

20. Post maintains that German–Soviet military cooperation reached the 'high water mark' in 1932. Post, ibid., p. 301.

21. On the subject of German–Soviet trade relations, see Dyck, *Weimar Germany*, p. 216.

22. On worsening diplomatic relations between Berlin and Moscow during the early Thirties, see Dyck, ibid.: 'The confusion of Germany's domestic scene had rendered the Rapallo front unstable, making the Soviets eager to reinsure their position against the possibility of German's defection.... An added incentive to take up the French offer [of a non-aggression] pact was a hardheaded assessment of the shifting power relations in Europe in the first four months of 1931, which seemed to favor France. To the USSR it appeared that her principal friend, Germany, was becoming infirm in her resolve and unsure of her goals at a time when her chief opponent, France, was moving from one foreign policy success to another....'

23. See in this regard C. Bloch, *Hitler und die europäischen Mächte 1933/34. Kontinuität oder Bruch* (Frankfurt a.M., 1966), p. 22; and now particularly Wollstein, *Weimarer Revisionismus, passim.*

Despite the protests, assertions and propaganda of the National Socialists, the appointment of Adolf Hitler as Reich Chancellor in a cabinet of 'national concentration' could hardly be described as a 'revolution'. To the satisfaction of most 'knowledgeable' political observers, Hitler had been 'positioned' (*eingerahmt*) within a conservative majority in the new cabinet and a 'taming' or 'domestication' (*Zähmung*)[24] of the National Socialist *Führer* and his mass party seemed to have been accomplished.[25] This 'positioning and taming' policy with respect to Hitler seemed to have been most clearly evident in the realm of foreign policy. Conforming to the wishes of Reich President von Hindenburg, Hitler agreed that von Neurath remain as Foreign Minister, which position he had held since May/June 1932 under both Papen and Schleicher. As an aristocrat and a conservative, Neurath enjoyed considerble trust from the 'old gentleman' Hindenburg.[26]

Following the appearance of Hitler in 1933 the traditional instrument of German foreign policy, the *Auswärtiges Amt*, remained almost completely unaffected in its personnel structure for the next five years, until well into 1938.[27] The result was that for the first five years of the National Socialist Reich the Prussian–German 'dualism' of statecraft and militarism — *Staatskunst und Kriegshandwerk*[28] — continued to color German foreign policy. Hillgruber noted the continuity of traditional diplomatic and military elites throughout the first half of the National Socialist Reich: 'The continuity of a politico-military accent in the formulation of foreign policy goals after 30 January was represented — most evidently — in the members of the

24. Bracher, *Auflösung*, pp. 632ff; K. D. Bracher, *The German Dictatorship* (New York, 1976), pp. 191ff.

25. That many, however, both within and outside the German government, viewed Hitler's assumption to power as a break with past events is reflected in the conversation between the head of the Third Section (Great Britain, America, the Orient and Colonial Affairs), Ministerialdirektor Diekhoff, and his State Secretary, von Bülow, in which Diekhoff described the change in governments as a National Socialist 'seizure of power'. 'Diekhoff war sich also darüber klar, dass außer dem Kanzlerwechsel vielleicht Schlimmeres drohte.' Cited in P. Krüger and E. J. C. Hahn, 'Der Loyalitätskonflikt des Staatssekretars von Bülow im Frühjahr 1933', *VZG*, 20 (1972), pp. 376–410, here, p. 381.

26. See Pfeiffer, *Deutsch-britische Beziehungen*, p. 3, who indicates that Neurath's appointment had also been calculated for its value in Anglo-German relations, since Neurath was seen in London as pro-British.

27. H.-A. Jacobsen, *Nationalsozialistische Außenpolitik, 1933–1938* (Frankfurt, a.M., 1968), pp. 20ff.; in addition, see P. Seabury, *The Wilhemstrasse* (Berkeley, 1954), *passim*; G. A. Craig, 'The German Foreign Office from Neurath to Ribbentrop', in Craig and Gilbert, pp. 406–36. See in this context, M. Funke, ed., especially the articles by K. D. Bracher, W. Michalka and H.-A. Jacobsen; and W. Michalka, ed., *Nationalsozialistische Außenpolitik* (Darmstadt, 1978).

28. Title of the four-volume opus of Gerhard Ritter on the relationship between statecraft and the military in modern German history: *Staatskunst und Kriegshandwerk* (Munich, 1957ff); English translation: *The Sword and the Scepter* (Miami, 1969ff.).

elite involved in German foreign policy: Neurath and Blomberg.'[29] Furthermore, during this period of transition from the beginning of his Chancellory until perhaps September 1933, Hitler himself appeared rather to be exercising restraint while the Foreign Ministry and the *Reichswehr* worked for the quickest possible collapse of the disarmament negotiations and pushed for an aggressive escalation of Germany's revisionist demands.[30] The reservation and temporizing with which the National Socialist *Führer* and Reich Chancellor approached foreign policy was directly related to domestic political considerations. Not only had Hitler agreed with Hindenburg to leave foreign policy in the aristocratic hands of the old conservative Neurath, he was preoccupied during the initial months of his government with domestic 'coordination' (*Gleichschaltung*). This process, through which Hitler intended to capture the most important institutions in the state by taking control of the key administrative posts in each agency, entailed the emasculation and destruction of all political parties except the NSDAP, all labor unions and other movements. *Gleichschaltung*, or the coordination of the state with the principles of the National Socialist movement, was the essential precondition for a revolutionary National Socialist foreign policy.

Such tactics, which 'closed ranks' in Germany, appealed to conservatives and traditional elites who during the latter years of the republic had felt that party factions and constantly changing governments had passed them by; politics of this nature, they believed too, enhanced the likelihood of communist victory with inevitable socialization and expropriation. Thus, the conservatives' fear of social revolution contributed to their support of terror tactics by the National Socialists during the early stages of the Hitler government.[31] Nevertheless, despite all apparent lines of continuity during the *Gleichschaltung* phase, a distinct qualitative change took place in political principles and methods as compared to those prior to 1933. This had particular significance for foreign policy, for following the National Socialist *Machtergreifung* in January 1933:

> . . . there was a return during the first phase of the National Socialist regime to a relationship between foreign and domestic policy strongly suggestive of prewar imperialist practice. While the prestige of the Wilhelmine Reich

29. Hillgruber, *Kontinuität*, p. 23.
30. *Ibid.*, see also G. Wollstein, 'Eine Denkschrift des Staatssekretärs Bernhard von Bülow vom März 1933. Wilhelminische Konzeption der Außenpolitik zu Beginn der nationalsozialistischen Herrschaft', *MGM*, 1 (1973), pp. 77 n. 3; Block, *Hitler*, pp. 22ff.
31. Of interest in this context is the attitude of von Bülow, whose justification for 'closed ranks' [*innere Geschlossenheit*] stemmed from his concern for the need for a domestic concensus in support of Germany's foreign policy; Krüger and Hahn, p. 397.

required, according to social-imperialist thinking, the subjugation of domestic dissidents, Hitler on the contrary saw in their literal destruction the precondition to any forceful political expansion.[32]

A second essential factor in Hitler's initially temperate conduct in foreign affairs was his anxiety to overcome the decidedly negative foreign reaction to the anti-parliamentarism and terror tactics associated with is 'seizure of power'. The increasing regimentation and militarization of everyday life in the Third Reich made a considerable impression on foreign observers, particularly from France and Poland, who seriously considered the possibility of a preventative war against Germany.[33] Hitler took great pains, through frequent newspaper interviews and speeches which continually returned to his peaceful intentions, to offset the unquestionably bad press which he and his government received abroad during his first year in office.[34]

Despite this policy, however, which gave the appearance of moderation and a commitment to peace, Hans-Adolf Jacobsen is correct when he asserts that rather than differentiating between revisionist and expansionist phases in National Socialist foreign policy during the period 1933 to 1939, one must 'separate much earlier a phase of concealed preparations for aggression until 1937, a period of open expansion through the threat of force from 1938 on, and the unleashing of war in 1939'.[35] Although Hitler almost immediately began preparations for an aggressive expansionist foreign policy, he was forced to conceal them, in part to escape other countries' notice, in part because of domestic political realities. Not the least of his political concerns was that, as an interloper, he found it at the outset impossible to do without the conservative elites, either in government administration, foreign policy or the economy. Before 1938, Hitler and his followers were 'neither able nor in the position to give rise to a new

32. H. Kaiser, 'Probleme und Verlauf der nationalsozialistischen Außenpolitik', *Politische Bildung* V, 1 (1972), p. 58.

33. Krüger and Hahn, p. 395: 'Immer häufiger liefen Berichte aus den wichtigsten Auslandsvertretungen ein, in denen die Feindseligkeit der öffentlichen Meinung and das Mißtrauen und die Abneigung der Regierungen gegen das nationalsozialistische System ausführlich dargestellt wurden....Man fing in Frankreich an, über einen Präventivkrieg nachzudenken. In Polen war die Stellungnahme noch entschiedener; auch hier, ja sogar in der Tschechoslowakei tauchten Präventivkriegsdenken auf....' Additional documentary evidence of German concern over the possibility of a preventive war can be found in *DGFP*, Series C, v/ I, 1, documents 70, 83, 105, 111, 120, 180, 239, 320: in addition, on Pilsudski's interest in a preventive war, see H. Roos, 'Die "Präventivkriegspläne" Pilsudskis vor 1933', *VZG*, 5 (1955), pp. 344ff.; and finally, Bloch, *Hitler*, pp. 34ff. and 84, n. 2.

34. On 'diplomacy by press interview', see W. W. Schmokel, *Dream of Empire. German Colonialism, 1919–1945* (New Haven, 1964), p. 88; Hildebrand, *The Foreign Policy of the Third Reich*, p. 28; Jacobsen, pp. 339ff.

35. Ibid., p. 613.

diplomatic elite parallel to the [existing] foreign service bureaucracy'.[36]

Finally, despite Weinberg's claims to the contrary, Hitler's abstinence from any significant foreign policy initiatives during the early months of his government was the result of a congruity of interests and a similarity of goals shared by the National Socialists and the representatives of almost every other political and economic group.[37] Hitler did nothing to alter the impression that his government would pursue foreign policy as previously laid down, that is, following the definitive settlement of the burdensome reparations problem, Germany would turn to intensive rearmament as the next step toward the revision of the Treaty of Versailles. In this fashion she would accomplish her rehabilitation as a legitimate Great Power and in this fashion Hitler could operate with the broad support of the German conservative ruling elite. Hitler and the conservatives agreed on the immediate goal of foreign policy — the recovery of diplomatic autonomy. It is important to note, however, that Stresemann had in fact already restored Germany's autonomy. Hitler, nevertheless, steadfastly insisted that the nation was still 'fettered' by the Versailles settlement. This agreement, then, between Hitler and the conservatives as to the need to reassert Germany's Great Power status,

... saved Hitler from having to chose between the different varieties of Prussian-German *'Weltpolitik'*, none of which at this time would have succeeded anyway. The initial phase of National Socialist foreign policy is thus distinguished by the high degree of agreement among the leaders [both conservative and National Socialist] of the 'new constellation of power'.[38]

The question remains, however, why the *Auswärtiges Amt* continued to serve the National Socialist government with almost undiminished loyalty. Did the Weimar diplomats remain faithful to Hitler because they viewed his foreign policy as a continuation of earlier policy? Or did they remain out of loyalty to the state and the

---

36. Ibid., p. 614.
37. Weinberg, and Bennett view Hitler's early months from opposite perspectives. Weinberg portrays Hitler as brushing the Weimar diplomats aside, choosing to tolerate the most pliable, the hapless Neurath for example, while charting his 'diplomatic revolution', See Weinberg, *Foreign Policy*, pp. 25–56. It is significant, however, to examine the degree to which Hitler's ideas and those of the career diplomats were consonant with one another. Bennett, among others, sees such consonance: 'While Hitler continued to pursue the broad military objective of rearmament, which had helped bring him to power, he also had the political sense to follow the policy of the German diplomats, that of concealing German armament plans as long as possible, rather than making threats of rearmament as Schleicher had done. This did not prevent Hitler from being strongly revisionist, as were the diplomats . . . [nevertheless,] serious military and diplomatic affairs continued to be conducted by the professionals of the old regime . . .'; Bennett, *Rearmament*, p. 508.
38. Kaiser, 'Probleme', p. 60.

bureaucracy? Ignoring the possibility of simple fear as a motive, Peter Krüger and Erich Hahn maintain that:

> In the highest administrative tradition of the Foreign Minister, the loyalty toward the state and its current leadership, also right-radically oriented — which naturally raises the question as to whether they would have remained loyal to a leftist government —' represents perhaps a stronger continuity than that of the immediately apparent similarity of foreign policy goals.[39]

It should not, therefore, be over-hastily assumed that during the first months of the Hitler government, the traditional diplomatic elite and the National Socialists shared identical goals, concepts and methods of foreign policy. In fact, the Wilhelmstraße and Hitler diverged in their views. The creation of a power base in Central Europe was a self-evident necessity to the diplomats, who without exception thought in traditional power-political terms. Hitler's mind, however, worked in distinctly non-traditional ways. To him, the creation of a German *Mitteleuropa* was merely one element — and by no means the most important — in his highly personal hierarchy of foreign policy goals, which, like the methods by which he sought to reach them, went far beyond traditional Prussian–German policy. Notably, Hitler incorporated in his plans the most extreme traditional aim, that of Ludendorffs *Ostraum*, along with a two-phase struggle for the recovery of German 'world power'. But, if his plans encompassed a German *Imperium*, like that suggested in 1918, they achieved a totally new quality when Hitler joined to them his radical racial ideology of universal antisemitism. Here was a program, then, only vaguely foreshadowed in the most extreme expansionist pipe dreams of 1914–1918 and clearly an escalation to a new stage in foreign policy development. Hitler's assumption of power, then, represented in Hillgruber's estimation both 'the triumph of the most radical champions of that militant rightist opposition to the official German foreign policy of the Wilhelmstrasse during the Weimar Republic', and a staggering escalation in foreign policy goals beyond those even of the most radical of his predecessors.[40]

Yet the differences between Hitler's conceptions and traditional German foreign policy were only dimly, if at all, perceived. Indeed, during the early months of his Chancellorship, officials in the Foreign Ministry explored various options open to Germany. There appeared to be a congruity of interests between traditional German Great Power policy and the racially motivated global policy of the National Social-

39. Krüger and Hahn, pp. 376f.
40. Hillgruber, *Kontinuität*, p. 23.

ists. The confusion of the conservative professional diplomats as to the exact nature of Hitler's foreign policy was heightened by the *Führer*'s reluctance during much of 1933 to allow himself to become involved in foreign policy beyond the occasional interview. What resulted, then, from discussion within the Wilhelmstraße, was the consensus that Germany should set her own diplomatic course, free from the influences of neighboring powers or international organizations.

The earliest indication of the nature of official German foreign policy after 30 January 1933 was the extensive statement by Foreign Minister von Neurath in cabinet session on 7 April.[41] Neurath's remarks not only defined his own foreign policy program, but also represented the views of most Wilhelmstraße officials, and those of influential elements of the economy and conservative political parties. In addition, his goals were shared both by the *Reichswehr* and by the right wing of the NSDAP, whom Hildebrand has termed 'Wilhelmine Imperialists'.[42] The intellectual father of Neurath's remarks was von Bülow who, from his advance to State Secretary in 1930 until his death in 1936, was perhaps the most influential figure in the Foreign Ministry.[43]

The Bülow–Neurath memorandum began with the assertion that although Germany remained isolated and weak, the new year — 1933 — represented a promising new beginning for her foreign policy.[44] Clearly, the two men sought to create an autonomous policy for the coming year which would overcome foreign mistrust and suspicion of the new Reich Chancellor's 'program'.[45] On the one hand, they hoped to counteract recent domestic events surrounding the *Machtergreifung* with a cautiously but purposefully executed foreign policy.[46] On the other hand, they intended thereby to reassert the function of the Foreign Ministry as the decisive foreign policy agency in the state, an obvious reaction to the very limited influence the Ministry felt it had

---

41. *DGFP*, Series C, v. I, document 142; Bloch, *Hitler*, pp. 22ff.; Wollstein, *Weimarer Revisionismus, passim*.

42. Hildebrand, *The Foreign Policy of the Third Reich*, p. 13.

43. DZA 60966, reproduced and analyzed by Wollstein, 'Eine Denkschrift', pp. 77–94; partially reproduced by Jacobsen and v. Bredow, pp. 85–93; see also Krüger and Hahn, *passim*.

44. Wollstein, 'Eine Denkschrift', p. 78.

45. Weidenfeld, *Englandpolitik*, p. 144: 'Im allgemeinen Rahmen der Verschiebung der Macht von der legislative zur staatlichen and privaten Bürokratie als Folge einer unzulänglichen parlamentarischen Regierungstätigkeit hatte sich das Auswärtige Amt eine Schlüsselposition im außenpolitischen Entscheidungsprozeß erarbeitet. Mit relativ großer Automatie widmete sich das Auswärtige Amt seinen vielfältigen Aufgaben, wobei das Parlament meist noch nicht einmal einer rein formalen Kontrolltätigkeit, wie bei anderen Ministerien, nachgekommen ist.'

46. Krüger and Hahn, p. 387.

possessed under Stresemann, Brüning and Papen.[47] Furthermore, in view of the apparent break in foreign policy which 1933 seemed to offer, the *Auswärtiges Amt* representatives intended to chart a new course, independent of previous policy. This seemed entirely justified, for Brüning, having capitalized on domestic unrest, had achieved a breakthrough on reparations and disarmament, thus opening new opportunities for German foreign policy. The continental perspective of Papen, his striving for cooperation between Germany and both France and Poland; the efforts of Schleicher to stabilize relations between Germany and France, and also between Germany and the Soviet Union: all seemed too rigid and unimaginative to von Bülow and von Neurath, who viewed Germany's diplomatic situation from the altered perspective of Hitler's seizure of power. They sought more effective means of enhancing Germany's strength.[48]

The essential element in every German foreign policy analysis since the collapse of 1918 had been the Versailles Treaty, which had channelled German foreign policy, limiting and inhibiting it. The primary task therefore, must be the final revision of that hated act (i.e., remilitarization of the Rhineland, rearmament, the recovery of the Saar and lost territories).[49] In this regard, given Germany's military weakness, the best weapon was her economy, which, Wollstein points out, Bülow felt might serve to exploit the weakness of the global economic system in an effort to overcome Germany's own economic limitations:

> In particular, Germany's central [geographical] position, the interest of her creditors in a functioning German economy, as well as a skilful, well-timed application of German economic potential in the commercial sector, should be used to secure a meaningful position for Germany, a position scarcely imaginable prior to the Depression.[50]

The weight given here to Germany's economic potential as a factor in German foreign policy is very reminiscent of the policies of both Stresemann and Brüning.[51] In contrast, however, the economic calcu-

---

47. Clearly, under Stresemann, but under Brüning and Papen as well, the *Auswärtiges Amt* had allowed '*Nicht-Diplomaten*' to influence foreign policy. The penetration of German foreign policy by non-professionals had an ample background during the decade preceding Hitler.
48. Wollstein, 'Eine Denkschrift', p. 78.
49. Ibid., p. 82.
50. Ibid., p. 79.
51. Quite interesting in this regard is the conclusion of Hentschel, who maintains that in economic and social policy during the late Weimar and early NS periods there were far stronger threads of continuity than signs of breaks. Relying on a mass of various economic and social data, Hentschel shows that traditional market and economic forces had much greater influence over German society than did National Socialist ideology, strengthening the lines of continuity from Republic to Third Reich: V. Hentschel,

lations of Bülow and Neurath were preparatory to a more far-reaching foreign policy. There is no doubt that territorial revision was at the heart of the foreign policy concepts of all four men. For Bülow it was a question of the 'adjustment of the eastern borders, at which point [we] demand the return of all the Polish territories in question simultaneously and reject partial or interim solutions (only after a partition of Poland)'.[52] Although Stresemann gave Eastern territorial revision a pivotal position in his foreign policy, and although he favored economic pressure on Poland as the means of extorting such revision, there was a profound qualitative distinction between his ideas and those of Bülow. The difference was summed up by Bülow in the one piquant phrase: 'Only after a *partition* of Poland.'[53] A policy calling for the fourth partition of Poland can under no circumstances be considered merely aimed at the revision of the Treaty of Versailles, which would have created the German frontiers of 1914. On the contrary, Bülow's thinking not only encompassed the war aims discussion of 1917–1918, which had conceived of a Polish client state subordinate to Prussia, but also embraced territorial expansion in the east as in 1918, when it had been sanctioned in the Treaty of Brest-Litovsk.

How far Bülow's goals were identical to those of Stresemann remains, of course, an open question. It is conceivable, however, that despite, or indeed because of, the failure of his economic offensive against Poland in 1925–1926, Stresemann never stated *expressis verbis* his Eastern territorial aims in their entirety. Nevertheless, the possibility cannot be excluded that Stresemann's aims in Poland were ultimately the same as those of Bülow, when, in his own words, 'Germany refuses to discuss the recognition of the borders [here he clearly was referring to the eastern borders], Germany refuses to discuss the renunciations of war and is only prepared to discuss other questions'.[54]

The revisionist objectives of Bülow and Neurath were in no sense limited only to Germany's eastern frontiers.[55] They included Danzig, Memel, the Hultschin District (Czechoslovakia), the eventual readjustment of the frontiers of Schleswig, the recovery of Malmédy; even the return of Alsace-Lorraine and German colonies was not excluded, nor the question of one day acquiring 'new colonies'. In the distant

---

'Wirtschafts- und sozialhistorische Brüche und Kontinuitäten zwischen Weimarer Republik und Drittem Reich', *Zeitschrift für Unternehmensgeschichte* XXVIII, 1 (1983) pp. 39–80.
52. Wollstein, 'Eine Denkschrift', pp. 79f.
53. Ibid.
54. Ibid., p. 79.
55. Ibid., p. 80.

future remained *Anschluß* with Austria. Alongside the 'traditional' goals of colonies, *Anschluß* and eastern territory, a new prospect was introduced, transcending the bounds of mere 'revision' and pointing to the next phase of German policy. Neurath advocated that 'Germany demand rejuvenation in all ways'. Exactly what he had in mind was not clear; he went on, however, to call for Germany to seize new markets and prevent the industrialization of Europe's agrarian economies, by which he meant Eastern Europe.[56] In this effort, the Foreign Minister believed, German settlers abroad *(Auslandsdeutschtum)* would be particularly helpful.

It is clear from the remarks of its two leading figures, Bülow and Neurath, that thinking in the Foreign Ministry followed the traditional path of Wilhelmine plans for a *Mitteleuropa*, which, despite Germany's defeat and the damage to her Great Power status, had never been written off entirely. It is equally clear that analogies in the foreign policy conceptions of leading German statesmen from Stresemann to Neurath point to an unbroken continuity in German foreign policy from the Wilhelmine era through the Weimar Republic and on into the early years of the Hitler regime.[57] That the National Socialist *Führer* merely had to take up earlier expansionist foreign policy goals is obvious.

Nevertheless, where there was apparent continuity, there was also qualitative difference. On key issues, traditional thinking of professional diplomats differed significantly from that of the National Socialist Reich Chancellor. Even in the early weeks of the new regime, such divergent thinking became evident with respect to the Soviet Union. Within the Wilhelmstraße, there was virtual unanimity on the tactical value of continued German–Soviet cooperation. Neurath was supported not only by his State Secretary, von Bülow, but by a strong cadre of 'Easterners' in the Ministry who argued for the continuation of Germany's traditionally close relationship to Russia. This view had held sway during the Weimar Republic and was now represented by Rudolf Nadolny, former candidate for Foreign Minister in 1930, leader of the German delegation at the Geneva Disarmament Conference and eventually German ambassador to Moscow for a brief period in late 1933 and early 1934,[58] and Herbert von Dirksen[59] who would succeed Nadolny as ambassador in Moscow. Russia, maintained the

---

56. Ibid., p. 87.
57. Bennett, *Rearmament*, p. 508: 'Taking account of both military and diplomatic policy, a further conclusion is that there was continuity in German history, not only between Wilhelminian Germany and the Nazi era, but also specifically at the critical junction of the end of the Weimar era with Hitler's new regime.'
58. See R. Nadolny, *Mein Beitrag* (Wiesbaden, 1955).
59. See H. v. Dirksen, *Moscow, Tokyo, London* (London, 1951).

traditionalists, was a vital link in Germany's Eastern policy, particularly in connection with Poland. As Bülow asserted in a memorandum to Neurath:

> With respect to Russia the most important fact is that we cannot dispense with her support against Poland. Especially important are our good relations with the Russian army, from which we can accurately gauge its level of armament, and which we cannot afford to drop, if we are to spare ourselves any unpleasant surprises.[60]

In addition to the military relationship, to which the Wilhelmstraße had not always been so favorably inclined, the question of close German–Soviet economic relations arose. The Foreign Ministry was reluctant to jeopardize these, since 'Russia . . . through her massive orders had become the greatest consumer of German industrial products'.[61]

Economically, politically and militarily, close relations with the Soviet Union were so important to Germany that Neurath and Bülow apparently felt it necessary to approach the Chancellor directly on the subject. Both nations benefited so much from continued cooperation, the two contended, that 'the energetic resistance to the communists and Bolshevization [in Germany] would, as shown in Italy, not necessarily hamper long-term German–Russian relations'.[62] Such an appeal contrasted sharply with Hitler's racially-determined concept of Russia: a vast expanse ready for colonization after the native sub-human population had been exterminated. The Soviet Union occupied a special place in Hitler's foreign policy concept, following axiomatically from his belief that National Socialism was engaged in a life-and-death struggle with the global Jewish conspiracy, the most virulent form of which was Bolshevism.[63] The contradiction between the views of the Foreign Ministry and the *Führer* surfaced in a *Chefbesprechung* on 26 September 1933. In this discussion, the chief 'Easterner' in the Wilhelmstraße, Rudolf Nadolny, found his own ideas to be so inconsistent with those of his Chancellor that he resigned within a few

60. Wollstein, 'Eine Denkschrift', p. 91.
61. Ibid.; on German–Soviet economic relations, 1932–1933, see Dyck, *Weimar Germany*, p. 216.
62. Wollstein, 'Eine Denkschrift', p. 91.
63. For Hitler's attitudes toward Russia, Bolshevism and the international Jewish conspiracy', see *Mein Kampf*, (Munich, 1925, 1929), which has appeared in numerous editions and translations: the present writers have used the version published in New York, 1943; see the provocative content analysis by R. A. Koenigsberger, *Hitler's Ideology. A Study in Psychoanalytical Sociology* (New York, 1975). See also Rudolf Binion, *Hitler Among the Germans* (New York, 1976) and Robert G. L. Waite, *Adolf Hitler. The Psychopathic God* (New York, 1977).

months of his posting as Ambassador to Moscow.[64]

Although the example of Nadolny illustrates the extreme difference in foreign policy goals between Hitler and the conservative professional diplomats, a serious divergence in views concerning Russia had already become evident. The apparent community of interests between the Chancellor and the Wilhelmstraße during the early months of the National Socialist regime was only partial at best and only temporary in duration. The conservative professionals of the Wilhelmstraße were tolerated until 1938, at which point Hitler finally consolidated his control over the Foreign Ministry. Although during the early years of his regime Hitler did not actually prevent the continuation of neutral and noncommittal German–Soviet relations, he rejected any suggestion of improving them. The relationship was symbolic of the long-term conflict between the *Führer* and the old professional elite which, Wollstein indicates, surfaced once Hitler embarked on aggressive expansion:

> Only in the phase of direct expansion policy were the grave differences between Hitler and the leading officials of the *Auswärtiges Amt* conceivable, since Hitler's program, which aimed at a world domination motivated by racist ideology, exceeded all bounds of revisionism [accepted by the Wilhelmstraße].[65]

In the initial phase of the National Socialist dictatorship, however, aggressive revisionist policy evident at least since the days of Brüning combined with a return to Wilhelmine foreign policy goals to form a common ground from which both conservative elites and National Socialists could together pursue a common foreign policy. The combination of traditional political goals and the dogma of Hitler's National Socialist racial ideology would have tragic and fateful consequences for Germany and the world.

64. Wollstein, 'Eine Denkschrift', p. 82; D. C. Watt, 'Hitler and Nadolny', *Contemporary Review*, 196 (1959), pp. 53–56; compare with Wollstein, *Weimarer Revisionismus*, pp. 263ff.
65. Wollstein, 'Eine Denkschrift', pp. 80f.

Conclusions
Leitmotif and Recitative:
Continuities and Breaks in
Weimar Foreign Policy

Achieved through political armistice in August 1914, the *Burgfrieden* delayed and ultimately prevented needed domestic political reform in Germany. During the First World War this truce prevailed, however, only at the cost of great personal and political sacrifice. Finally, long overdue constitutional reform could no longer be offset and blocked by further escalation in war aims or lavish expectations of victory. Although the military collapse of the German *Kaiserreich* marked an end to the world war, for the Germans it merely altered the conflict from distant and external events to an internal and immediate crisis. Naval mutinies, the establishment of short-lived soviet republics, *putsches* and terrorism all signalled the outbreak of domestic warfare. Within such an environment, reform politics stood little chance.

The Social Democratic Party, the protagonist of parliamentarization and democratization of the German Empire, was forced in the very hour of birth of the republic to enter into an alliance with the conservative leadership of the Wilhelmine Reich in order to preserve the infant republic from the attacks of both left-wing and right-wing extremists. According to the conditions of this political truce, essential reforms representing part of the traditional SPD platform were postponed, indeed completely discarded. In this sense, one can speak of a certain domestic continuity, for in 1919 the German Left, like their predecessors during the *Reichsgründungszeit*, sacrificed liberal principles for the sake of national unity. In 1919 national emergency created the unusual alliance of former enemies and the paradox by which, despite 'revolution', traditional ruling elites not only survived, but became key supporters of the republic. Thus, throughout the 'revolution', German social order remained unaltered and in principle intact. Without doubt, then, this continuity in personnel from *Kaiserreich* to republic had far-reaching significance for Weimar foreign policy. In this context, the formulation of foreign policy goals was critical, especially as it developed from the war aims debate during the early stages of the war to late 1917 or early 1918, when those aims were at least partially realized. Wilhelmine concepts of Germany's Great Power status and her position as a 'world power' remained intact beyond 1918 to influence Weimar foreign policy in varying degrees.

Such traditional foreign policy goals, however, inevitably collided with the spirit of the Versailles Treaty and indeed the new European constellation of power as shaped at the Paris Peace Conference. Guided by their various and distinct national interests, the victorious Allies attempted to construct a new international system which would assure peace and in which Germany, potentially just as much a Great Power as ever, posed no aggressive threat. To insure Germany's continued pacification, the elaborate treaty mechanism imposed on her a variety of controls: territorial loss, disarmament and international control, occupation of strategic German territory, and burdensome reparations. In addition, from the ruins of the Habsburg and Romanov empires rose a series of lesser states some of which, as members of the French alliance system, would provide additional security against Germany. Finally, by means of collective security, it was hoped the League of Nations would maintain the newly created structure of peace and make possible the equitable settlement of international interests.

As the United States withdrew from European affairs and the Soviet Union assumed the role of outsider, it became increasingly clear that the newly fashioned European order came closer to serving the national interests of the victors rather than satisfying Woodrow Wilson's ideal of a society forever free from conflict. Germans of every political hue rejected the treaty as an affront to national honor and an unjustly dictated settlement. The treaty thus virtually eliminated the possibility of political understanding and cooperation between victors and vanquished and strengthened the German will for the earliest possible revision. The failure to reach an equitable settlement at the Paris Peace Conference sharpened international tensions and extended hostile prewar constellations into the postwar world.

How much freedom of diplomatic action did the Weimar Republic have in the wake of the Versailles settlement and what foreign policy concepts emerged to enhance German diplomatic autonomy in the future? Although militarily almost defenseless and despite territorial losses, Germany was able to maintain the national state almost intact and above all conserve her economic potential so that to some degree — albeit very limited — it still was possible to pursue a foreign policy. In contrast to the situation before 1914, the newly-created states in Eastern and Southeastern Europe offered the German economy a virtually unlimited sphere of influence, which could be exploited not only for its commercial and economic value but also for its political advantages. What had been conquered by force of arms in 1917 to 1918, and described in the war aims debate as the *Ostreich*, could now be reconquered with the help of the German economy. Hitler's goal of acquiring *Lebensraum* in the east by force was in part already anticipated and realized here in the form of an economic 'informal empire'. Following the Great Crash, Berlin concentrated both economic and foreign policies on Eastern and Southeastern Europe, so that Hitler had only to take up the threads of this policy.

It was no accident that the first steps toward an 'active' foreign policy in the Weimar Republic came from the German economic sector, where heavy industrialists strove to accelerate the transition from wartime to peacetime economy, in order to maintain a high production and sales level. Exchange and cooperation between foreign firms and individual branches of industry offered an ideal means to coordinate such a transition. From these tentative private contacts developed the original initiatives for new foreign policy alternatives, in particular three closely related elements which would have a decisive influence. Firstly, Germany appeared ready to cooperate with foreign private industrial interests in an effort to stabilize and expand her own economy, the ultimate goal being to make other foreign economies dependent upon German industry. Secondly, there was the closely related intent of gaining by economic means what German arms had failed to achieve. Thirdly, financial and political pressure might accomplish the recognition of Germany as a Great Power, and might undermine and ultimately destroy the victorious coalition.

Although German financial and industrial initiatives aroused the interest of both Britain and France, America proved the key to success, for the German economy offered her an overwhelmingly attractive opportunity for economic penetration of Western Europe. The United States' economic policy in Europe directed vast amounts of capital into Germany; with this, Germany, looking the American model, sought to create a 'penetrating system' of investment and economic influence in Eastern and Southeastern Europe.

It was soon recognized in Berlin that the American policy of 'peaceful change' was incompatible with French security policy, which sought to preserve the *status quo* established by the Treaty of Versailles, thus promising France a hegemonic position in Europe. Washington, on the other hand, was committed to the peaceful settlement of European disputes through negotiated adjustment, in order to preserve this stability of Western European markets. The German government, grasping these underlying differences, skilfully sought to exploit them by offering America virtually limitless market and investment opportunities. Thus, American financial assistance enabled Germany not only to recover from the disastrous postwar inflation but also successfully to combine German and American financial and commercial interests in Western Europe. The United States thus became the most important partner (not, however, to be termed 'an ally') in Germany's policy of revision. This strategy succeeded within the framework of a policy of peaceful cooperation. With the onset of global depression and the rise of new, more 'active' German foreign policy goals, however, this harmony of German and American aims came to an end. It is, however, interesting in regard to the question of continuity in German foreign policy from Bismarck to Hitler, that such a close economic and political cooperation with the United States constituted a new dimension in German policy and consequently a distinct break in its method. While this discontinuity in political methods and strategy may be apparent, however, in no sense was there an evident break as regards foreign policy goals. For Germany, financial and political cooperation with the United States was simply a means of accomplishing traditional aims not achieved by military means in the First World War.

Quite another partner, but no less important to Weimar foreign policy, was the Soviet Union. Like Germany, the USSR was an outcast from the postwar international order and similarly isolated by the Versailles system. The two countries were thus thrust together by circumstances and a community of (negative) interest. As mutual tensions stemming from wartime enmity and ideological differences subsided, prewar economic relations resumed. In addition, contacts between the Reichswehr and Red Army proved an important element in improving relations. But the most important point of agreement, masking the considerable ideological and power-political antagonism between the two regimes, lay geographically between the two: Poland. Ultimately the cementing link in German–Soviet relations was that shared hostility. Influential circles in both the *Reichswehr* and the *Auswärtiges Amt* favored joint German–Soviet action in an 'active' (that is to say, military) policy of revision with respect to Poland. During the Weimar republic, the concept of military power had absolutely no value to German foreign policy; it represented the idle dreams (*Wunschträume*) of conservatives who had long since relinquished the military base of German foreign policy. Foreign Minister Gustav Stresemann in particular scrupulously avoided allowing German foreign policy to become biased toward the Soviet Union. On the contrary, he was at great pains to pursue a policy of balance between East and West, in order to win the greatest freedom of movement for his most urgent priority: treaty revision in the West. Eastern territorial revision would follow later.

Bilateral relations with America on the one hand and the Soviet Union on the other served German foreign policy in several important ways. First, Germany was able to break out of the diplomatic isolation imposed by the Versailles system. Second, Washington and Moscow provided a crucial counterweight to the combined influence exerted by the treaty guarantors. To this combination of cooperation in two directions, a third element — Great Britain — represented an additional important factor in Weimar foreign policy.

Great Britain was perhaps the only nation in the First World War to realize her most important war aim: her chief naval and colonial rival and greatest economic-commercial threat, Germany, was defeated. Despite this power-political victory, however, the Empire was far from secure: beginning well before the end of the war and rising to a crescendo during the next decade, political change gripped the Empire, eventually to replace it by the Commonwealth. Britain's postwar imperial decline was accompanied by serious social and economic crisis. The result, diplomatically, was a return to traditional 'balance of power' politics in Europe and the consequent adoption of a policy of appeasement. London sought to pacify Europe in order to devote complete attention to domestic matters. The increasingly insular nature of Britain's foreign policy was already evident during the Paris Peace Conference. It did not long survive, however, for the Ruhr Crisis forced a reluctant Whitehall to play a more direct role in continental affairs. Germany could not fail to recognize a foreign policy opportunity in London's evident confusion and uncertainty. It was clear that British policy was not in complete conformity with France's policy of *sécurité*. This obvious disharmony seemed to offer the perfect chance gradually to drive the two former allies apart and in the process perhaps ruin the victorious coalition. In this regard, German policy was less fruitful in reality than in dreams, and in the end could show few concrete results. Its evident miscalculation of Whitehall's continental policy, especially toward Germany, moreover, must be viewed within the continuity of German foreign policy from Bismarck to Hitler. In this context one may justifiably speak of a 'continuity of error', a consistent misreading from 1870 to 1945: over this period, German foreign policy alternated between efforts to induce Britain to enter into a bilateral union and equally mistaken attempts to intimidate her into accepting German continental domination.

Of central importance to Germany during at least the first half of the 1920s was, of course, French foreign policy, with its attempts to secure and project France's apparent hegemonic position in Europe following the German defeat of 1918. This seemed possible only if Germany could be kept militarily, politically and economically weak. The means to accomplish this task were at hand: the Treaty of Versailles, an alliance system with the treaty states of Eastern and Southeastern Europe, and the League of Nations. Through reparations, France could directly influence economic and financial developments in Germany. Finally, occupation of German territory afforded additional security. Failing all else, France could still have recourse to intervention, a measure finally resorted to in 1923.

France's policy of *sécurité* and Germany's policy of revision were almost totally at odds with one another. From the outset, then, the threat of conflict colored postwar politics. Few people on either side were under any illusion as to the underlying nature of Franco-German antagonism, and the confrontation prolonged the struggle of the First World War into the 1920s. The Ruhr Crisis manifestly reflected the true warlike nature of the confrontation, yet it also clearly demonstrated the limits of policy in Berlin, as well as in Paris. Under extreme pressure from both the United States and Great Britain, each was forced to modify their positions and to seek settlement by other means. First 'fulfilment' and then after 1923 'understanding', which reached a high point at Locarno and Thoiry, and then again at Geneva in late 1929, marked this shift in international relations in Europe which lasted for the remainder of the decade. Neither *Verständigung* nor *Erfüllung* could overcome the basic disparity in economic potential between two protagonists, however; thus the root cause for mutual suspicion and hostility was never addressed. Nevertheless, by the late 1920s an era of negotiation and peaceful settlement of disputes seemed to have dawned.

In Germany, the outbreak of global depression and with it the radicalization of domestic conditions brought an abrupt end to the years of consolidation and stability. Due to her heavy dependence on American capital, the Wall Street Crash was even more serious for Germany than for other Western economies. From the local *Stammtisch* to the floor of the Reichstag, social and economic crises were attributed to the Treaty of Versailles; resentment against the treaty pervaded the day-to-day politics of the nation, increasing existing anti-democratic tendencies, so that a stabilizing domestic or foreign policy was scarcely possible. Before 1930 American financial assistance had fuelled economic prosperity, enabling German governments to pursue revisionist foreign policy with certain success, thus channelling and postponing domestic conflict. Now, in the wake of Western economic collapse, as American capital no longer flooded the German market, German foreign policy lost the only weapon in its arsenal: a vigorous economy. Thus, it was no longer able to secure revision of the Versailles system as compensation for the policy of fulfilment.

Conclusions

Following the death of Stresemann and the Wall Street Crash, then, the Reich government had to find either a new reward for the German people or a new foreign policy.

The result of the search for a new policy was an escalation in revisionist demands and the formulation of new diplomatic goals. And here the foreign–domestic policy nexus of late Weimar Germany is very suggestive of that of Wilhelmine Germany. By the late 1890s, Prussian Finance Minister Johannes Miquel's politics of national consolidation (*Sammlungspolitik*) had failed to integrate agrarian and industrial interests in Germany into a social-political concensus. *Sammlungspolitik* was followed by *Flottenpolitik* and *Kolonialpolitik*, in which, according to social-imperialist strategy, escalated naval and colonial propaganda would unite disparate national interests in a national consolidation. Just as Miquel's *Sammlungspolitik* had to give way to a more strident and aggressive foreign policy aimed at integrating diverse domestic interests, so, too, following the Wall Street Crash the mere revision of the Treaty of Versailles was no longer enough to integrate divergent and conflicting German national interests. New strategies for compensation, integration and national consolidation were necessary. Indeed, Krüger argues that after 1930 Germany sought to free herself from the restrictions of the Locarno system and return to the more free-wheeling states system of the late 19th century.[1] In the name of autarky, the Brüning government sought to extend German influence in Eastern and Southeastern Europe, so as to create that long-contemplated *Ostreich*, if not in name, in commercial and political influence. Such an Eastern empire would ensure Germany's victorious survival in the inevitable war to come, an idea which anticipated Hitler's need for *Lebensraum*. Thus compensated, divergent segments of the national polity would close ranks in a new domestic *Burgfrieden*. But if, strategically, Brüning's chosen course was suggestive of *fin-de-siècle* Wilhelmine policy, in 1930 the price of this domestically-oriented foreign policy threatened to be every bit as high as in 1900. Following the collapse of *Sammlungspolitik*, naval and colonial rivalries poisoned Anglo–German relations before 1914. So, too, after 1930 did the shift in German foreign policy produce a radical cooling of relations with the Soviet Union and the United States.

In their demands for political *Gleichberchtigung* the German leaders wanted to put an end to reparations, and bring about armament parity — that is, rearmament — and the fulfilment of territorial claims. After 1930 these aims could only be realized through confrontation and

---

1. Krüger even argues that after 1930 a *Freie-Hand-Politik* dominated German thinking, a policy reminiscent of Caprivi and the early 1980s. Krüger, *Außenpolitik*, pp. 522–3.

threat, for throughout the West, social and economic crisis imposed a sense of urgency and immediacy on foreign affairs. The European diplomatic climate became increasingly tense. Simultaneously, German policy-makers aimed to exploit the depression, first for an immediate end to reparations and second in order to make the less-industrialized European economies more dependent upon the German economy. Here their gaze fell most fixedly on Eastern and Southeastern Europe, where the opportunities for influence were the greatest. Not surprisingly, signs that Germany intended to 'open up' the agrarian states to the east provoked resistance, in particular from France, which took immediate steps to buttress her eastern flank with renewed bilateral commitments.

Yet escalation in the methods and goals of German foreign policy after 1930 could not keep pace with the radicalization of German domestic conditions. The polarization of Right and Left crippled parliamentary politics, necessitating an autocratic presidial government under the emergency provisions of Article 48 of the Weimar constitution. Hitler, whose National Socialists seemed to offer the most acceptable formula for the integration of disparate elements in German society, could portray himself as the knight in shining armor. Diplomatically, his takeover of power had the effect of confirming the need for a more extreme foreign policy, a policy which of late had borne fruit: an end of reparations and the acquisition of *Gleichberechtigung*. National Socialist *Gleichschaltung* produced the people's community, or *Volksgemeinschaft*, which galvanized the national will for an escalated policy of revision which, from the very outset, signified a policy of expansion on the grandest scale.

What for Stresemann, even for Brüning, had served as the final goal, was for Hitler only the jumping-off point: a rearmed Germany tore up the Treaty of Versailles, scrapped carefully-negotiated security pacts, and in the *Blumenfeldzug* of March 1938 annexed Austria. Great Britain and France stood meekly by, registering only paper protests; everything seemed to confirm the validity of Germany's more aggressive foreign policy.

The ultimate foreign policy goals of the Weimar Republic had been achieved. But in this field the initial similarity of objectives between the conservative elite and the National Socialists soon proved chimerical. The violation of treaties; terror; discrimination; brutality in the name of an ideology bent on creating a biological superior race; and the extermination of the Jews; all these signalled Germany's departure from traditional foreign policy to something totally new, throwing every belief open to question, perverting every civilized German value and ending only in the ruins of the Second World War.

Chronology

1916	*December*	German peace feelers without specific conditions
1917	*January*	Declaration of unrestricted submarine warfare
		Wilson's 'peace without victory' speech
	March	First Russian Revolution
	March–April	German strategic withdrawal in the West
	April	American entry into the war
	July	Russian offensive
		Bethmann Hollweg's fall, Michaelis successor
		Peace Resolution in *Reichstag*
		Ludendorff dictatorship
	November	Bolshevik Revolution
	December	Opening of peace negotiations between Russia and the Central Powers
1918	*January*	President Wilson's Fourteen Points
	March	Treaty of Brest-Litovsk
	March–April	German offensive in the West
	August–September	Allied counter-offensive
	September	Ludendorff demands acceptance of allied Armistice conditions
		Fall of the Imperial Government
	October	New government; Max von Baden Chancellor
		Resignation of Ludendorff Allied advances
	November	Sailors' mutiny at Kiel
		Revolution in Munich
		Abdication of the Kaiser
		Scheidemann (Majority Socialist) proclaims a republic
		Armistice
1919	*January*	Opening of the Paris Peace Conference
		Spartakus revolt in Berlin
		Murder of Karl Liebknecht and Rosa Luxemburg
	February	Opening of the National Assembly in Weimar

March	Second *Spartakus* revolt in Berlin
April	*Putsch* in Bavaria
June	Bauer cabinet; Müller Foreign Minister
	Signature of the Treaty of Versailles
July	Proclamation of the Weimar Constitution

1920 *January* — Versailles Treaty comes into force

February	Cession of North Schleswig to Denmark under plebiscite
	Allied occupation of Silesia
March	Kapp *Putsch*
	Spartakus revolt in the Ruhr
	Müller cabinet; Köster Foreign Minister
April	Occupation of Frankfurt by French troops
June	Fehrenbach cabinet; Simons Foreign Minister
July	Reparations Conference in Spa
September	Cession of Eupen and Malmédy to Belgium

1921 *March* — Allied occupation of Düsseldorf, Duisberg and Ruhrort

April–May	London Reparations Conference (London Ultimatum)
May	Wirth cabinet; Rosen Foreign Minister
	German–Soviet trade agreement
	German acceptance of Allied reparations conditions
August	Separate peace between Germany and USA
	Murder of Erzberger
October	Wirth cabinet; Wirth Foreign Minister; Rathenau Foreign Minister (January–June 1922)
November	Washington Conference

1922 *April* — Genoa Conference

	Rapallo Treaty
June	Assassination of Rathenau
August	Balfour Note
	Mark begins to fall
	London Conference on German reparations default
November	Cuno cabinet; Rosenberg Foreign Minister
December	REPKO declares Germany in default

1923 *January* — Paris Reparations Conference

	Repeated declaration of German default
	Occupation of the Ruhr by French and Belgian troops
	German declaration of passive resistance
August	Stresemann cabinet; Stresemann Foreign Minister
September	End of passive resistance
October	Declaration of a separate Rhenish Republic
November	Hitler *Putsch* in Munich

		Rentenmark and the first stabilisation of German currency Marx cabinet; Stresemann Foreign Minister
1924	*April*	Dawes Plan
	July–August	London Reparations Conference
	October	Geneva Protocol
	November	Withdrawal of occupation forces from the Ruhr
1925	*January*	Luther cabinet; Stresemann Foreign Minister
	February	Death of President Ebert
	April	Election of Hindenburg as President
	August	Evacuation of last occupation troops from the Ruhr
	October	Locarno Conference
	December	Signature of Locarno Treaties in London
1926	*January*	Luther cabinet; Stresemann foreign minister; Withdrawal of troops from the First Rhineland Occupation Zone
	March	German entry into the League of Nations postponed
	April	Treaty of Berlin
	May	Opening session of the Preparatory Disarmament Commission Marx cabinet; Stresemann Foreign Minister
	September	German entry into the League of Nations Thoiry
1927	*January*	Withdrawal of the IMCC from Germany Marx cabinet; Stresemann Foreign Minister
	September	German signature of the Optional Clauses
1928	*June*	Müller cabinet (Great Coalition); Stresemann Foreign Minister
	August	Kellogg–Briand Pact
1929	*January*	Creation of Young Commission on Reparations
	January–June	German minorities offensive at League of Nations
	June	Young Plan
	August	First Hague Conference
	September	Pan-European plan of Briand
	October	Death of Stresemann; Curtius Foreign Minister; Wall Street Crash
	November	Withdrawal of troops from the Second Rhineland Occupation Zone
	December	Young Plan Referendum
1930	*May*	Presidial cabinet of Brüning; Curtius Foreign Minister
	June	Withdrawal of troops from the Third Rhineland

		Occupation Zone
	September	Reichstag elections; NSDAP gains (107 seats)
1931	*March*	German–Austrian Customs Union Plan
	May	Collapse of Austrian *Creditanstalt*
	June–July	Hoover moratorium
	October	Presidial cabinet of Brüning; Brüning Foreign Minister
1932	*February*	Opening session of Geneva Disarmament Conference
	April	Hindenburg elected President for second term
		Ban on SA and SS
	May	Fall of Brüning
		Presidial cabinet of von Papen; von Neurath Foreign Minister
	June	Lausanne Conference
		Ban on SA and SS lifted
	July	Reichstag elections; NSDAP gains (230 seats)
	September	Dissolution of *Reichstag*
		German withdrawal from Geneva Disarmament Conference
	November	Reichstag elections; NSDAP losses (196 seats)
		Fall of von Papen
	December	Presidial cabinet of von Schleicher; von Neurath Foreign Minister
		Recognition of German *Gleichberechtigung*: German return to Geneva Disarmament Conference
1933	*January*	Hitler cabinet; von Neurath Foreign Minister
	July	Four-Power Pact
	September	German withdrawal from League of Nations and Geneva Disarmament Conference
1934	*January*	German–Polish Non-Aggression Pact

Appendices

All statistics are from B. R. Mitchell, *European Historical Statistics, 1750–1970* (New York, 1976).

A. External trade aggregate current value for Germany (in millions of Marks)

Year	Import	Export
1913	10,751	10,097
[1914–19 no figures given]		
1920	3,929	3,709
1921	5,732	[2,976]
1922	6,301	6,188
1923	4,808	5,338
	6,150	6,102
1924	9,132	6,674
1925	12,429	9,284
1926	9,984	10,415
1927	14,114	10,801
1928	13,931	12,055
1929	13,359	13,486
1930	10,349	12,036
1931	6,713	9,592
1932	4,653	5,741
1933	4,199	4,872
1934	4,448	4,178

B. Balance of payments; German (in million of Marks)*

Year	VB	IB	OCB
1913	−673	+1,612	+939
[1914–24 no figures given]			
1925	−2,444	+456	−1,988
1926	+793	+359	+1,152
1927	−2,960	+300	−2,660
1928	−1,311	+109	−1,202
1929	−44	−88	−132
1930	+1,558	−462	+1,096
1931	+2,778	−750	+2,038
1932	+1,052	−635	+417
1933	+666	−385	+281
1934	−373	−161	−534

* VB = Visible balance IB = Invisible balance OCB = Overall current balance

C. Germany's external trade with main trading partners (in millions of Marks)

	Austria-Hungary		Belgium		France		Italy		Netherlands		Russia		Sweden		UK		USA	
	I	E	I	E	I	E	I	E	I	E	I	E	I	E	I	E	I	E
1913	827	1,105	345	551	584	790	318	394	333	694	1,425	880	224	230	876	1,438	1,711	713
1914	—	—	—	—	—	—	—	—	—	—	—	—	—	—	—	—	—	—
1915	—	—	—	—	—	—	—	—	—	—	—	—	—	—	—	—	—	—
1916	—	—	—	—	—	—	—	—	—	—	—	—	—	—	—	—	—	—
1917	—	—	—	—	—	—	—	—	—	—	—	—	—	—	—	—	—	—
1918	—	—	—	—	—	—	—	—	—	—	—	—	—	—	—	—	—	—
1919	—	—	—	—	—	—	—	—	—	—	—	—	—	—	—	—	—	—
1920	—	—	—	—	—	—	—	—	—	—	—	—	—	—	—	—	—	—
1921	—	—	—	—	—	—	—	—	—	—	—	—	—	—	—	—	—	—
1922	Austria —	—	—	—	—	—	—	—	—	—	—	—	—	—	—	—	—	—
1923	131	305	85	112	186	67	150	245	201	685	92	73	95	271	1,015	557	1,172	475
1924	134	313	204	106	694	114	372	240	426	648	126	89	121	286	827	612	1,709	491
1925	176	320	415	344	558	489	496	425	743	996	205	250	269	342	944	937	2,196	604
1926	116	311	343	418	378	670	388	486	543	1,127	323	266	234	401	576	1,163	1,603	744
1927	211	366	548	441	806	562	528	462	698	1,119	433	330	370	409	963	1,178	2,073	776
1928	232	425	474	489	741	693	467	547	710	1,175	379	403	253	431	894	1,180	2,026	796
1929	202	441	447	609	642	935	443	602	701	1,355	426	354	350	476	865	1,306	1,790	991
1930	181	360	325	601	519	1,149	365	484	561	1,206	436	431	304	494	639	1,219	1,307	685
1931	114	275	222	464	342	834	268	341	384	955	304	763	158	424	453	1,134	791	488
1932	65	160	146	302	190	483	181	223	273	633	271	626	95	228	259	446	592	281
1933	58	121	139	278	184	395	166	227	232	613	194	282	103	191	238	406	483	246
1934	66	107	161	236	177	282	185	246	264	482	210	63	134	198	206	383	373	158

D. External trade with Germany, by country (in millions of currency)

	Austria (schillings)		Belgium (francs)		Bulgaria (lev)		Czechoslovakia (koruna)		Hungary (penges)		Poland (Zloty)		Romania (lei)		Russia (rubles)		Yugoslavia (dinars)	
	I	E	I	E	I	E	I	E	I	E	I	E	I	E	I	E	I	E
1913			762	940	37	17							183	47	512	356		
1914													89	176				
1915																		
1916																		
1917																		
1918																1		
1919			100	667			—	—	—	—								
1920	—	—	952	1,282			5,604	3,331	41	21			4	41	5	—	50	99
1921	—	—	1,409	1,097			5,862	3,061	78	27	—	—	134	353	43	—	174	397
1922	575	248	[870]	[609]	870	713	3,700	4,118	104	35	312	324	1,087	822	[66]	[7]	462	311
1923	508	228	916	458	1,014	286	4,488	3,205	70	24	487	605	2,422	1,788	48	34	724	339
1924	537	279	1,614	1,576	1,126	867	6,435	4,131	102	53	510	547	4,429	1,615	36	52	682	389
1925	479	316	1,640	1,829	1,430	1,131	7,140	5,347	132	89	511	559	5,051	2,462	81	69	866	637
1926	483	222	2,504	2,487	1,369	1,095	5,635	4,780	157	114	367	573	4,996	—	138	88	918	724
1927	543	412	3,610	4,521	1,290	1,529	6,539	5,721	216	107	737	805	—	7,096	127	138	899	679
1928	667	440	3,994	4,246	1,494	1,739	7,410	5,670	237	98	903	859	7,645	—	195	152	1,067	779
1929	704	374	4,908	3,812	1,850	1,912	7,675	4,691	213	121	850	877	7,135	8,005	153	169	1,188	675
1930	581	333	5,181	2,987	1,065	1,621	6,011	3,572	175	94	606	627	5,777	5,364	197	161	1,221	791
1931	495	224	4,047	2,390	1,084	1,748	4,791	2,493	131	73	359	315	4,589	2,543	322	101	925	543
1932	290	139	2,748	1,553	900	880	2,869	1,454	74	51	173	176	2,832	2,054	257	79	506	345
1933	236	130	2,473	1,448	841	1,025	1,774	1,170	62	44	146	168	2,181	1,503	116	67	379	471
1934	209	145	2,004	1,628	902	1,083	1,707	1,618	63	90	109	162	2,048	2,264	23	77	497	598

Abbreviations

AA	Political Archive of the German Foreign Ministry
ADAP	*Akten zur Deutschen Auswärtigen Politik*
BA	German Federal Archives (Koblenz)
CEH	*Central European History*
DBFP	*Documents on British Foreign Policy*
DGFP	*Documents on German Foreign Policy*
DZA	German Central Archive (Potsdam)
FAZ	*Frankfurter Allgemeine Zeitung*
FRUS	*Foreign Relations of the United States*
GWU	*Geschichte in Wissenschaft und Unterricht*
HZ	*Historische Zeitschrift*
IMCC	International Military Control Commission
JCH	*Journal of Contemporary History*
JMH	*Journal of Modern History*
LoN	League of Nations Archive (Geneva)
MGM	*Militärgeschichtliche Mitteilungen*
NPL	*Neue Politische Literatur*
PRO	Public Record Office (London)
QdO	French Foreign Ministry Archive (Paris)
VZG	*Vierteljahrshefte für Zeitgeschichte*
ZfG	*Zeitschrift für Geschichtswissenschaft*

Select Bibliography

Many works cited in the footnotes do not appear in this bibliography, in particular memoirs and articles.

I. Bibliographic Aids

Bracher, K. D., Jacobsen, H.-A., and Funke, M., eds. *Bibliographie zur Politik in Theorie und Praxis*, rev. ed. (Düsseldorf, 1976).
Vogelsang, Th., ed., *Bibliographie zur Zeitgeschichte. Beilage der Vierteljahrshefte für Zeitgeschichte* (Stuttgart, 1953 et seq.); also as Th. Vogelsang and H. Auerbach, eds., *Bibliographie zur Zeitgeschichte 1953–1980* (Munich, 1982, 1983).

II. Government Publications

Germany. *Akten der Reichskanzlei. Weimarer Republik* (Boppard, 1968 et seq.).
Germany. Auswärtiges Amt: *Akten zur Deutschen Auswärtigen Politik, 1918–1945*, Series A: 1919–1925; Series B: 1925–1933 (Gottingen, 1968 et seq.).
Great Britain. Foreign Office: *Documents on British Foreign Policy, 1919–1939* (London, 1946).
France. Ministère des affaires étrangères. Commission de publication des documents relatifs aux origines de la guerre 1939–1945: *Documents diplomatiques français* (Paris, 1964).
United States. Department of State: *Papers Relating to the Foreign Relations of the United States* (Washington, D.C., ongoing).

III. General Surveys of Interest

Becker, J., and Hildebrand. K., eds. *Internationale Beziehungen in der Weltwirtschaftskrise 1929–1933* (Munich, 1980).
Craig, G. A., *Germany, 1866–1945* (Oxford, 1978).
Holborn, H., *A History of Modern Germany, 1840–1945* (New York, 1969).

167

Kennedy, P., *The Realities Behind Diplomacy: Background Influences on British Foreign Policy, 1865–1950* (London, 1981).

Opitz, R. *Europastrategien des deutschen Kapitals 1900–1945* (Cologne, 1977).

Zahniser, M. R., *Uncertain Friendship — American-French Relations Through the Cold War* (New York, 1975).

IV. General Studies of the Weimar Republic

Bariéty, J., and Droz, J., *Rèpublique de Weimar et régime hitlérien, 1918–1945* (Paris, 1973).

Bracher, K. D., *Die Krise Europas 1917–1975* (Frankfurt, 1976).

Conze, W., *Die Zeit Wilhelms II. und die Weimarer Republik: Deutsche Geschichte, 1890–1933* (Tübingen and Stuttgart, 1964).

Dederke, K., *Reich und Republik: Deutschland 1917–1933* (Stuttgart, 1969).

Erdmann, K. D., *Die Zeit des Weltkrieg*, in Vol. IV of: *Bruno Gebhardts Handbuch der deutschen Geschichte*, Grundmann, H., ed. (Stuttgart, 1973).

Eyck, Erich. *A History of the Weimar Republic*, 2 vols. (Cambridge, Mass., 1962–1963).

Heiber, H., *Die Republic von Weimar* (Munich, 1974).

Kolb, E. *Die Weimarer Republik* (Munich, 1984).

Michalka, W., and Niedhart, G., eds, *Die Ungeliebte Republik* (Munich, 1980).

Rosenberg, A., *Geschichte der Weimarer Republik* (Frankfurt a.M., 1961).

Ruge, W., *Deutschland von 1917 bis 1933. Von der Großen Sozialistischen Oktoberrevolution bis zum Ende der Weimarer Republik* (Berlin, 1974).

Schulz, G., *Deutschland seit dem Ersten Weltkrieg, 1918–1945* (Göttingen, 1976).

V. General Studies of Weimar Foreign Policy

Hiden, J., *Germany and Europe, 1919–1939* (London, 1977).

Krüger, P., *Die Außenpolitik der Republik von Weimar* (Darmstadt, 1985).

Zimmerman, L., *Deutsche Außenpolitik in der Ära der Weimarer Republik* (Göttingen, 1958).

VI. General Studies of International Relations in the Inter-War Era

Graml, H., *Europa zwischen den Kriegen* (Munich, 1969).

Kennedy, P. M., *Strategy and Diplomacy, 1870–1945* (London, 1983).

Marks, S., *The Illusion of Peace. International Relations in Europe, 1918–1933* (London and New York, 1976).

Schmidt, G., ed., *Konstellationen internationaler Politik 1924–1932* (Bochum, 1983).

Sontag, R., *A Broken World, 1919–1939* (New York, 1971).

VII. On Continuity in Recent German History

Berghahn, V. R., *Germany and the Approach of War in 1914* (New York, 1973).

Blackbourn, D., and Eley, D., *The Peculiarities of German History* (Oxford, 1984).

Calleo, D., *The German Problem Reconsidered: Germany and the World Order 1870 to the Present* (Cambridge, 1978).

Elben, W., *Das Problem der Kontinuität in der deutschen Revolution. Die Politik der Staatssekretäre und der militärischen Führung vom November 1916 bis Februar 1919* (Düsseldorf, 1965).

Fischer, F., *Bündnis der Eliten. Zur Kontinuität der Machtstrukturen in Deutschland 1871–1945* (Düsseldorf, 1979).

——, *War of Illusions. German Politics from 1911 to 1914* (New York, 1975).

——, *World Power or Decline?* (New York, 1974).

Hillgruber, A., *Kontinuität und Diskontinuität in der deutschen Außenpolitik von Bismarck bis Hitler* (Düsseldorf, 1969).

Wehler, H.-U., *The German Empire* (Leamington Spa and Dover, N.H., 1985).

VIII. Noteworthy Monographs and Topical Studies

1. On German War Aims in the First World War

Fischer, F., *Germany's War Aims in the First World War* (New York, 1967).

Rössler, H., ed., *Weltwende 1917. Monarchie, Weltrevolution, Demokratie.* (Göttingen, 1965).

Schieder, W., ed., *Erster Weltkrieg. Ursachen, Entstehung, Kriegsziele.* (Cologne, 1969).

2. On the Peace Negotiations, 1918–1919

Haupts, L., *Deutsche Friedenspolitik* (Düsseldorf, 1976).

Krüger, P., *Deutschland und die Reparationen, 1918/1919. Die Genesis des Reparationsproblems in Deutschland zwischen Waffenstillstand und Versailler Friedensschluss* (Stuttgart, 1973).

Hovi, K., *Cordon Sanitaire ou Barrière de l'Est? The Emergence of the New*

French Eastern European Alliance Policy, 1918–1919 (Turku, Finland, 1975).

Kolb, E., ed., *Vom Kaiserreich zur Weimarer Republik* (Cologne, 1972).

Marks, S., *Innocent Abroad. Belgium at the Paris Peace Conference of 1919* (Chapel Hill, 1981).

Mayer, A. J., *Politics and Diplomacy of Peacemaking. Containment and Counterrevolution at Versailles, 1918–1919* (New York, 1969).

McDougall, W. A., *France's Rhineland Diplomacy, 1914–1924. The Last Bid for a Balance of Power in Europe* (Princeton, 1978).

Rössler, H., ed., *Die Folgen von Versailles, 1919–1924* (Göttingen, 1969).

Schulz, G., *Revolution und Friedensschlüsse, 1917–1920* (Munich, 1974).

Schwabe, K., *Deutsche Revolution und Wilson-Frieden. Die amerikanische und deutsche Friedensstrategie zwischen Ideologie und Machtpolitik. 1918/19* (Düsseldorf, 1971).

Trachtenberg, M., *Reparations in World Politics: France and European Economic Diplomacy, 1916–1923* (New York, 1980).

3. On the German Economy during the Weimar Republic

Aldcroft, D. J., *From Versailles to Wall Street, 1919–1929* (Berkeley, 1977).

Beitel, W. & Nötzold, J., *Deutsch-sowjetische Wirtschaftsbeziehungen in der Zeit der Weimarer Republik* (Baden-Baden, 1979).

Borchardt, K., *Wachstum. Krisen. Handlungsspieträume der Wirtschaftspolitik*, (Göttingen, 1982).

Feldman, G. D., *Iron and Steel in the German Inflation 1916–1923* (Princeton, 1977).

——, and Homberg, H., *Industrie und Inflation* (Hamburg, 1977).

Fink, C., *The Genoa Conference. European Diplomacy, 1921–22* (Chapel Hill, 1984).

Fischer, W., *Deutsche Wirtschaftspolitik, 1918–1945* (Opladen, 1968).

Glashagen, W., *Die Reparationspolitik Heinrich Brünings 1930–1931* (Bonn, 1980).

Hollferich, C.-L., *Die deutsche Inflation 1914–1923* (Berlin, 1980).

Kindleberger, C. P., *The World Depression, 1929–1939* (Berkeley, 1973).

Link, W., *Die amerikanische Stabilisierungspolitik in Deutschland, 1921–1932* (Düsseldorf, 1970).

Maier, C. S., *Recasting Bourgeois Europe. Stabilization in France, Germany, and Italy in the Decade After World War I* (Princeton, 1975).

Mommsen, H., Petzina, D., and Weisbrod, B., eds., *Industrielles System und politische Entwicklung in der Weimarer Republik* (Düsseldorf, 1974).

Petzina, D., *Die deutsche Wirtschaft in der Zwischenkriegszeit* (Wiesbaden, 1977).

Ránki, G., *Economy and Foreign Policy. The Struggle of the Great Powers for Hegemony in the Danube Valley, 1919–1939* (Boulder, Colorado, 1983).

4. On German Ostpolitik

Campbell, G. F., *Confrontation in Central Europe. Weimar Germany and Czechoslovakia* (Chicago, 1975).

Dyck, H. L., *Weimar Germany and Soviet Russia, 1926–1933. A Study in Diplomatic Instability* (New York, 1966).

Hildebrand, K., *Das deutsche Reich und die Sowjet-Union im internationalen System, 1918–1932. Legitimität oder Revolution?* (Wiesbaden, 1977).

Linke, H. G., *Deutsch-sowjetische Beziehungen bis Rapallo* (Cologne, 1972).

Meyer, H. C., *Mitteleuropa in German Thought and Action, 1914–1945* (The Hague, 1955).

Riekhoff, H. von., *German-Polish Relations, 1918–1933* (Baltimore, 1971).

Suval, S., *The Anschluss Question in the Weimar Era. A Study of Nationalism in Germany and Austria, 1918–1932* (Baltimore, 1974).

Walsdorff, M., *Westorientierung und Ostpolitik in der Locarno-Ära* (Bremen, 1971).

5. On the Ruhr Conflict

Cornebise, A. E., *The Weimar Crisis. Cuno's Germany and the Ruhr Occupation* (Washington, 1977).

Rupieper, H. J., *The Cuno Government and Reparations 1922–1923: Politics and Economics* (The Hague, 1979).

Schuker, S. A., *The End of French Predominance in Europe. The Financial Crisis of 1924 and the Adoption of the Dawes Plan* (Chapel Hill, N.C., 1976).

Zimmermann, L., *Frankreichs Ruhrpolitik. Von Versailles zum Dawes-Plan* (Göttingen, 1971).

6. On Westpolitik and Locarno

Jacobson, J., *Locarno Diplomacy. Germany and the West, 1925–1929* (Princeton, 1972).

Maxelon, M.-O., *Stresemann und Frankreich. Deutsche Politiker der Ost-West-Balance* (Düsseldorf, 1972).

Megerle, K., *Deutsche Außenpolitik 1925. Ansatz zu aktivem Revisionismus* (Frankfurt, a.M., 1974).

Michalka, W., and Lee, M., eds., *Gustav Stresemann* (Darmstadt, 1982).

Rössler, H., ed., *Locarno und die Weltpolitik, 1924–1932. Vorträge und Diskussionen einer Tagung in Eichstätt, 1966* (Göttingen, 1969).

Salewski, M., *Entwaffnung und Militärkontrolle in Deutschland, 1919–1927* (Bonn, 1966).

Weidenfeld, W. J., *Die Englandpolitik Gustav Stresemanns. Theoretische und praktische Aspekte der Außenpolitik* (Mainz, 1972).

Select Bibliography

7. On German League of Nations Policy and Minorities Policy

Kimmich, C. M., *Germany and the League of Nations* (Chicago, 1976).

Krekeler, N., *Revisionsanspruch und geheime Ostpolitik der Weimarer Republik. Die Subventionierung der deutschen Minderheit in Polen, 1919–1933* (Stuttgart, 1973).

Pieper, H., *Die Minderheitenfrage und das deutsche Reich, 1919–1933/34* (Frankfurt a.M., 1974).

Spenz, J., *Die diplomatische Vorgeschichte des Beitritts Deutschlands zum Völkerbund, 1924–1926. Ein Beitrag zur Außenpolitik der Weimarer Republik* (Göttingen, 1966).

8. On the German Military and Military Policy

Bennett, E. W., *German Rearmament and the West 1932–1933* (Princeton, 1979).

Carsten, F. L., *The Reichswehr and Politics 1918–1933* (Oxford, 1966; Berkeley, 1973).

Dülffer, J., *Weimar, Hitler und die Marine. Reichspolitik und Flottenbau 1930–1939* (Düsseldorf, 1973).

Gatzke, H. W., *Stresemann and the Rearmament of Germany* (New York, 1954).

Geyer, M., *Deutsche Rüstungspolitik 1860–1980* (Frankfurt a.M., 1984).

——, *Aufrüstung oder Sicherheit. Die Reichswehr in der Krise der Machtpolitik* (Wiesbaden, 1980).

Hansen, E. W., *Reichswehr und Industrie. Rüstungswirtschaftliche Zusammenarbeit und wirtschaftliche Mobilmachungsvorbereitungen 1923–1932* (Boppard, 1978).

Müller, J.-K., and Opitz, E., eds., *Militär und militärismus in der Weimarer Republik* (Düsseldorf, 1978).

Post, G., *The Civil–Military Fabric of Weimar Foreign Policy* (Princeton, 1973).

9. On the Last Phase of the Republic and Its Collapse

Bracher, K. D., *Die Auflösung der Weimarer Republik. Eine Studie zum Problem des Machtverfalls in der Demokratie* (Villingen, 1971).

Conze, W., and Raupach, H., eds., *Die Staats- und Wirtschaftskrise des Deutschen Reiches, 1929–1933* (Stuttgart, 1967).

Grübler, M., *Die Spitzenverbände der Wirtschaft und des erste Kabinett Brüning* (Düsseldorf, 1982).

Helbig, W. J., *Die Reparationen in der Ära Brüning. Zur Bedeutung des Young Plans für die deutsche Politik, 1930 bis 1932* (Berlin–Dahlem, 1962).

Hermens, F. A., and Schieder, T., *Staat, Wirtschaft und Politik in der Wei-*

marer Republik. Festschrift für Heinrich Brüning (Berlin, 1967).

Hörster-Philipps, U., *Konservative Politik in der Endphase der Weimarer Republik*. (Cologne, 1982).

Jasper, G., ed., *Von Weimar zu Hitler* (Cologne, 1968).

Nadolny, S., *Abrüstungsdiplomatie 1932/33. Deutschland auf der Genfer Konferenz im Übergang von Weimar zu Hitler* (Munich, 1978).

10. On the Machtergreifung and Initial Phase of National Socialist Foreign Policy

Bracher, K. D., Sauer, W., and Schulz, G., *Die nationalsozialistische Machtergreifung*, 3 vols. (Berlin, 1974).

Funke, M., *Hitler, Deutschland und die Mächte* (Düsseldorf, 1976).

Hildebrand, K., *The Foreign Policy of the Third Reich*, (Berkeley, 1973).

Jacobsen, H.-A., *Nationalsozialistische Außenpolitik, 1933–1938* (Frankfurt a.M., 1966).

Michalka, W., ed., *Nationalsozialistische Außenpolitk* (Darmstadt, 1978).

Schreiber, G., *Hitler. Interpretationen 1923–1983* (Darmstadt, 1984).

Weinberg, G. L., *The Foreign Policy of Hitler's Germany. Diplomatic Revolution in Europe. 1933–1936* (Chicago, 1970).

Wollstein, G., *Vom Weimarer Revisionismus zu Hitler. Das Deutsche Reich und die Großmächte in der Anfangsphase der nationalsozialistischen Herrschaft in Deutschland* (Bonn, 1973).

Index

Index

175

Index

85–111, 127, 134f., 137, 150, 154
Assembly, 89, 93, 100ff., 112, 124
Charter (Covenant), 47, 66, 81, 85, 89
    Art. 8, 98f.
    Art. 16, 86f.
'collective security', 89, 137
Council, 87ff., 93ff., 101f.
    Crisis of 1926, 88
    membership, 87
    German policy toward, 87ff., 103
disarmament, 81, 97–111, 112
    Comité d'arbitrage et de sécurité,
    101
    France, 81
    General Act for the Pacific
      Settlement of International
      Disputes, 101ff.
    Geneva Protocol, 81f.
    Germany, security proposals, 90
    Model Treaty to Strengthen the
      Means of Preventing War, 102
    Preparatory Commission on
      Disarmament, 99f., 102
Germany and, 85–111
    advantages to Germany, 31
    Anglo-French domination, German
      belief in, 89
    entry, 8, 66, 85, 87ff., 98, 104, 123
    revisionist policy toward, 89f.
    Stresemann's ambivalence toward,
      90f.
Japan, withdrawal from, 103
Manchurian Incident, 103
minorities
    German policy toward, 85ff., 92ff.,
      95, 112
    Poland, 93
    Upper Silesia, 93
    Russia, absence of, 88
    Upper Silesia, partition of, 51
    Woodrow Wilson and, 21
Lebensraum, *see* Hitler
Lenin, Vladimir I., 11
Link, Werner, 63, 69f., 104, 117
Linke, Horst G., 65
Lloyd George, D., 55, 65f.
London Reparations Conference, *see*
    reparations
Locarno, Pact of (Rhineland Pact), 8,
    82ff., 86ff., 89f., 95f., 98, 104, 123,
    126, 154f.
    Annex F, 86
    benefits of for Germany
      (*Rückwirkungen*), 85

Eastern Locarno (*Ostlocarno*), 83,
    124f.
    era of, 98
    origins of, 46, 82ff.
    signature of, 84
    Thoiry, 104f., 124, 133, 154
Ludendorf, General Erich, 13f., 16f.
    foreign policy concepts similar to
      Hitler, 14
Lüdtke, A., 5
Lugano, 93, 95
Luther, Hans, 74

Machtergreifung, *see* National Socialists
Madrid, 94
Maltzan, Ago von, 60, 65
Manchurian Incident, 103
Marks, Sally, 26, 47, 84
Maxelon, Michael-Olaf, 75, 96f.
Mayrisch, Emile, 135
McDougall, Walter, 23
MICUM, *see* Ruhr
Miquel, Johannes, 155
    Sammlungspolitik, 155
Mirbach-Harff, Count Wilhem von, 49,
    92
Mitteleuropa, *see* German foreign policy,
    imperialism
Mosse, George, 4
Müller, Hermann, 93
Mussolini, Benito, 84

Nadolny, Rudolf, 146ff.
National Socialists, 116, 130f., 135, 137f.,
    143, 148, 156
    coordination policy (*Gleichschaltung*),
      139, 156
    electoral gains in 1930, 114–15
    foreign policy
      aggression, plans concealed until
        1937, 140
      goals, 141
      January 1933, 137
      racial ideology of, 148
      seizure of power (*Machtergreifung*), 6,
        135, 137ff., 140, 142ff.
Neurath, Konstantin von, 60, 136, 138f.,
    143f., 146f.

OHL, *see* German army, High
    Command
Optional Clauses of the Permanent
    Court of International Justice at The
    Hague, 100

Index

Index

Index